Carol Costa

Alpha Teach Yourself

Bookkeeping

in 24 hours

ALPHA A member of Penguin Group (USA) Inc.

ALPHA BOOKS

Published by the Penguin Group

Penguin Group (USA) Inc., 375 Hudson Street, New York, New York 10014, USA

Penguin Group (Canada), 90 Eglinton Avenue East, Suite 700, Toronto, Ontario M4P 2Y3, Canada (a division of Pearson Penguin Canada Inc.)

Penguin Books Ltd., 80 Strand, London WC2R 0RL, England

Penguin Ireland, 25 St. Stephen's Green, Dublin 2, Ireland (a division of Penguin Books Ltd.)

Penguin Group (Australia), 250 Camberwell Road, Camberwell, Victoria 3124, Australia (a division of Pearson Australia Group Pty. Ltd.)

Penguin Books India Pvt. Ltd., 11 Community Centre, Panchsheel Park, New Delhi—110 017, India

Penguin Group (NZ), 67 Apollo Drive, Rosedale, North Shore, Auckland 1311, New Zealand (a division of Pearson New Zealand Ltd.)

Penguin Books (South Africa) (Pty.) Ltd., 24 Sturdee Avenue, Rosebank, Johannesburg 2196, South Africa

Penguin Books Ltd., Registered Offices: 80 Strand, London WC2R 0RL, England

International Standard Book Number: 978-1-59257-695-1
Library of Congress Catalog Card Number: 2007932633

658.1
COS OCLC 1/3/08

10   09   08   8   7   6   5   4   3   2   1

Interpretation of the printing code: The rightmost number of the first series of numbers is the year of the book's printing; the rightmost number of the second series of numbers is the number of the book's printing. For example, a printing code of 08-1 shows that the first printing occurred in 2008.

Printed in the United States of America

Publisher
Marie Butler-Knight

Editorial Director
Mike Sanders

Managing Editor
Billy Fields

Acquisitions Editor
Tom Stevens

Development Editor
Lynn Northrup

Senior Production Editor
Janette Lynn

Copy Editor
Michael Dietsch

Cover Designer
Kurt Owens

Book Designer
William Thomas

Indexer
Angie Bess

Layout
Brian Massey

Proofreader
Aaron Black

To my family, who is a constant source of love and support

Overview

Contents

Appendixes

Introduction

Everyone needs some degree of bookkeeping knowledge. Individuals need to keep track of their income and expenses in order to maintain the lifestyle they wish to lead, obtain credit, and file an income tax return at the end of each year.

There are many computerized programs that can be used to collect and report bookkeeping data. Keep in mind, that although these programs are great time-savers, the reports that they generate are only as accurate as the information that has been keyed into them.

Business owners must keep a set of books themselves or employ other people to do it for them. The size of the business and the products or services it provides dictate the amount of work it takes to develop a sound bookkeeping system that allows the company to operate smoothly and profitably.

This book provides basic bookkeeping information that covers personal finance tasks, large corporate bookkeeping procedures, and everything in between.

In the business world there are different categories of bookkeepers and each category entails its own duties and responsibilities. At the same time, different types of business entities require different types of book-keeping systems. Much attention to detail has gone into the writing of this book to supply the reader with an understanding of each book-keeping category and the work required to manage the job successfully. In addition to the fundamental elements of bookkeeping used by every business, there is an overview of the functions unique to a variety of specialized business operations.

The information is offered in a friendly, easy to understand format that allows the reader to absorb the knowledge at his or her own pace. At the end of each chapter, a short quiz helps the reader review the lessons presented in the preceding pages.

Whether you want to balance your checking account, run a home-based business, or keep the books for a large corporation, you will find the basic information you need in this book. It will also show you how to track and store the personal financial data you need for your federal and state tax returns. Having this information readily available whenever it is needed for credit applications or a review of your personal financial status saves time and energy.

If you have specific areas of interest, you will like the convenience this book provides. You will be able to pick and choose the lessons set forth in the text to fulfill your particular needs.

Long after you have gone through the lessons in this book, you will want to keep it on your desk or in your bookcase as a reference guide. Although payroll tax rates and forms may be updated from year to year, the principles of bookkeeping and the accepted methods used in managing financial information do not change. So any time a question arises or you want to review any of the rules or procedures presented in the book, you can be sure that the basic information will always be valid.

Another feature of this book is the inclusion of helpful hints, shortcuts, and additional tips spread throughout the text. Watch for the following:

GO TO ▶

This sidebar directs you to another chapter or section of the book to learn more about a particular topic.

JUST A MINUTE

 This sidebar offers advice or teaches an easier way to do something.

TIME SAVER

 Here you'll find information on a faster way to do something.

PROCEED WITH CAUTION

 These are warnings that caution you about potential problems and help you steer clear of trouble.

FYI These are quick references to direct you toward further reading and examples in other sources.

STRICTLY DEFINED

 These boxes offer definitions of terms you may not know.

All in all, this book is intended to be both a learning tool and a reference guide you will use over and over again.

About the Author

Carol Costa is a professional writer with a business background in accounting, taxes, and real estate. She has owned and managed a bookkeeping and income tax service, worked as a staff accountant at a CPA firm, and managed accounting systems for a variety of small and large businesses. A number of firms have hired her to assess and analyze their accounting/bookkeeping systems in order to bring them up to date, unravel problems, and correct errors.

Her bookkeeping and tax preparation experience includes work for individuals, businesses, and major corporations. Her experience includes managing the books in the following types of business operations: Insurance, Auto Repair, Auto Sales, Law Firms including Patent Attorneys, Internet Technology, Real Estate Sales, Property Management, Gold Mining, Retail, Contractor, Literary Agent, Entertainment Industry, Manufacturing, Medical, Food Processing, and more.

Carol currently serves as the Treasurer of two nonprofit organizations and is responsible for all accounting functions.

Carol is the author of *Alpha Teach Yourself Accounting in 24 Hours*, editions 1 and 2 with Wes Addison, CPA; *The Complete Idiot's Guide to Surviving Bankruptcy* with James Beaman J.D.; and several other nonfiction books and novels.

Acknowledgments

Thanks to my agent, Andree Abecassis of Ann Elmo Agency, for her friendship and guidance.

Thanks to my editors, Tom Stevens, Lynn Northrup, Anthony Offret, and the editorial staff of Alpha Books for their help and expertise.

Special Thanks to the Technical Editor

Alpha Teach Yourself Bookkeeping in 24 Hours was reviewed by an expert who double-checked the accuracy of what you'll learn here, to help us ensure that this book gives you everything you need to know about bookkeeping. Special thanks are extended to Anthony J. Offret.

Anthony J. Offret is Chair of the School of Business, ITT Technical Institute in Tucson, Arizona. His experience in the financial services industry spans 25 years, including banking, investments, and small business lending. Anthony received his Bachelor's degree in Liberal Arts from the University of Arizona and his Master's degree from the University of Oklahoma. He has been the treasurer of several nonprofit and service organizations.

Trademarks

All terms mentioned in this book that are known to be or are suspected of being trademarks or service marks have been appropriately capitalized. Alpha Books and Penguin Group (USA) Inc. cannot attest to the accuracy of this information. Use of a term in this book should not be regarded as affecting the validity of any trademark or service mark.

Duties and Responsibilities of Organizing and Managing a Bookkeeping System

Part I

Bookkeeping Job Titles, Duties, and Responsibilities

Chapter Summary

In this hour you will learn about …

- Employment categories
- Bookkeeping duties and responsibilities
- Personal record keeping
- Assistant bookkeepers and clerks
- Full-Charge Bookkeepers

Bookkeepers and accountants are closely related because they use the same basic principles and procedures for establishing and running a system that records financial data. The differences lie in the way they work within that system.

A bookkeeper is a person who handles the day-to-day transactions and records the information into the accounts required by the business or individual. While most accountants, especially *Certified Public Accountants (CPAs)*, do not handle the day-to-day transactions of their employers or clients, they do analyze, verify, and report the data in financial statements or in the annual tax returns. They also advise their clients in tax matters and other economic decisions.

STRICTLY DEFINED

 In most states, a **Certified Public Accountant (CPA)** has a Bachelor's degree in accounting and has passed a rigorous examination in order to be certified to handle public and private financial matters.

There are a number of different job titles that fall into the bookkeeping category. Each has its own particular area of expertise and each has its own set of duties and responsibilities.

Employment Categories

The employment section of a daily newspaper is a good place to start when considering a career in bookkeeping. Regardless of the size of the city you live in, ads for bookkeeping positions are usually displayed. That's because all business entities require some sort of bookkeeping help; many require several people to fill various positions within their financial systems.

Bookkeeping is a skill that will always be in demand. Therefore learning how to manage a set of books or becoming adept at some of the tasks performed by assistants and clerks within a large bookkeeping system will increase your employment choices and opportunities.

As you review the employment opportunities for bookkeepers you should note the assortment of jobs that employers are trying to fill. Payroll clerks, assistant bookkeepers, and cashiers are examples of the types of bookkeeping personnel that are sought on a regular basis. The salaries offered for these positions are usually determined by the amount of work and the degree of skill required for each individual job.

Even if you are not interested in pursuing a career in bookkeeping, studying the methods used in overseeing a set of books or the individual tasks performed within a bookkeeping system will help you manage your business and personal finances more efficiently.

Bookkeeping Duties and Responsibilities

You may have heard the term *cash flow*. Cash flow is the primary concern and responsibility of a bookkeeper. Cash flow in general refers to all the money that comes in and goes out of a bookkeeping system. The system can be as small as an individual's household account or as large as the operations of a giant corporation.

Under the heading of cash flow are a number of different areas that must be defined and managed by the bookkeeper. Money coming into the system is income from outside sources that can be received daily, weekly, or monthly. The same time frames may apply to the money going out of the system for expenses or other on-going obligations. However, most individuals and companies pay their bills on a monthly basis. That allows them time to accumulate enough income to pay their bills.

Income is usually categorized as sales, commissions, or wages earned from a job or profession. As this income is collected it is usually deposited into a bank account or put aside so it can be easily disbursed to pay the bills.

The responsibilities with regard to cash flow are twofold:

- The bookkeeper must monitor and record the cash that flows into the system.
- The bookkeeper must handle the disbursements, paying the bills in an accurate and timely manner.

The bookkeeper must also look ahead to the end of the month to ascertain whether the cash that is flowing in will be sufficient to cover the bills that are scheduled to be paid out.

A positive cash flow normally means the enterprise is profitable. In other words, there is enough money flowing into the system to pay the bills and still have money in the bank account at the end of the month.

Management of the cash flow is a form of budgeting. This duty is especially important when working in an enterprise where the income fluctuates due to seasonal demand or other market factors. For example, a company that sells patio equipment may experience a drop in sales during the winter months. Because normal overhead such as rent and utilities will still have to be paid during the slow sales period, a budget is developed and excess cash flow is put aside to keep the company solvent despite the temporary reduction in income.

TIME SAVER

 An informal budget can be as simple as keeping a running total of the bills as they come in, so there are no surprises at the end of the month.

Keep in mind that business owners, especially those who double as sales people, often rely on their bookkeepers to advise them of cash flow problems. Reporting any inkling of trouble to the owner may be one of a bookkeeper's most important duties. This allows the owner to find ways to increase income or arrange for loans to keep the business running smoothly.

A good credit rating and history is very important because it allows a business to buy the inventory and supplies needed to produce income and pay for those items after the income has been earned. We will discuss the specific details of obtaining and offering credit in business operations in later chapters. For now, just remember that managing the cash flow efficiently makes it possible to pay bills in a timely manner and maintain a good credit rating.

Depending on the type of business you keep the books for, other duties and responsibilities may be considered part of the job. However, no business can operate without money, so a bookkeeper's first and foremost responsibility will always be keeping a close eye on the dollars that flow in and out of the company's accounts.

Personal Bookkeeping Duties

Managing and monitoring the cash flow in your personal finances can be difficult if you have not established a bookkeeping system for yourself. Let's be honest. Many people don't even take the time to balance their checking accounts on a regular basis. With *ATMs* on every corner and the speed of electronic check processing, not knowing exactly how much money you have in your account can spell disaster.

STRICTLY DEFINED

 ATM is the acronym for Automated Teller Machine used in electronic banking.

To complicate matters, there are some banks that encourage customers to do all their banking through ATMs. These banks actually charge a fee to go inside the bank and deal with a real person rather than a computer. If you do business with this type of financial institution, be aware that there can be a downside to the convenience and speed of automation.

When you make a deposit or a withdrawal through the ATM, it prints out a receipt for the transaction you have just completed. It also shows the balance in the account you accessed. That is all well and good except you must bear in mind that the balance printed on the receipt may not include the deposit you just made and does not reflect any outstanding checks that have not yet cleared your account. As the term implies, an outstanding check is a check you have written and mailed that has not yet been received by your bank. Therefore the balance on the ATM receipt may not be accurate. This is one of the reasons it is prudent to balance your operating account on a regular basis.

At the same time, be aware that many companies process the check you send them electronically. That means the day they receive the payment, it gets charged against your bank account.

In the past, individuals and businesses operated on what was commonly known as "float." This was the time between the date you mailed your payment to the creditor and the date the amount of the check was actually charged against your bank account. This "float" time could be anywhere from a few days to a week. It depended on how long it took for the mail to be delivered to the creditor, how long it took the creditor to post the payment to their books, deposit the check, and the time it took their bank to process the check and send it on to the payer's bank to be processed.

This time lapse prompted some people and businesses to issue checks before the money to cover the check was actually in their bank accounts. Using "float" time assumed that by the time the check actually cleared an account, the money to cover it would be earned and deposited.

Those days are gone forever, and it's probably a good thing. Many people got into financial trouble by overestimating the "float" time and having their checks returned for insufficient funds. Nothing will ruin your monthly budget faster than having a check returned for insufficient funds because of the hefty bank fees, the late charges assessed on the original bill, and the fact that late charges and late payments are quickly reported to the credit bureau, lowering your credit rating and making it more difficult and expensive to obtain future credit.

A good credit rating is just as important to an individual as it is to a major corporation, so your financial plan should include ways to establish credit. That doesn't mean you should accept every credit card offer that appears in your mailbox. On the contrary, be sensible and only take what you need without getting yourself into debt.

As you have learned, the business bookkeeper is responsible for preparing budgets and planning ahead for the bills that must be paid at the end of the month. Your personal cash flow should be managed in the same way. Knowing how much money is in your account and meeting your monthly obligations on time is your responsibility.

GO TO ▶
Hour 10 where you will find detailed instructions for balancing the bank account used for personal or business transactions.

By setting up your personal bookkeeping plan you will avoid late fees on bills, eliminate bank charges for returned checks, and establish yourself as a credit-worthy individual.

The following guidelines can help you stay on your projected budget and eliminate personal financial problems:

- **Avoid impulse buying.** There will always be times when you are tempted to buy a luxury item that you don't really need. If you have the extra cash flow to make the purchase, it's not a problem. Using a credit card for such a purchase may be okay, too, unless the amount of the purchase causes you to exceed your credit limit or raises your monthly payment so that it jeopardizes the other bills you have to pay each month.
- **Pay necessary living expenses first.** Your rent or mortgage payment and utility bills are priority items that must be figured into your budget and paid promptly. Food is another necessary living expense. If you are short of funds, find ways to economize, such as cooking at home instead of going to restaurants or taking your lunch to work instead of eating out.
- **Never write a check unless there is enough money in your account to cover it.** It is better to be late with a bill than to risk having a check returned and incurring bank fees along with the late charges on the bill. Often you can call a creditor and obtain an extension so you will not have a late fee.

As you move forward in this book, you will learn a number of ways you can streamline and organize your personal bookkeeping plan. Remember that when it comes to personal finances, all the responsibility rests with you.

Assistant Bookkeepers and Clerks

Depending on a company's bookkeeping system, there may be more than one person responsible for its functions. Usually there is a supervising bookkeeper who assigns work and oversees the assistant bookkeepers.

For example, a company that employs outside sales people often gives those sales people expense accounts to cover auto expenses and other normal costs associated with selling. This creates an additional duty for the primary bookkeeper that could be assigned to an assistant.

Expense accounts are usually treated as a separate area of the bookkeeping system. An assistant would have the responsibility of collecting reports and checking them for accuracy. Once all the reports are verified, the information is entered into the bookkeeping system either by the assistant or the supervisor.

GO TO ▶

Hour 11 to find detailed instructions on expense accounts and how they are reconciled and balanced within the bookkeeping system.

While the assistant bookkeeper is not expected to have as much education or experience as the supervisor, this is not a position for a rank beginner. Most companies expect the assistant bookkeeper to have enough knowledge to be able to handle a variety of functions within the bookkeeping system. Working as an assistant is an opportunity to learn more about bookkeeping and how all the functions used by a particular business come together at the end of the month to report the financial status of the company.

Studying the basics of bookkeeping is an important part of the learning process, but the hands-on experience of actually working with an established and smooth-running bookkeeping system is invaluable.

Clerks fall into their own special category because they are often totally responsible for the area of the bookkeeping system they handle. Again, depending on the workload, there may be one or several clerks assigned to handle certain functions of the bookkeeping system that need special attention. Some of these specialized areas are:

- Inventory
- Purchasing
- Accounts Payable
- Accounts Receivable
- Billing
- Payroll

All of these areas will be discussed in detail in later chapters. For now, the terms are introduced so you can understand why they are sometimes handled as separate departments. You will also get some insight into the responsibilities assigned to the clerks who work in these departments.

Inventory

A retail enterprise, such as Wal-Mart, sells hundreds of products. All the products sold by Wal-Mart are part of the company's inventory. It's easy to see why Wal-Mart or any large retail chain would need a special department to keep track of all the merchandise that moves in and out of its stores. Also, when there are so many categories of products to keep track of, the Inventory Department itself may be divided into several different departments, such as food, clothing, toys, tools, garden, and electronics.

Overall, the Inventory Department is responsible for checking in merchandise, sending it to a warehouse or to a retail outlet, and keeping count of the items in stock and their value.

For the bookkeeping clerk, it is still a matter of numbers. A home-based retail business may just keep track of the numbers on a pad of paper. The industry giants, of course, have computerized systems that keep track of the inventory, but sitting at those computers inputting the data is a bookkeeping clerk who has the responsibility of entering the numbers accurately.

Purchasing

In smaller retail outlets, the Purchasing Department and the Inventory Department are often the same. Larger companies separate them into two departments, although it is necessary that they work in conjunction with one another.

A purchasing clerk usually works directly with the *vendors* that sell wholesale merchandise. Sometimes those vendors are the manufacturers that actually make the products; sometimes they are wholesalers that handle products for a variety of manufacturing companies. Again, it is a bookkeeping function where the clerks check prices and estimate profits before purchases are finalized.

STRICTLY DEFINED

 Companies or individuals that sell products or services in the business world are known as **vendors.**

Accounts Payable

This brings us to Accounts Payable clerks. Obviously all the vendors that sold merchandise or services to a business want to be paid. Small businesses often have to pay for merchandise and services when they are received. However, most companies have established that good credit rating mentioned earlier and the vendor allows them to pay for goods and services some time after they are received.

Accounts Payable clerks process all the invoices for merchandise and services and issue the checks to the various vendors. The clerk has the responsibility of checking the invoices for mathematical accuracy, verifying the payment terms, and paying the bills in a timely manner. The clerk may also be responsible for paying the normal overhead expenses of rent and utilities and any other bills that are sent to the department.

Accounts Receivable

One of the most important functions in a large company may be the work performed by the Accounts Receivable Department. Most businesses allow their customers to buy goods or services today and pay for them sometime in the future. Accounts Receivable clerks bill the customers and collect the payments. It is their responsibility to make sure the customer's billing information is correct and that the invoices or statements they send to the customers are accurate.

GO TO ▶
Hour 7 to learn about credit sales and how they are tracked and collected through Accounts Receivable.

Billing

Usually customer bills are issued by the Accounts Receivable Department. However, in very large companies, the billing may be done by a separate Billing Department. Duties may also be split among various clerks. For example, one clerk may handle the billings for the customers whose names begin with the letters A to I, another with the letters J to N, and so on. Again it depends on the size and the amount of work generated by the volume of credit sales.

Payroll

Last but certainly not least is the Payroll Department. Payroll clerks have a number of duties and shoulder a lot of responsibility. If the company is large enough to have a Human Resources Department, all the employee information and forms will be completed by the people that work in that department. However, often it is the Payroll Department that must meet with new employees and make sure all the paperwork is completed correctly.

In addition to the paperwork that must be kept on each employee, the payroll clerks are responsible for seeing that wages and taxes are computed correctly and paychecks are issued and distributed on time.

Perhaps the biggest challenge for the Payroll Department is reporting the taxes associated with the salaries and wages. Federal and state requirements are stringent and must be followed precisely to avoid penalties.

FYI Federal tax reporting requirements, along with forms and instructions, can be reviewed at the Internal Revenue Service (IRS) website, www.irs.gov.

All in all, clerks in any bookkeeping department are expected to handle a variety of tasks with knowledge and competence. Because clerks work mainly within their own specialized area of the bookkeeping system, it is not required that they know how it all comes together at the end of the month. They just need to accomplish their own duties efficiently and in a timely manner so that it can be transferred into the main system. That said, remember that learning the basics of bookkeeping makes you more valuable as an employee, affords you the opportunity for advancement in the company, and helps you manage your personal finances as well.

Full-Charge Bookkeepers

There are many small- to medium-size firms that only employ one bookkeeper. That bookkeeper performs all the functions we have just reviewed that are handled by assistant bookkeepers and specialized clerks in larger companies.

If you want to do the books for your own home-based business, you will have to become a Full-Charge Bookkeeper. You will have to handle Inventory, Purchasing, Accounts Payable, Accounts Receivable, Billing, and if applicable, Payroll and Payroll tax reporting. While this may sound daunting, once you learn the basic procedures of general bookkeeping, all the tasks can be handled with a minimum of effort.

Even if you do not want to handle your own bookkeeping, you should still become acquainted with the process and understand the reports and the information they impart. You should never leave your finances, personal or business, totally in someone else's hands. It is an area of your life you must always monitor. There have been many instances where celebrities have left all the bookkeeping to an accountant or manager and subsequently found themselves in deep financial trouble.

Going back to the employment ads in the daily newspaper, you will often see a listing that says Bookkeeper, *Full-Charge through Financial Statements.*

STRICTLY DEFINED

 Full-Charge through Financial Statements means that the bookkeeper handles all the day-to-day transactions of the company and at the end of the month puts all the information together to issue Financial Statements.

Some Full-Charge Bookkeepers do not issue the company's Financial Statements. After they have completed all the transactions for the month, the data is turned over to a professional accounting firm or a Certified Public Accountant hired by the company who reviews the bookkeeper's work and issues the Financial Statements.

The owner of the company determines whether the in-house bookkeeper will do the company's Financial Statements or whether they will be completed by a Certified Public Accountant.

A Financial Statement prepared by a Certified Public Accountant is usually required by banks or other financial institutions when a business is applying for a credit line or for loans. This is not to suggest that the company's Full-Charge Bookkeeper is not capable of preparing and issuing accurate Financial Statements. It is simply a requirement of the bank or lending institution. The CPA or other outside professional serves as an independent, unbiased third party that the bank can call for clarification or additional information.

The job opportunities for a Full-Charge Bookkeeper are many and varied. These bookkeepers can work directly with one company or be self-employed and do the books for a number of companies.

GO TO ▶

Hour 13 for an overview of payroll services and the advantages of using one for a business.

Some Full-Charge Bookkeepers work for CPA firms doing the end of the month work for a variety of clients. Other Full-Charge Bookkeepers run payroll services for a number of different companies.

Now that you have learned about the different titles assigned to bookkeepers and the duties and responsibilities that go along with them, you are ready to move ahead. In the next hours you will study the individual functions that must be handled on a daily basis within a bookkeeping system. You will learn how those daily tasks vary or are expanded to fit the needs of different types of business entities.

Once you have completed all the lessons in this book, you should be able to do your own set of books manually or enter the financial data into a computerized bookkeeping program.

Hour's Up!

Try to answer the following questions based on the information in this hour without looking back at the text.

1. What is the main factor that has eliminated the use of "float" time?
   a. Faster mail deliveries
   b. Electronic check processing
   c. Late fees

2. What does the acronym ATM stand for?
   a. At The Movies
   b. Ask The Manager
   c. Automated Teller Machine

3. Which departments in a bookkeeping system are the most connected?
   a. Accounts Receivable and Accounts Payable
   b. Inventory and Purchasing
   c. Payroll and Accounts Payable

4. Expense accounts are usually treated as a separate area of the bookkeeping system.
   a. True
   b. False

5. What is one of a bookkeeper's primary duties?
   a. Paying bills
   b. Recording income
   c. Monitoring cash flow

6. A positive cash flow normally means:
   a. Sales are swift
   b. The business is profitable
   c. A good credit history

7. What tasks are performed by Accounts Receivable Clerks?
   a. Billing customers
   b. Sales
   c. Cash Disbursements

8. Full-Charge Bookkeepers are often on staff at CPA firms.
   a. True
   b. False

9. Writing a check when there is no money in the bank can result in:
   a. Late fees on the bill being paid
   b. Bank charges
   c. A derogatory report to the credit bureau
   d. All of the above

10. Individuals who sell products or services in the business world are known as customers.
   a. True
   b. False

Organization and Bank Accounts

Chapter Summary

In this hour you will learn about …

- Calendar or fiscal year
- Organizing a bookkeeping system
- Personal Banking
- Business Bank Accounts
- Trust Accounts

Contractors don't start building a house until the blueprints have been drawn up for it. The same should be true for a bookkeeping system. Before any transactions are completed or recorded, a preliminary plan should be worked out and some sort of a filing system organized.

Fortunately, building a record-keeping system doesn't involve pouring cement that would have to be broken up with a jackhammer if the plan is not structured properly. You can always make changes in a bookkeeping system if it does not suit your personal needs or the needs of the business operation. The important thing is to organize the accounts where the financial data will be recorded and establish a filing system to store the work papers generated by the business activities.

In a computerized bookkeeping program the accounts where business activity is posted are assigned numbers and titles. The numbers allow the computer to access and post the figures to the proper accounts as they are entered by the bookkeeper. For example, the Sales or Income Account is usually Account Number 4000. The data entry person has only to type in that account number and the computer will automatically bring up the Sales Account for posting.

The numbered accounts are stored in the computer and are called the *Chart of Accounts*. Additions or changes can be made to the Chart of Accounts as needed.

The **Chart of Accounts** is simply a listing for the accounts available for use in the bookkeeping system. Once the accounts are actually put into use they become the General Ledger where all transactions are posted.

Calendar or Fiscal Year

All bookkeeping systems are set up for a period of twelve months. Individuals and many businesses begin their annual record keeping on January 1st of each year and close the books on December 31st. This means they are operating in accordance with the calendar year. While income-earning individuals are required to file an income tax return based on the calendar year, businesses such as partnerships and corporations are allowed to operate on what is known as a fiscal year.

Like the calendar year, the fiscal year is twelve months long. The difference is that a fiscal year begins on the first day of any month and ends twelve months later on the last day of that month. So, for example, if a corporation begins its bookkeeping year on October 1st of this year, the fiscal year ends on September 30th of the following year. It is still a twelve-month period, but it is spread over more than one calendar year. Tax returns for fiscal year filers are due approximately three months after the end of the fiscal year.

PROCEED WITH CAUTION

Tax due dates for business operations can vary depending on the type of corporation and are subject to change. Check with a tax professional or with the IRS (www.irs.gov) to determine the date the tax return must be filed to avoid penalties.

Organizing a Bookkeeping System

Organization is the backbone of any first-rate bookkeeping system. The accounts that are initially set up will be structured to suit the needs of the daily business activity. The filing system will serve as a backup to those accounts and will store financial data such as invoices, inventory records, and client and customer information. A proper filing system allows you to access the information you need quickly and easily. It also provides hard copies of the data you may need to answer questions for clients, prove that a bill was paid, or provide receipts to the IRS if your tax return is audited.

GO TO ▶

Hour 10 for more information and details on audits.

Even if you are using a computerized bookkeeping program to store data and issue Financial Statements, you must still have an orderly filing system in place to store the paperwork generated by the company's activities.

Take the time to sit down and review the business operation. Answer a few simple questions to determine exactly what will be needed before you try to set up the books and a filing system:

- What twelve-month period will be used for recording the financial data?
- What is the size of the business entity?
- Is the business income based on sales or services?
- Are there employees?
- What type of equipment is needed to operate the business?

A home-based business will usually require a simpler bookkeeping system and fewer files than a larger company. Some small businesses are also partnerships. However, the books and the files would be set up the same as a single-owner company. It isn't until the end of the tax year that the net profit or loss from a partnership is divided among the owners for tax purposes. You will need to set up a file folder for each partner in the business to keep track of any money the partners have drawn from the business during the year.

FYI Publications on forming partnerships and the rules and regulations regarding taxes can be obtained from the IRS by calling 1-800-829-1954. Your legal advisor should also be consulted.

In a manual bookkeeping system the accounts can be set up in bound books or on individual ledger sheets that are sold in tablets in office supply stores. For clarity and to avoid confusion, use one ledger sheet for each account. Each account sheet will have five columns titled as follows: Date, Description, Debit, Credit, and Balance. The same information is already programmed into the account ledgers of computerized systems.

GO TO ▶

Hours 3 and 4 to learn about the accounts that can be set up and used in a bookkeeping system.

By going through the steps to set up books manually, you will gain a greater understanding of the basic procedures of bookkeeping. This is knowledge you should have before you attempt to post financial data into a computer. Remember that the basic principles and procedures are used in all bookkeeping systems regardless of the size of the business.

Financial Statements are divided into two sections: the Balance Sheet and the Profit & Loss Statement. Every account set up in a bookkeeping system is either a Balance Sheet account or a Profit & Loss account.

Accounts

To ease you into the process of setting up accounts, we will start with a very simple set of books and indicate the section of the Financial Statement where each item would be found at the end of the month or year.

Let's look at a home-based business, Cakes by Claire, that sells beautifully decorated cakes for all occasions. The accounts you would set up to track income and expenses might include the following:

Cash in Checking (Balance Sheet)

Cash in Savings (Balance Sheet)

Sales (Profit & Loss)

> Birthday Cakes
> Wedding Cakes
> Anniversary Cakes
> Miscellaneous Cakes

Cost of Sales (Profit & Loss)

> Baking Ingredients
> Decorating Supplies
> Boxes and Platters

Expenses (Profit & Loss)

> Advertising
> Delivery Expense
> Equipment
> Office Expense
> Miscellaneous Supplies
> Telephone Expense
> Website

Retained Earnings (Balance Sheet)

Capital (Balance Sheet)

Every bookkeeping system begins with the bank accounts. The checking account is where the money the business generates is deposited and then disbursed to pay the company's expenses. Most businesses also have a savings account where excess funds are deposited. The system will also have a Capital account as every new business must have money in its bank account to begin operating.

For this sample business let's assume that Claire provided $1,000. in cash to begin her business. $900. was deposited into the checking account and the balance of $100. was used to open the savings account.

Every business must also have a Retained Earnings account where the *Net Profit or Loss* is recorded.

STRICTLY DEFINED

 The **Net Profit or Loss** of a business is obtained by subtracting the totals recorded in the Cost of Sales and Expense Accounts from the totals recorded in the Sales or Income accounts.

Notice that under the heading of Sales, there are four different accounts. Every time a cake is sold, the amount is recorded on the appropriate ledger sheet. This allows the owner to keep track of the total sales in four key areas of the business and indicates which cakes are the best sellers. This information then helps the owner determine the supplies that are needed most and also serves as a guideline for ordering the proper quantities.

Cost of Sales covers the cost of the items directly related to the products (cakes) that are being sold. All three accounts in this section of the ledger are direct costs related to the sales. Most purchases would be recorded in one of these three accounts.

The Expenses section of this bookkeeping system is broken down into the general operating expenses of running a business. As these expenses are paid, the amount of each is recorded on the corresponding ledger sheet.

At the end of each month or at the end of the tax year all the ledger sheets are totaled and a simple Balance Sheet and Profit & Loss Statement can be issued based on those figures.

GO TO ▶
Hour 16 to see samples of Financial Statements and learn how the information is recorded and reported.

Files

Once the accounts have been established, the files that support them can be set up. Standard manila folders that can be purchased in any office supply store are used to hold the files. You will also need a file drawer, a file cabinet, or a stand-alone file holder to place on a table or desk to hold the files. Again, the quantity of files and the storage space for them depends on the size of the company you are organizing.

Put the files in alphabetical order or in the same order as you have placed the accounts you set up on the ledger sheets.

The larger the company, the more files and accounts that will need to be established. For the cake company, we will begin with the accounts and files that are needed to process the daily transactions and monitor the cash flow and profitability of the business operation.

Based on the accounts established for the cake business, the filing system set up to keep the paperwork in order would include the following folders:

- A folder that holds all the bank account information, including the monthly bank statements must be established. It might be labeled Bank Statements or could be labeled with the name of the bank where the account is housed.
- Orders: This file would contain information on cake orders that had not yet been baked and delivered.
- Sales Invoices: Paid invoices for cakes delivered and paid for by customers are stored in this folder. Note that this is not the type of business that would handle credit sales. Cakes would be paid for in advance or upon delivery.
- Bills to Pay or Accounts Payable: All outstanding bills would be filed in this folder. This would include cost of sales' items and general expenses.
- Paid Bills: As the bills are paid, the number of the check that was used to pay each and the date would be marked on the invoice and it would be filed in this folder. This type of business would probably pay cash for some supplies and the receipts for those expenditures could also be filed in this folder or a separate folder for cash payments could be set up.

The amounts for the cash expenditures would be recorded on the Cost of Sales ledger sheets or on one of the expense account sheets before being filed away.

You might also want to have a file folder containing information on the current customers and other folders containing information on vendors or potential customers.

Service Business

If the small business offers a service rather than a tangible product, the accounts and files would suit the needs of that business. For example, a person who edits manuscripts for a living might establish the following accounts:

Cash in Checking (Balance Sheet)

Cash in Savings (Balance Sheet)

Income (Profit & Loss)

    Editing Fees
    Consultations

Expenses: (Profit & Loss)

    Advertising
    Office Expense
    Telephone
    Website

Retained Earnings (Balance Sheet)

Capital (Balance Sheet)

JUST A MINUTE

 The terms Income and Sales are interchangeable as Sales are income to most businesses. Many computer programs only use Sales as the account heading for income in general. If that term is built into the program, it cannot be changed, and that is not a problem.

There are two categories under the Income heading. Editing fees are the monies collected from a client for going through a manuscript, line by line, and correcting things such as typographical errors, grammar, and punctuation.

Depending on the editor's prior experience, some writers may want to consult with the editor before beginning a project to get an opinion as to its marketability or appeal to the public. Thus, there is a second income category titled, Consultations.

Notice that there are no Cost of Sales accounts because there are really no purchases to be made that directly reduce the income accounts.

The accounts set up for recording expenses in this example are general and can be expanded as the need arises.

The files to support these accounts for a service business would include file folders for bank statements and information, invoices presented and paid by editing clients, and files for unpaid bills and paid bills.

As you can see, setting up the books and a filing system for a small company is not difficult. Once these things are in place, the bookkeeping itself becomes easier and the business owner has instant access to information whenever it is needed.

If you are hired to do bookkeeping for an existing company, there will already be a bookkeeping system and a filing system in place. Take some time to review the system and become familiar with it before you actually start using it.

If you walk into a new job and find the bookkeeping office messy and disorganized, it is in your best interest to take the time to clean it up and organize it properly. Bookkeepers often tell stories about the companies they had to put into order. Sorting through the mess often uncovers unpaid bills, undeposited checks and cash, and a multitude of other things that needed immediate attention.

PROCEED WITH CAUTION

 If you encounter an existing system that is a mess, study the checkbook and see what checks were written. Then search the office and make sure the checks were actually mailed out to the vendors so if a vendor calls and inquires about a payment, you can provide the correct information.

Bookkeeping is a precise, orderly process. Granted some businesses run at a fast pace, but chaos on the sales floor should not keep the bookkeeping system from running smoothly and efficiently if it is properly organized.

Personal Banking

An individual's bank account is where all the income and expenses of that person are recorded. Ideally, people should have a savings account and a checking account.

There are a lot of choices when it comes to savings accounts. Here are a few of the accounts you may want to consider for your excess funds.

- **Regular Savings Account:** Standard interest rates apply and there are usually no minimum balances.
- **Money-market Accounts:** Interest rates are based on short-term investments, such as Treasury Bonds. There are minimum balance requirements.
- **Individual Retirement Accounts (IRAs):** Intended to be long-term accounts to supplement retirement income. Tax credits may be available for yearly deposits and there are penalties and tax liabilities for withdrawing funds before the age of 59½.
- **Certificates of Deposit:** Interest rates are based on the amount of the balance and the term of the CD. Penalties exist for early withdrawal of funds.

FYI For more information on savings accounts, interest rates, and terms, contact your local bank or access information from either of these online banking sites: www.chase.com or www.bankofamerica.com.

Some checking accounts also pay interest on the average balance maintained month to month, but the main function of a checking account is to monitor cash flow, not to earn interest.

As noted in Hour 1, some banks do not encourage their customers to come into the bank to do business and you may want to avoid doing business with those types of financial institutions. This is especially true for people who have not organized their personal bookkeeping system.

Using ATMs to withdraw cash from your accounts is fine. If you don't have enough money to cover the withdrawal, the machine will refuse the request. It's the deposits you make to your savings or checking accounts that sometimes constitute a need to actually talk to a person, a live teller working inside the bank. One of those times is when you are depositing a check from an insurance company for a claim. Most of those checks are not credited to your account when they are deposited. Banks often put a hold on insurance claim checks and the bank's ATMs may not be equipped to advise you of that delay in crediting the amount of the check to your account.

Refunds of certain escrow amounts relating to real estate deals may also have a hold placed on them. Refunds of federal or state income tax are also checks that may require special endorsements or handling.

When you deposit a check like the ones just described, the teller will advise you of when the funds will actually be credited to your account. That means that you may not withdraw any portion of that deposit money or write checks against that amount until the holding period has ended and the amount has actually been credited to your bank account.

Consider the problems that could arise if you don't know there is a hold on a deposit you have put into your account. If for instance, you write a check against that amount and that check arrives at your bank before the holding period expires, your bank will return the check to the payee's bank for insufficient funds. Bank charges will accrue on both sides and everyone will be unhappy.

Another area that must be addressed in the area of personal banking is the misconception that exists regarding postdated checks. First of all, writing a postdated check is illegal. Secondly, postdating a check does not stop creditors from depositing that check into their bank accounts and does not stop your bank from charging the amount of the check against your account. Like the old "float" game discussed in Hour 1, postdated checks should never be written and mailed off; they only lead to trouble in the form of bank charges and late fees.

You should also monitor the checks you deposit into your account. If someone gives you a bad check it will be returned and charged back against your account and can result in additional bank fees as well.

PROCEED WITH CAUTION

 Be wary of any creditor who asks you to write a postdated check, and be suspicious of anyone who asks you to take a postdated check.

The bank you choose for your personal accounts should be convenient to your home or office. It should also be a bank that offers good customer service. That doesn't mean that the bank gives new customers a gift for opening an account. It means that the bank has employees who are ready and willing to answer questions and discuss quickly and courteously any problems that arise.

Work with a bank or credit union that offers the services that you need to monitor your own cash flow and keep track of your income and expenses. Some of the services that you should look for when choosing a bank include the following:

- No charges to use the bank's ATM.
- Monthly bank statements mailed to customers
- Online banking and bill-paying capabilities
- No fees on savings accounts regardless of the balance
- Reasonable fees on checking accounts
- Automatic transfers between savings and checking accounts to cover insufficient funds

Some of these services may or may not be important to you, but the last service is one that everyone should have set up with their bank. Automatic transfers between savings and checking accounts mean that if you should make a mistake and overdraw your checking account, the bank will automatically transfer the funds from your savings account to cover the overdraft. This avoids returned checks and the fees associated with them. Of course, you must have enough funds in the savings account to cover the needed transfer amount.

An individual's bank accounts are the primary components of a personal bookkeeping system. Check registers are actually a mini-set of financial books. Learn to use the check register to record every deposit and every check that is written. You must also record every ATM withdrawal from your checking account. If you use a *debit card*, you must enter the amounts you have charged against your account with the card each time you use it.

STRICTLY DEFINED

 A **debit card** is issued to you by your bank. You will also receive a personal identification number (PIN) that verifies that you are the one authorizing a debit card purchase. The debit card works like a credit card except that the amount of the purchase is instantly withdrawn from your checking or savings account.

Duplicate checks have been around for a while and they too can be useful tools in tracking your expenses. The original checks each have a carbon copy that is automatically filled in whenever you write a check.

Most banks no longer include copies of the checks that have cleared your account and appear on your monthly statement. Using duplicate checks provides you with those copies. However, a carbon copy of the check is not enough to prove that a bill has been paid, only a canceled check—the original check that was written by you and processed and canceled by the bank can do that.

GO TO ▶
Hour 10 to find more information on canceled checks.

Duplicate check copies are a convenient way to track expenses that are tax deductible, such as charitable donations and medical bills.

JUST A MINUTE

 Using duplicate checks and keeping your check register updated gives you quick access to your financial data. Going through the duplicates and pulling out items you paid for that are tax deductible provides an easy way to gather information for your annual tax return.

Keeping your check register up to date gives you a running total of your bank balance allowing you to keep a close watch on your personal cash flow.

Business Bank Accounts

Business bank accounts are basically the same as personal bank accounts. However, it is assumed that a business account has more activity and more money flowing in and out of it. Because banks use their depositors' money to make loans and investments that earn money for the bank, they often give business customers free checking accounts and some other services not extended to individuals. However, service charges on business accounts vary depending on the balances maintained and the activity in the business accounts.

Just as individuals should check out the services of a bank before opening an account, businesses should do the same and make sure the business services offered by the bank fit the company's needs.

Many banks have tellers who handle only deposits and other transactions of the bank's business customers. This makes a trip to the bank quicker as the business customer can bypass the line of people waiting to do their personal banking.

Night depository boxes are also important to companies that have business hours that extend past the time the bank is open to accept deposits. The bank provides numbered lock bags in which to place deposits that can then be put into an outside receptacle that drops the bag into the bank's vault. The following day, business tellers count and verify the deposit and issue deposit slips to the company showing the amounts that were added to the company's account. Of course the company's bookkeeper should have already double-checked the deposit and entered the amount in the company's check register.

For the convenience of some retail establishments, banks often use armored car services to deliver the change needed for cash registers directly to the stores and pick up the deposit bags containing the prior day's receipts when the change funds are delivered. Again the retail establishments' bookkeepers should have already verified the deposit amounts and entered them into the company's check register.

Of course there is a charge for the change service. The bookkeeper or head cashier tells the bank how much change is needed for each register and the type and quantity of the currency and coins needed. When the change is delivered it is ready to be placed in the cash registers, saving a lot of time and energy.

GO TO ▶

Hour 6 for instructions on how to balance a cash drawer at the end of the business day.

Most businesses strive to have a checking account where funds from sales or services are deposited and used to pay the liabilities and expenses of the business operation. If the business is profitable, it would also have one or more savings accounts. The types of accounts are the same as the ones previously listed and described for personal banking.

As you have learned, keeping a company's checking account updated is imperative, and it's the surest way to monitor cash flow and profitability.

Trust Accounts

Trust accounts are used by businesses that service clients, such as law firms and property management companies. They can be checking accounts, but they are separate from the checking and savings accounts that belong to the business.

Rental property owners often hire a property management firm to handle the rental property for them. The property management firm advertises the property, screens potential tenants, collects rents, and handles repairs and maintenance. The money collected from the tenants on the owners' behalf is deposited into the company's trust account and held for a predetermined period of time. In other words, the property owners are "trusting" the management company to collect and hold their money. The rents collected less the management fees are paid out to the owners on an agreed-upon date. Once all the rents are paid out, the property management company can transfer the management fees earned for that month into its operating account. Any security deposits or cleaning deposits are usually kept in the trust account until the current tenant moves out.

Trust accounts are often subject to audit by state authorities to ensure that they are in balance and that the funds accurately reflect the deposits shown on the company's books. For example, a property management company's trust account would be examined and audited by the Real Estate Commission in the state where its business is conducted.

Whether you are doing bookkeeping for yourself or are employed by a business, you will usually be the one who handles the bank accounts. Understanding the various accounts and their function within the bookkeeping system is important because it is the bank accounts that reflect the financial stability of an individual or a company.

Setting up books, files, and bank accounts for your personal finances or a business entity may seem a little daunting if you have had no prior experience. However, with some forethought and planning, the tasks can be accomplished with a minimum of effort. Remember, the purpose of a bookkeeping system is to record financial data and it does not have to be elaborate or complicated. It does have to be organized and updated regularly.

Hour's Up!

The following questions are a short review of the information provided in this chapter.

1. What is the Chart of Accounts?
    a. A list of customers
    b. A method to track sales
    c. A list of bookkeeping accounts

2. If a fiscal year begins on June 1, 2007, when does it end?
    a. May 31, 2008
    b. June 30, 2008
    c. December 31, 2007

3. What is the Capital account used for?
    a. Recording of funds needed for a new business
    b. Recording of profits
    c. Recording of sales

4. Cost of Sales accounts are directly related to the Expense accounts.
    a. True
    b. False

5. Banks usually place "holds" on deposits of
    a. Payroll checks
    b. Insurance claim checks
    c. Postdated checks

6. Income accounts are often broken down into specific categories.
    a. True
    b. False

7. When should you write a postdated check?
    a. When a creditor requests it
    b. When a bill is overdue
    c. Never

8. A debit card works exactly like a credit card.
    a. True
    b. False

9. What does IRA stand for?
    a. Internal Revenue Association
    b. Individual Retirement Account
    c. Interest Reduction Act

Review

10. A duplicate check is not the same as a canceled check.
   a. True
   b. False

The Balance Sheet Accounts

Chapter Summary

In this hour you will learn about …

- Assets
- Liabilities
- Equity

- Opening entry
- Net Worth

It is important to know and understand the different types of accounts that are used to record the day-to-day activities of a business. In the last hour, you learned how to set up accounts and files for two very simple business entities. This was a way to ease you into the process, as well as an introduction to the more complex structures of bookkeeping systems that are necessary for larger companies.

You have also reviewed the various types of bank accounts that are used for businesses and personal finances. Remember that the bank account is the center of all bookkeeping systems because it tracks the cash that flows in and out of the system providing an easy way to monitor the overall financial status of a business or household.

As you move forward in this book, you will find that each hour builds on the information previously presented. This design is to help you learn the basic procedures and tasks necessary to develop and maintain a bookkeeping system that can be expanded to suit the needs of a growing enterprise.

Assets

Assets are all the items of value owned by an individual or a business. While some of the assets are tangible holdings, such as cash and property, others are items that do not have a physical or material basis. For example, when a business is up for sale, the owners often add the account Goodwill to their list of Assets and assign a value to it. Potential buyers who examine the company's books see this account as a positive feature of the business enterprise. An intangible asset can simply be the good reputation earned by a business for treating its customers fairly. While this is not something that can be touched, it can be a valuable asset as it keeps existing customers coming back and recommending the business to others.

Because everyone wants to put their best foot forward, Assets are always listed first on a Balance Sheet beginning with the cash accounts. In a computerized system, the Asset accounts begin with the number 1000, and end with 1999. Most of the time all of the numbers in between that are not used as many items are grouped together into one account.

Here is a sample listing of accounts that may be found in the Asset section of a company's Balance Sheet. It includes the account numbers that would be in a computerized bookkeeping program.

Account Number	Name
1000	Cash in Checking
1010	Cash in Savings
1020	Cash on Hand
1100	Accounts Receivable
1200	Inventory
1350	Prepaid Expenses
1500	Land
1510	Buildings
1511	Accumulated Depreciation-Buildings
1570	Equipment
1571	Accumulated Depreciation-Equipment
1580	Furniture & Fixtures
1581	Accumulated Depreciation-Furniture & Fixtures
1650	Vehicles
1651	Accumulated Depreciation-Vehicles
1800	Deposits
1810	Other Assets
1850	Organizational Costs
1851	Accumulated Amortization-Organizational Costs

The sample list of accounts is standard for retail and wholesale operations and manufacturing companies. However, other than the Cash in Checking account, it contains accounts that may or may not be used by other types of businesses.

Remember that the nature of the business and the type of activity that takes place day-to-day and month-to-month determine the accounts that will be set up and used to record the financial data.

You have already received detailed information on the Cash in Checking account. Now, to give you an idea of how to pick and choose the other accounts that may be needed for a particular business, you need to understand what type of financial data would be recorded in each one listed on the sample.

Cash in Savings is used to hold excess funds not needed to operate the business. Deposits and withdrawals would be posted to this account.

Cash on Hand is the amount of change necessary to run the cash registers in a retail operation. It is usually a set amount that includes various currency denominations and coins. The actual money in the Cash on Hand account may be deposited and replaced on a daily basis, but the amount in the account doesn't change unless it is determined that more or less cash is needed for the registers. This account can also be used to record the amount of Petty Cash kept on hand for small expenditures.

GO TO ▶
Hour 15 to find a detailed explanation of the use and reconciliation of a petty cash fund.

Accounts Receivable is where all credit sales are recorded. If the business does not extend credit to its customers, this account would not be needed. Accounts Receivable is automatically included in the Balance Sheet accounts in a computerized system. It is considered a control account and cannot be deleted from the system. However, as long as the account is not used and has a zero balance it will not be included when a Balance Sheet is printed.

When credit sales are processed by a business, Accounts Receivable becomes as important as the cash accounts. The sales must be correctly posted to Accounts Receivable and ledgers must be set up for each customer that purchased merchandise or services on credit.

GO TO ▶
Hour 7 to learn the procedures and checks and balances needed to handle Accounts Receivable.

Inventory is the account where the total value of the products manufactured or held for sale or resale is recorded. The balance in this account should be updated as often as needed to keep track of the inventory on hand. Companies that manufacture or sell goods, raw materials, food, and products would need this account in their bookkeeping system.

Prepaid Expenses is an Asset account because it reflects money that has been paid out in advance for products or services. A good example of an expense that would be posted to this account is an annual insurance premium. If no advance payments have been made, this account is not needed.

Land with a building on it is usually priced as one real estate parcel. However, in the Balance Sheet accounts the two are valued separately because buildings can be *depreciated*, but land is never depreciated.

STRICTLY DEFINED

 Depreciation is a federal tax deduction for property used to produce income. There are rules and regulations that govern the useful life of an asset and how much can be deducted each tax year. Usually, the depreciation is calculated and written off monthly to make gathering the end of the year tax data easier.

The next four accounts are depreciable assets and each one is used to record the original cost of tangible property used in the business. Buildings, Equipment, Furniture & Fixtures, and Vehicles are all expensive items and the cost of these items is usually written off based on the tax rules and regulations.

GO TO ▶

Hour 15 to see how depreciation schedules are created and how this deduction affects the value of the Assets.

An account for Accumulated Depreciation is usually assigned to each of the depreciable assets as in the sample accounts. The amounts in the Accumulated Depreciation account are subtracted from the amount shown for the asset, thereby reducing its value on the Balance Sheet.

The account titled Deposits is used to record money paid in advance for rent, utilities, or other expenses. The difference between this account and Prepaid Expenses is that the amounts held for Deposits remain in the account until they are returned to the payer after a specified time period.

Other Assets is an account that can be included to record assets that do not fall into the other major categories.

Organizational Costs are mainly intangible assets, such as Franchise Fees or License Fees. Because these costs are often sizeable, they are written off over a longer period of time.

Only tangible property can be depreciated, but the costs of intangible assets can be amortized. Accumulated Amortization follows the asset it modifies in the Balance Sheet just as the Accumulated Depreciation accounts follow the depreciable asset accounts.

Assets are a vital part of the financial stability of any individual or company. They should be repaired and maintained as needed in order to make sure they keep their value.

Many assets are purchased on credit and the loan or credit agreement leads us to the next section of the Balance Sheet. Protecting the company or individual's asset includes the responsibility of handling the liability connected to it.

Liabilities

There are two types of *liabilities* and knowing the difference between the two types is just as important for an individual as it is for a business owner.

STRICTLY DEFINED

A **liability** is a loan or debt owed to a person or company. Automobile loans, mortgages, utility bills, and credit card debt are all liabilities. The person who has incurred the liability is called the payer, the person who collects on the liability is called the payee.

There are secured liabilities and unsecured liabilities. A secured liability is one that has an asset of value guaranteeing the repayment of the debt. A mortgage is a secured liability. Auto loans are secured liabilities.

With a secured liability the amount of the loan is usually dependent on the value of the asset. A house selling for $100,000. on the real estate market may be mortgaged for a percentage of that amount. The buyer's financial status and credit rating determine the loan to value ratio. For example, a qualified buyer may obtain a mortgage for $90,000. That means the buyer will only have to come up with a down payment of 10 percent on the house. The difference between the loan amount and the value of the asset is called equity and will be discussed in detail later in this hour. If a buyer or payer defaults on a secured loan the lender or payee can seize the property that guarantees that liability. This process is called repossession.

An unsecured liability is any loan or credit agreement that is not insured by an item of value. The most common unsecured loan is credit card debt.

The liability accounts in a computerized bookkeeping program are numbered from 2000 to 2999. The following chart includes the most commonly used liability accounts.

Account Number	Name
2000	Accounts Payable
2010	Credit Card-Visa
2090	Note Payable-Short Term
2100	Employee Health Insurance Payable
2105	Employee Dental Insurance Payable
2110	401k Payable
2120	Customer Security Deposits
2190	Sales Tax Payable
2200	Federal Withholding Tax Payable
2210	Social Security Tax Payable
2212	Medicare Tax Payable
2220	State Withholding Tax Payable
2280	FUTA Payable
2290	SUTA Payable
2300	Notes Payable-Long Term
2500	Corporation Taxes Payable
2900	Notes Payable-Officers

Again, the number of liability accounts listed on the company's Balance Sheet depends on how many outstanding debts the company is paying. If there are employees, liability accounts must be added to cover payroll taxes and employee benefit programs. With this in mind, let's examine the accounts in this example and explain when they are needed and what financial data is recorded in each.

Accounts Payable is an account used to record all products and services purchased on credit. This would include merchandise, raw materials, and expenses for rent, utilities, and supplies.

GO TO ▶

Hours 8 and 9 to learn more about Accounts Payable and how bills are processed through this account and posted into the bookkeeping system.

Credit Card accounts can be identified by the type of credit card used to make the purchases recorded in it. In the sample, we used Credit Card-Visa, but it could have been Credit Card-MasterCard or Credit Card-American Express. It could even be identified with the name of the bank that issued the credit card to the business or individual. This is a personal choice of the company or the bookkeeper that sets up the account on the books. The idea is to differentiate the accounts so that they are easily recognizable.

Note Payable-Short Term is used to record debts that are expected to be paid in full in a year or less. Like the credit card accounts, Note Payable can be identified by the name of the lender if desired.

The next three accounts, Employee Health Insurance Payable, Employee Dental Insurance Payable, and 401k Payable, are used to record benefits paid by the employer on behalf of the employees. In most cases the employees will also be contributing to these benefits and would do so through payroll deductions. In other words, these contributions would be subtracted from their Gross Wages along with payroll taxes. These accounts are used to separate these funds from the other company funds so that they can be tracked and paid out in a timely manner.

FYI A 401k is a retirement plan that is based on the contributions made by employees and can also receive funds from the employers. For more information, visit the 401k Help Center online at www.401Khelpcenter.com.

Customer Security Deposits is a liability for the business owner as the money collected and recorded in this account will have to be returned to the customer at some point in time. Rental agencies and utility companies are the primary users of this type of account.

Sales Tax Payable is used by retail outlets, restaurants, and any other business that is required to charge sales tax to its customers. The sales tax collected is recorded and held in this account until it is paid out to the city or state where business is conducted.

Payroll taxes must be collected and held by the employer so that the taxes can be remitted to the various government agencies according to the payment times set by those agencies. Some companies use a general account titled Payroll Taxes Payable and record all the taxes in that one account. However, it is much more efficient to have a separate liability account for each type of tax because it makes it easier to monitor the different types of tax and do the reports that must be filed with Federal, State, and Local taxing entities.

Federal Withholding Tax Payable is deducted from the employees' wages and recorded in this account.

Social Security Tax Payable is the United States government's mandated retirement and disability system. A percentage of employees' wages is calculated and deducted from their paychecks. The amounts are then recorded in this account. A matching amount must also be contributed by the employer and recorded in this account.

Medicare Tax Payable is part of the Social Security system and provides medical benefits to the retired or disabled. Like the Social Security tax it is based on a percentage determined by the Federal government and the employees' contribution must be matched by the employer who is obligated to remit the collected tax revenue in full and on time.

TIME SAVER

 There are a number of computerized payroll programs that allow the user to program in the tax rates so that all the employee and employer deductions are done automatically and the required tax reports are also generated by the computer at the designated time.

State Withholding Tax Payable is used to record the advance tax payments employees are required to make in states where there is a personal income tax.

FUTA stands for Federal Unemployment Tax and SUTA stands for State Unemployment Tax. These taxes must be paid by the employer. Both taxes are based on a certain percentage of the employees' wages and can be paid monthly or annually depending on the number of employees and the amount of the tax liability.

Notes Payable-Long Term is an account that holds the amount of a loan or debt that has a payback schedule longer than a year. An example of this type of debt would be a mortgage or an auto loan. Notes Payable is a generic term and often the liability account bears the name of the lender and specifies the type of loan, such as Auto Loan Payable-Sunset Bank. Again, these account titles are determined by the business owner or the bookkeeper and are used to make accounts easily identifiable.

Corporation Taxes Payable is an account that is used to record a company's tax liability at the end of the tax year even though the tax won't be paid until the next tax year. It's simply a way of recording an expense that applies to the year that is ending.

Often the owners of corporations invest funds into the business to get it started or to keep it going during a temporary financial crisis. This money is considered a loan to the company and is recorded in Notes Payable-Officers. Once the company is stabilized and profitable, the officer can withdraw the money without being subject to payroll taxes as this money was taxed when the officer earned it initially from other sources.

Liability accounts must be closely monitored and maintained so that the balances they hold are always current and payments are made in a timely manner. Individuals and companies often depend on loans or credit cards to maintain their financial stability. A good credit rating enables them to borrow funds when needed, and avoiding overdue bills and late charges protects that credit rating as well as the assets the liability has financed.

Equity

Equity accounts in a computerized system are numbered from 3000 to 3999. The following sampling lists the main accounts you would use in this third and final section of the Balance Sheet.

Account Number	Name
3010	Common Stock
3040	Retained Earnings
3210	Capital
3220	Drawing

An account for Common Stock is normally only found on the books of corporations that sell stock in the corporation in order to raise funds. The amount recorded in this account reflects the value of the stock issued to the stockholders.

Common Stock becomes more valuable as the issuing corporation becomes more profitable. It sometimes takes several years for stockholders to realize a gain or receive dividends on the stock purchased from a new corporation. If the corporation fails, the stock often becomes worthless.

Retained Earnings is the account where the net profit or loss realized from a company's operation is recorded and accumulated from month to month and year to year. Obviously, this is the account that reflects the overall financial strength of the company.

The initial investments put into a business to get it started and additional sums added during its operation are all recorded in the Capital account. Normally, these investments are in the form of cash but the value of other items, such as property or machinery needed to run the business, may also be recorded in this account.

The Drawing account is used to record any funds withdrawn by the owners or officers of a company.

Many businesses, especially partnerships, have Capital and Drawing accounts set up in the Equity sections for each partner or owner. This would make it possible for the bookkeeper to monitor each individual's investments and withdrawals.

The sample accounts do not include multiple accounts for officers and partners. This information and explanation is provided only to make you aware of what you could encounter if you were to work as a bookkeeper in a large corporation.

The Balance Sheet is the first financial report that can be generated by a new business. Even if the company has not yet begun operations it may still have Asset, Liability, and Equity accounts.

Opening Entry

A business that is just starting might have a Balance Sheet that looks like the following:

Assets:

Cash in Checking	$5,000.00
Equipment	$1,500.00
Inventory	$1,000.00
Total	$7,500.00

Liabilities & Equity:

Loan Payable-Sunset Bank	$3,000.00
Capital	$4,500.00
Total	$7,500.00

Note that the total Assets match the total Liabilities & Equity. The owner has started the business with $7,500. worth of Assets. Of that amount, $3,000. was borrowed from Sunset Bank and the balance of the funds were contributed by the owner.

It is also possible for individuals to prepare a similar report for their personal finances. Indeed, when you complete a loan application, you are sharing the same type of information that would be found on a Balance Sheet.

Net Worth

Individuals and all businesses, large or small, use some form of the Balance Sheet accounts to calculate their *Net Worth*. So, even if you are just organizing your own financial data, learning how this is done will be beneficial to you.

STRICTLY DEFINED

 Net Worth is the difference between the Assets and Liabilities of an individual or company. If your Liabilities are greater than your Assets, your Net Worth is zero.

To demonstrate how Net Worth is determined, let's study the Balance Sheet of a fictional bookstore, called Buy the Book.

Buy the Book
Balance Sheet
June 30, 2007

Assets:	
Cash in Checking	$6,100.00
Cash in Savings	$575.00
Cash on Hand	$100.00
Inventory	$15,000.00
Furniture & Fixtures	$3,300.00
A/D Furniture & Fixtures	$(800.00)
Total Assets	**$24,275.00**
Liabilities:	
Accounts Payable	$4,350.00
Credit Card-Visa	$900.00
Total Liabilities	**$5,250.00**
Net Worth	**$19,025.00**

Net Worth does not take the profitability of the bookstore into consideration. However, based on the fact that the store has sufficient funds in the checking account to meet the liabilities that have to be paid, it can be assumed that the bookstore is earning a profit.

The same type of report can be completed for individuals and, as mentioned earlier, is actually done every time a loan application is filled out. The following report is for a fictional couple, Martin and Mabel Mason, who are retired and own a home and two automobiles.

Martin and Mabel Mason
June 30, 2007

Assets:	
Cash in Checking	$940.00
Cash in Savings	$7,002.00
3-Bedroom Residence	$250,000.00

continues

(continued)

1999 Volvo	$2,500.00
2007 Ford Sedan	$21,565.00
Furniture	$5,600.00
Jewelry	$10,750.00
Other Assets	$3,000.00
Total Assets	$301,357.00

Liabilities:

Mortgage-Sunset Bank	$78,000.00
Auto Loan-Mira Bank	$15,725.00
Credit Card-Visa	$642.00
Credit Card-MasterCard	$1,351.00
Total Liabilities	$95,718.00
Net Worth	$205,639.00

Like the bookstore, the income and expenses of the Masons are not reflected in their statement of Net Worth.

Neither of these samples are a completed Balance Sheet because they don't report the monthly profit or loss generated by their income and expenses. An individual's or company's Net Worth is not the same as the Net Profit or Loss. In the next hour we will examine the accounts that are set up and used to calculate that.

The accounts included in the Balance Sheet section of the Financial Statements provide vital information. The stability of an individual or company is reflected by the value of their assets as opposed to the amount of debt incurred. The bookkeeper must monitor all the liability accounts to make sure they are updated properly when a payment is made so that the information on the Balance Sheet is current and correct.

GO TO ▶
Hour 16 to learn how the information for the Balance Sheet is gathered and reported during any given month.

Hour's Up!

Test the knowledge you gained in this chapter by answering the following questions.

1. Assets are the items of value owned by a company or individual.
   a. True
   b. False

2. What is an example of an intangible asset?
   a. Land
   b. Equipment
   c. Goodwill

3. What is depreciation?
   a. A reduction in sales
   b. A tax deduction
   c. A large expenditure

4. How does an account with a zero balance appear on the Balance Sheet?
   a. In brackets
   b. Last
   c. Not at all

5. What is an example of a secured loan?
   a. Mortgage
   b. Credit card debt
   c. Loan from a friend

6. What is a 401k?
   a. An expense account
   b. A safe deposit box
   c. A retirement plan

7. Retail operations collect and pay sales tax.
   a. True
   b. False

8. What happens to the common stock of a failed corporation?
   a. It is sold
   b. It becomes worthless
   c. It is redeemed

9. A Net Worth Statement is similar to what?
    a. A Profit & Loss Statement
    b. A Chart of Accounts
    c. A Balance Sheet

10. When is a short-term liability expected to be paid off?
    a. Two years
    b. Less than twelve months
    c. Five years

The Profit & Loss Accounts

Chapter Summary

In this hour you will learn about …

- Income accounts
- Cost of Sales accounts
- Selling Expenses
- General Expenses
- Other Income accounts
- Net Profit or Loss

The accounts a bookkeeper works with the most are the accounts contained within the second section of the Financial Statements. Along with the Cash in Checking account, these are the accounts where the majority of the day-to-day business transactions are recorded.

All the income generated by the business activity of an individual or company and all the costs and expenses incurred and paid out are posted to these accounts. The particular needs of the business entity are reflected in the type of accounts that are set up for the company or individual.

In Hour 2, you learned how to set up accounts and files for two very simple businesses. In this hour we will move on to review an expanded listing of accounts and explain the purpose of each within the bookkeeping system.

There can be up to five separate sections used in the Profit & Loss section of the Financial Statements. Once again, the number of sections and the types of accounts used are determined by the size of the company and the amount of detailed financial data desired by the principles of the business.

Income Accounts

The Income or Sales accounts are always listed first. The numbers for the Income accounts in a computerized system range from 4000 to 4299. Let's start with the accounts that would be listed for a business where the primary source of income is sales.

Account Number	Name
4000	Sales
4250	Sales Discounts
4270	Sales Returns & Allowances

In this example there is just one account to record the sales of all products and merchandise. However, like the home-based cake business in Hour 2, a number of sales accounts used to record sales of different products can be set up and used to provide more detail on the Financial Statements.

GO TO ▶

Hour 6 to learn how discounts and returns and allowances are posted and how they affect the Sales account.

The purpose of the next two accounts is to record adjustments that affect the Sales account. Sales Discounts is used to record any price reductions applied to the products or merchandise sold by the business. Sales Returns & Allowances captures refunds made to customers and may also be used to record special reductions in price due to damage or other circumstances that prevent the merchandise from being sold at the regular price.

If the primary business activity involves services rather than sales, Account Number 4000 would probably just be titled Income. Again, if the owner wants to track the income related to a variety of different services an account could be set up for each one. For example, an accounting firm might set up an Income account for General Accounting and another for Tax Return Preparations to monitor how much of the firm's income is earned from each activity.

Cost of Sales

The Cost of Sales accounts are directly related to the Income accounts. Therefore, in a computerized system the numbers assigned to these accounts are also within the 4000 range. The following is a list of some of the most common accounts used in this area of the financial system.

Account Number	Name
4300	Purchases
4310	Purchase Discounts
4320	Purchase Returns & Allowances

The account titled Purchases is used to record any of these transactions:

- The cost of merchandise intended for resale
- Raw materials used in the manufacture of goods
- Food products used in the restaurant business or used to prepare goods sold in grocery stores
- Any other purchases directly related to the sale or manufacturing of goods or products

Usually, businesses that derive their income from services to consumers do not have Cost of Sales accounts on their books.

Purchase Discounts and Purchase Returns & Allowances serve the same purpose in the Chart of Account to Purchases as the Sales Discounts and Sales Returns & Allowances do with the Sales accounts and are posted in the same way.

STRICTLY DEFINED

 Purchase Discounts are often extended by vendors to companies that pay their invoices within a specified time period, usually a 2 percent discount is allowed for invoices paid within 10 days. You may see 2/10 noted on an invoice to confirm these payment terms.

Selling Expenses

Numbers assigned to Selling Expenses are numbered from 5000 to 5999 in the computerized programs. However, these accounts are not always used because the same expenses can be included in the General Expenses section of the Profit & Loss accounts and others can be added to the Cost of Sales accounts.

The use of these accounts is usually determined by the owner of the company's personal preference in the way the financial data is presented at the end of the month or year.

The following is a list of accounts used to record expenses directly related to the Sales or Income accounts.

Account Number	Name
5000	Salaries-Sales
5050	Commissions
5100	Advertising
5150	Brochures & Catalogues
5230	Travel
5550	Miscellaneous Expense-Sales
5650	Payroll Taxes-Sales
5660	Freight & Delivery

Salaries-Sales would be used to record the salaries of the sales force only. Other employees' wages would be recorded in the General Expenses account for salaries and wages. It is much easier and more prudent to record all salaries in the General Expenses account. Having it all in one account eliminates the possibility of overlooking information needed for the payroll tax reports. The payroll ledgers can be noted as to which amounts are salary and which are commission checks and if desired a separate report could be issued from the ledgers.

Commissions would also be paid to the sales force personnel and would only be recorded in this special account if the company wanted it set up that way.

Some companies feel that the money spent on advertising is directly related to the income generated by sales. In that case, the Advertising account would be included in this area of the Chart of Accounts. Otherwise, it would be listed in the General Expense section. Advertising expenses can include a variety of items that promote a business venture, make the public aware of the company's products and services, and generally keep the company in the public eye.

The same is true for accounts titled Brochures & Catalogues, Travel, and Miscellaneous Expense-Sales. If the financial data recorded in these accounts is considered to be directly connected to Sales, the accounts would be listed as Selling Expenses instead of General Expenses.

Payroll Taxes-Sales is another account that really should be lumped into the General Expenses account for Payroll Taxes, but if the Salaries and Commissions accounts are set up in this section of the Profit & Loss accounts, the taxes related to those accounts should be here also.

If the books you manage are set up with separate payroll and payroll accounts for the sales force, take extra care when calculating the tax payments to make sure you have included all the data necessary to arrive at the correct amount to avoid penalties and interest charges.

The account for Freight & Delivery may be included in Cost of Sales, Selling Expenses, or General Expenses, but regardless of where it is located, it serves the same purpose. It holds the amounts paid for transporting merchandise either to or from the company.

Other accounts may be included in Selling Expenses at the discretion of the owners or officers of the business. Once you learn how an existing system is set up, you will be able to perform the required functions and tasks. However, if you are the person who initially sets up the bookkeeping system, keep it as simple and streamlined as possible. While certain information is nice to have at the end of the month, remember that your time and effort are valuable also. Setting up a system that is easy to manage may not provide as many financial details, but it will help you avoid errors and wasted time.

General Expenses

Account numbers for General Expenses range from 6000 to 6999 in a standard computer program. Many companies list these accounts in alphabetical order, but that is not necessary.

All the accounts covered under Selling Expenses can be included in the General Expenses section, but because they have already been explained, they will not be repeated in the sample list that follows.

Account Number	Name
6000	Salaries & Wages
6100	Auto Expenses
6120	Bank Service Charges
6140	Contributions
6150	Amortization Expense
6160	Depreciation Expense
6180	Dues & Subscriptions

continues

(continued)

Account Number	Name
6200	Equipment Rental
6220	Utilities
6230	Insurance-Employees Group
6240	Insurance-General
6250	Insurance-Officers Life
6255	401k Expense
6260	Interest Expense
6270	Legal & Accounting
6280	Miscellaneous Expense
6300	Office Expense
6310	Outside Services
6340	Postage Expense
6360	Rent Expense
6380	Repairs & Maintenance
6440	Supplies
6480	Real Estate Taxes
6490	Payroll Taxes
6500	Other Taxes
6520	Telephone
6540	Travel & Entertainment
6550	Bad Debts

As you can see, the General Expenses section contains a variety of accounts that apply to most businesses whether they are large corporations or small home-based operations. Although many of the account titles are familiar terms, let's look at them one at a time and briefly explain their purpose in the bookkeeping system. It is learning how and why each account is used to record certain data that allows you to work comfortably and confidently with them.

Salaries & Wages is used to record the gross earnings of all the company's employees. The gross wages are the amount an employee earns before taxes and other items are deducted.

GO TO ▶

Hour 11 to learn the procedures a bookkeeper must perform in order to meet the responsibilities and requirements related to employees.

Rather than post to separate accounts for expenditures related to company vehicles, such as gasoline, repairs, maintenance, and parking fees, all the expenses are posted to a catchall account, Auto Expenses. This account would also be used to post amounts reimbursed to employees for the use of their personal vehicles for business.

Bank Service Charges is obviously used to record any charges the bank imposes on the company bank accounts. If the company allows customers to pay for merchandise or services with credit cards, there will be additional charges for processing the credit cards through the bank. A separate account called Credit Card Fees could be set up to record those charges or they can just be posted to the Bank Service Charges account.

Gifts to charities are tax deductible for individuals and businesses and the account titled, Contributions, is used to keep track of these donations.

Amortization Expense and Depreciation Expense are the accounts that work in connection with the Accumulated Amortization and Depreciation accounts in the Balance Sheet. Instructions for posting to these accounts will be covered in the next hour.

Many business people belong to organizations that allow them to network with potential customers or provide information that helps them learn more about their business and issues related to it. The membership costs associated with these organizations and any printed materials are recorded in the Dues & Subscriptions account.

Renting equipment from outside sources is sometimes necessary and the rental fees for this expense are posted to Equipment Rental.

Utilities can be another generic account where all the bills incurred for electricity, water, and gas are posted. Some companies have a separate account for each utility, but that is not necessary.

There are three insurance accounts included in many bookkeeping systems. They are Insurance-Employees Group where the cost of any insurance plans that benefit the employees is recorded. Insurance-General is for the costs related to any type of liability insurance, fire insurance, and general business insurance. Insurance-Officers Life is often paid for by the company because the loss of an officer can cause a reduction in revenue for the company. This is especially true in small firms where only one or two people are depended on to produce most of the income.

As explained previously, a 401k is a retirement plan that covers employees. Employer contributions to the plan are an expense to the company and would be recorded in this account along with any administration fees.

While the principle payments on mortgages or other loans are not a deductible expense to an individual or business, the interest paid on such liabilities is deductible. Interest Expense is used to record the interest that is calculated and paid on the debt.

Legal & Accounting is the account where the expense related to the services of lawyers and accountants is posted.

Miscellaneous Expense covers a broad area of small incidental expenditures for supplies and services.

Office Expense is self-explanatory. The cost of supplies needed to run the office are posted to this account.

Outside Services is an account that may or may not be used. The cost for temporary workers who perform a necessary function for the business would be included under this account heading.

Any mailing expenses may be posted to a separate account, titled, Postage Expense. However, if there is not a large expenditure for postage, it is often recorded in the account for Office Expense.

The Rent Expense account would only be used by companies that do not own the property where their business operation is located.

TIME SAVER

 If the company conducts business from rented facilities, there will usually be a lease in force. This is a legal document that may have to be referred to on a regular basis, so it should be kept in a special file where it is easily accessible.

Repairs & Maintenance can be used to keep track of any expenses for work that is done to fix and care for buildings and equipment owned by the company. This could include such things as landscaping and refuse services.

Supplies is another one of those broad accounts that can be used to record the cost of business items that don't fall into one of the other account categories.

Real Estate Taxes is used to record taxes on land or buildings used for the business. However, if the property is mortgaged these taxes would be paid by the financing institution and included in the monthly payment. That's not to say that the amount of the real estate taxes could not be isolated from the principle, interest, and insurance and recorded in this account each month.

Payroll Taxes is the account where the expenses an employer incurs in relation to the wages paid to the company's workers are posted.

Some states impose a Personal Property tax on business property such as equipment, computers, and furniture. Other Taxes would be the place to post any miscellaneous taxes such as that.

JUST A MINUTE

 Some states, like Arizona, calculate the annual license fees based on the value of a vehicle. This is considered Personal Property Tax and the amount is a tax-deductible expense for individuals as well as businesses.

Most businesses cannot operate without telephone service. The Telephone account receives the posting for all the expenses local and long distance related to the company's phone service.

Travel & Entertainment is another deductible business expenditure. All costs for these activities are recorded in the designated account. However, keep in mind that Internal Revenue Service has restrictions on how much can be deducted on the company's annual tax return.

The last account shown on our list is labeled Bad Debts. Businesses who extend credit to their customers may find it impossible to collect from some people and will have to write off the uncollected amounts as Bad Debts.

GO TO ▶
Hour 15 to read instructions for handling and posting Bad Debts.

Other Income

The last group of accounts that can be found within the Profit & Loss section of the Chart of Accounts is not always used. It is presented here so that if you step into a position with an established bookkeeping system that includes this group you will recognize the accounts and understand their purpose. If these accounts were used in a computerized program they would range from 7000 to 7300.

Account Number	Name
7030	Interest Income
7100	Finance Charge Income

Both Interest Income and Finance Charge Income are usually included in the 4000 accounts established for income in general. Interest Income is where any interest earned on bank accounts is posted. Finance Charge Income would be a main income account for credit card companies and various lending institutions.

For a simpler bookkeeping system, these accounts should be moved and reclassified as regular Income accounts. However, if they are already established in an existing system, working with them should be no problem. The main difference will be the place the amounts in them print out on the Financial Statements.

One final account should be mentioned before we leave this section, and that is Account Number 9999 Temporary Distributions. This account does not often appear in a bookkeeping system but it can be added any time it is needed. The purpose of the Temporary Distributions account is to post an entry for income or expenses that have not yet been categorized within the bookkeeping system.

PROCEED WITH CAUTION

 Using the Temporary Distributions account can lead to problems if it is not noted that the amounts posted there are indeed temporary and need to be reposted to the correct accounts as soon as possible.

The Balance Sheet accounts and the Profit & Loss accounts make up the Chart of Accounts in any bookkeeping system. For the most part the accounts presented are in the proper order, but remember that the Chart of Accounts is there to provide the financial information needed by the individual or company. Therefore, accounts can be added, deleted, and moved (with some restrictions) to suit the needs and specifications of the business.

Net Profit or Loss

The profit or loss of a company is determined by totaling the Income accounts and then subtracting the amounts posted to the Cost of Sales accounts and the Expense accounts. If Other Income accounts are used they would be added to the profit or loss at the end of the statement rather than being added in with the main Income accounts.

If the income exceeds the cost of sales and expenses, the statement will show a profit. If the costs and expenses are more than the income, the end result will be a loss. You will see samples of other combined Financial Statements with a Balance Sheet and a Profit & Loss Statement later in this book as you study the bookkeeping procedures for more complex businesses.

To conclude this lesson, study the following sample of a Profit & Loss Statement for the home-based cake company. This report is often referred to and titled an Income Statement.

Cakes by Claire
Profit & Loss Statement
July 31, 2007

Sales		
Birthday Cakes	$650.00	
Wedding Cakes	$600.00	
Anniversary Cakes	$50.00	
Miscellaneous Cakes	$300.00	
Total Income	$1,600.00	
Cost of Sales		
Baking Ingredients	$345.00	
Decorating Supplies	$62.00	
Boxes and Platters	$48.00	
Total Cost of Sales	$455.00	
Gross Profit	$1,145.00	
Expenses		
Advertising	$25.00	
Delivery Expense	$40.00	
Equipment	$30.00	

continues

(continued)

Office Expense	$5.00
Miscellaneous Supplies	$3.00
Telephone Expense	$38.00
Website	$23.00
Total Expenses	$164.00
Net Profit (Loss)	$981.00

Notice that the Gross Profit of the business for July is obtained by subtracting the Total Cost of Sales from the Total Income. The Net Profit is obtained by subtracting the Total Expenses from the Gross Profit.

In the next hour, you will learn how to work within the bookkeeping system and see how all the day-to-day business transactions are handled, posted, and reported.

Hour's Up!

The Profit & Loss Statement accounts are many and varied. See if you can answer the following questions about them.

1. Sales Discounts and Sales Returns and Allowances adjust the balance in the Sales Accounts.
   a. True
   b. False

2. Which accounts are usually not needed for a service business?
   a. Selling Expenses
   b. Cost of Sales
   c. Other Income

3. Which of the following accounts could be categorized as Selling Expenses or General Expenses?
   a. Bank Service Charges
   b. Utilities
   c. Advertising

4. All expenses for Travel & Entertainment are tax deductible.
   a. True
   b. False

5. What portions of a mortgage payment are tax deductible?
  a. Interest and taxes
  b. Principle and interest
  c. Late fees and principle

6. Which expenses can be posted to the Repairs & Maintenance account?
  a. Interest
  b. Landscaping
  c. Legal fees

7. What account is used to post delinquent customer accounts?
  a. Bad Debts
  b. Sales Returns and Allowances
  c. Cost of Sales accounts

8. All the accounts under Selling Expenses could be listed under General Expenses instead.
  a. True
  b. False

9. The Gross Profit on the Cakes by Claire Profit & Loss Statement is obtained by subtracting
  a. Total Expenses from Total Income
  b. Cost of Sales from Total Expenses
  c. Cost of Sales from Total Income

10. How many sections can be included in the Profit & Loss Statement accounts?
  a. Three
  b. Five
  c. Four

Working Within the Bookkeeping System

Chapter Summary

In this hour you will learn about …

- Adding and deleting accounts
- Debits and credits
- Posting daily transactions
- Cash and accrual accounts
- Related accounts
- Posting monthly adjustments

You now have a general idea of how to set up the basic accounts and files for a bookkeeping system. You have also become familiar with the different types of bank accounts that can be used to handle the money that flows in and out of a business or an individual's household.

The Chart of Accounts for general business activities has been presented with explanations of these accounts and how and why they function within a bookkeeping system. Remember that once the Chart of Accounts has been created it becomes the General Ledger. The next step is learning more about the procedures that enable a bookkeeper to manage the General Ledger.

You may have already heard some of the terms defined in the following pages. You may have also performed some of the tasks described. From this point on, you should think of these basic tasks as the bookkeeper's tools. Implementing them will keep your books and financial data in balance and in order.

Adding and Deleting Accounts

The accounts initially set up in a bookkeeping system can be altered to meet the changing needs of a business. If a company takes on a new liability, an account can be set up in the Balance Sheet section to record the amount of the liability and the checks written to reduce it. The same is true for all sections of the Chart of Accounts. The bookkeeper can add accounts at any time.

Deleting accounts can be done at any time in a manual system, but in a computerized system there are safeguards built into the program that often prevent the bookkeeper from deleting certain accounts. This is not a problem as there are many accounts automatically set up in a computerized system that are not needed. As long as there are no amounts posted to the account, they remain dormant and will not affect any part of the bookkeeping system.

Debits and Credits

In the world of bookkeeping, every transaction posted into the General Ledger must have debits and credits of equal value. Because the books should always be kept in balance, it is necessary to make sure that all the credits in the system equal all the debits in the system. Debits are considered plus figures (+); credits are minus figures (–). So, when the debits are added and the credits subtracted the end result should be zero.

GO TO ▶

Hour 17 to learn more about the Trial Balance that reports the balances of all the accounts in the General Ledger. If the books are in balance the ending total on this report will be zero.

To maintain the perfect balance, every transaction posted as a credit to an account must also be posted as a debit to another account. In other words, each posting will have two sides to it so that one side of the transaction offsets the other side of the transaction. The term "double-entry bookkeeping" is derived from this concept. The trick is to learn which accounts should receive the credits and which accounts should receive the offsetting debits.

Generally speaking, income accounts used to record all the money that comes into the business or household from sales or services should have a credit balance. The accounts used to record the money going out of the system should have a debit balance.

This brings us back to the bank accounts reviewed in the last hour. Also, as you may recall, the first account set up in either a sales or service business is the one labeled Cash in Checking. Whenever you are posting cash transactions, Cash in Checking (or Cash in Bank, as it is sometimes titled) is the account where the offsetting amount is normally posted.

Here is the Chart of Accounts discussed in Hours 3 and 4 with a notation next to each account that shows whether the account is expected to have a debit or credit balance within the General Ledger.

Balance Sheet Accounts

Assets

Cash in Checking-Debit
Cash in Savings-Debit
Cash on Hand-Debit
Accounts Receivable-Debit
Inventory-Debit
Prepaid Expenses-Debit
Land-Debit
Buildings-Debit
Accumulated Depreciation-Buildings-Credit
Equipment-Debit
Accumulated Depreciation-Equipment-Credit
Furniture & Fixtures-Debit
Accumulated Depreciation-Furniture & Fixtures-Credit
Vehicles-Debit
Accumulated Depreciation-Vehicles-Credit
Deposits-Debit
Other Assets-Debit
Organizational Costs-Debit
Accumulated Amortization-Org. Costs-Credit

Liabilities

Accounts Payable-Credit
Credit Card-Visa-Credit
Note Payable-Short Term-Credit
Employee Health Insurance Payable-Credit
Employee Dental Insurance Payable-Credit
401k Payable-Credit
Deposits-Credit
Sales Tax Payable-Credit
Federal Withholding Tax Payable-Credit
Social Security Tax Payable-Credit
Medicare Tax Payable-Credit
State Withholding Tax Payable-Credit
FUTA Payable-Credit
SUTA Payable-Credit
Notes Payable-Long Term-Credit

Corporation Taxes Payable-Credit
Notes Payable-Officers-Credit

Equity

Common Stock-Credit
Retained Earnings-Credit
Capital-Credit
Drawing-Debit

Profit & Loss Statement Accounts

Income

Sales-Credit
Sales Discounts-Debit
Sales Returns & Allowances-Debit

Cost of Sales

Purchases-Debit
Purchase Discounts-Credit
Purchase Returns & Allowances-Credit

Sales/Direct Expenses

Salaries Sales-Debit
Commissions-Debit
Advertising-Debit
Brochures & Catalogues-Debit
Travel-Debit
Miscellaneous Expense Sales-Debit
Payroll Taxes-Sales-Debit
Freight & Delivery-Debit

General Expenses

Salaries & Wages-Debit
Auto Expenses-Debit
Bank Service Charges-Debit
Contributions-Debit
Amortization Expense-Debit
Depreciation Expense-Debit
Dues & Subscriptions-Debit
Equipment Rental-Debit

Utilities-Debit
Insurance-Employees Group-Debit
Insurance-General-Debit
Insurance-Officers Life-Debit
401k Expense-Debit
Interest Expense-Debit
Legal & Accounting-Debit
Miscellaneous Expense-Debit
Office Expense-Debit
Outside Services-Debit
Postage Expense-Debit
Rent Expense-Debit
Repairs & Maintenance-Debit
Supplies-Debit
Real Estate Taxes-Debit
Payroll Taxes-Debit
Other Taxes-Debit
Telephone-Debit
Travel & Entertainment-Debit
Bad Debts-Debit

Other Income

Interest Income-Credit
Finance Charge Income-Credit

In general you should realize that most of the Asset accounts are debits, and the Liability and Equity accounts are credits. That allows the total Assets to be offset by the Liability and Equity accounts, hence the name of the report is the Balance Sheet.

JUST A MINUTE

 The Accumulated Depreciation accounts in the Assets section have credit balances because their purpose is to reduce the value of the Asset for tax purposes. However, when you subtract the Accumulated Depreciation from the Asset it modifies, you will still have a debit balance for the Asset.

The accounts in the Profit & Loss section of the General Ledger do not offset each other. Their purpose, as you learned previously, is to calculate a Net Profit or Loss. Therefore, the Income accounts are credit accounts and all the accounts that would reduce that income are debit accounts.

A good way to remember what gets posted as a credit and what gets posted as a debit is to think about the two most common business or personal transactions and their effect on the balance in the checking account.

The Cash in Checking account in the General Ledger should always be a debit. If in reality a bank account in the General Ledger has a credit balance, it means the account is overdrawn and you may be in financial trouble. Deposits to the bank account are debits as they should increase or add to the debit balance already there. Checks written from the bank account are credits as they decrease the amount of money in the account. So, when posting a cash transaction it follows that a debit (deposit) to the bank should be offset with a credit to another account. A credit (a check or a withdrawal) to the bank account should be offset with a debit to another account in the General Ledger.

The following are simple examples of daily business transactions and how they would be recorded in the General Ledger. The owner of Cakes by Claire delivers an anniversary cake and collects $100. for it. The money is deposited into the company's checking account and recorded as follows:

Cash in Checking

Date	Description	Debit	Credit
2-1-07	Deposit	100.00	

Sales-Anniversary Cakes

2-1-07	Johnson-Cake		100.00

Note that the money collected for the anniversary cake has been recorded in two different accounts. One account receives a debit entry, the other a credit entry so that when the two postings are added together they equal zero. Also, note that one of the accounts posted, Cash in Checking, is a Balance Sheet account, while the Sales account falls under the Income section of the Profit & Loss accounts.

A few days later, the owner of the cake company writes a check to pay for the plastic forks sometimes supplied to customers. The check would be recorded on the books as follows:

Cash in Bank

Date	Description	Debit	Credit
2-4-07	Check # 2800		22.00

Miscellaneous Supplies

Date	Description	Debit	Credit
2-4-07	Check # 2800	100.00	

Some transactions require that amounts be posted to more than two accounts. This does not alter the rule that the debits posted must equal the credits. Note that the description entered on both General Ledger accounts refers to the number of the check written for the payment.

Assume that the owner of the cake company goes to a wholesaler and purchases decorating supplies and boxes for the business. One check is written for all the merchandise purchased and would be recorded on the books as follows:

Cash in Bank

Date	Description	Debit	Credit
2-8-07	Check # 2801		36.00

Decorating Supplies

Date	Description	Debit	Credit
2-8-07	Check # 2801	26.00	

Boxes and Platters

Date	Description	Debit	Credit
2-8-07	Check # 2801	10.00	

Note that the two Cost of Sales accounts that are debited equal the amount of the credit posted to the bank account.

PROCEED WITH CAUTION

 Don't be confused by the fact that your bank will refer to the deposits you make as credits to your account and checks or withdrawals as debits. That's because in the bank's bookkeeping system the money coming in is considered income to the bank (a credit account) and the money going out is an expense (a debit account).

Cash and Accrual Accounts

So far, all the transactions have been cash transactions involving money coming in or going out of the checking account. Some businesses operate on a cash basis. This means that the income shown on their books has already been received and put into their bank account. It also means that the expenses that reduce that income have already been paid out of the bank account.

Usually cash-basis bookkeeping systems are used by smaller enterprises that do not extend credit to their customers and do not seek credit from their suppliers. However, most businesses today operate on what is called an accrual basis. The accrual form of bookkeeping allows a company to recognize income and expenses before the money has actually been received or paid out. Under this type of bookkeeping a sale is posted into the General Ledger as income even though the money has not been deposited into the bank account. The same is true for expenses that are deducted from the income before they have actually been paid out of the bank account.

There are specific General Ledger accounts that must be included and used to accommodate the accrual system of bookkeeping. In the Chart of Accounts and General Ledger just reviewed, the accrual accounts will be found in the Balance Sheet section.

In the Asset section, the main accrual account is Accounts Receivable. The total in this account reflects the total of credit sales that are outstanding. In other words, these are sales that have been recognized as income even though the customers have not yet remitted the money for them.

In the Liability section there are a number of accrual accounts. They all have the words "payable" or "accrued" in their title. The balances in these accounts reflect amounts that have been posted into the General Ledger, but have yet to be paid out of the bank account.

GO TO ▶

Hour 19 to review specific information and instructions for filing business tax returns for both cash and accrual basis bookkeeping systems.

Take some time to review the Chart of Accounts listed in this hour and note that receivable accounts carry a debit balance, while payable or accrual accounts should carry credit balances in the General Ledger.

A cash or accrual bookkeeping preference is accepted by the IRS as the method used to calculate taxable income. There is a place on the tax forms where the taxpayer indicates which method was employed for that tax year.

Related Accounts

When you are reviewing the Chart of Accounts list, you should see the connection that exists between accounts in the Balance Sheet sections with accounts in other areas of the General Ledger. Most of the related accounts share similar account titles making it easier to match them up.

Accumulated Depreciation accounts are connected to Depreciation Expense. These might also be considered accrual accounts, if the depreciation expense is written off monthly. However, because the depreciation expense is determined by government rules and regulations, it does not always provide an accurate value of the assets eligible for this tax deduction.

For example, according to the government rules, a building can be depreciated. That is, the cost of the building can be written off over a specified time period. This write-off reduces the tax liability of the owner. It also reduces the value of the building as reported on the Balance Sheet, when in reality the building may have grown in value as most real property does if it is properly maintained. For this reason, many companies do not post the Accumulated Depreciation or the Depreciation Expense into the General Ledger until the end of the tax year.

Also, remember that for accounting purposes, the original cost of the building is retained on the Balance Sheet regardless of whether the property has become more valuable over time.

Let's assume the company is writing off the depreciation on an annual basis. For this sample, we'll use Accumulated Depreciation-Equipment to show how the posting would be done for these two related accounts.

Accumulated Depreciation-Equipment

Date	Description	Debit	Credit
12-31-07	2007 Write-Off		352.00

Depreciation Expense

Date	Description	Debit	Credit
12-31-07	2007 Write-Off	352.00	

Be aware that each Accumulated Depreciation account would be posted separately, but the total of all four of them could be posted to Depreciation Expense in a lump sum.

GO TO ▶

Hour 15 where information on the rules that govern the Depreciation Expense are explained and samples of Depreciation Schedules can be found.

GO TO ▶

Hour 12 where you'll find explanations and samples showing how to post payroll checks.

TIME SAVER

 In a computerized system the entry to post Depreciation Expense on a monthly basis can be set up as a recurring entry. That means at the end of each month, it would be automatically posted by the computer to the proper accounts.

The work associated with Depreciation Expense is normally done by the tax accountant at the end of the tax year. However, a bookkeeper should be familiar with the terms and understand how to post the information set up on the Depreciation schedules that will exist for each Asset.

Accumulated Amortization and Amortization Expense are two more accounts that are related. These accounts exist so the costs of intangible assets, those that can't be depreciated, can be written off over time.

Employee Health Insurance Payable and Employee Dental Insurance Payable are related to the account in the General Expense section, Insurance-Employees Group.

401k Payable is related to 401k Expense account and is handled like the insurance accounts. All the accrual accounts for Payroll are related to the Payroll Expense account. The payroll deductions that cover the employees' portion of the benefits are posted when the payroll checks are issued during the month.

Posting Monthly Adjustments

At the end of the month, the employer's portion of the benefits is posted to the accrual accounts so it can be expensed in the month it is incurred even though the benefit payments will not be made until after the first of the following month. The entry to post the employer's expense for the 401k accounts would be posted like the following example:

401k Payable

Date	Description	Debit	Credit
2-28-07	Employer Portion		2,356.00

401k Expense

2-28-07	Employer Portion	2,356.00	

When the check is issued to make the 401k payment the entry to post the check will be a credit of $2,356.00 to Cash in Checking and a debit to 401k Payable to clear the accrual amount from that account.

It is very important when posting checks for accrued expenses to post the debit to the accrual account, not the expense account where it has already been posted. That would double the amount of the expense for that year and reduce the company's Net Profit in error.

 After an expense has been posted as an accrual it is a good idea to make a notation on the invoice showing where the check should be posted when the payment of that invoice is made the following month. This will help you avoid posting the payment to the expense account twice.

There are often several adjustments that must be made on the books at the end of the month. The bookkeeper should take the extra time needed to make sure that all the adjustments are made before issuing the Financial Statements.

Computerized programs enable the bookkeeper to go back and forth between the current month and the past month to make entries into the General Ledger. This allows you to work in the current month while waiting for the bank statements or other data to close out the prior month and issue accurate Financial Statements.

Hour's Up!

To see if you have retained the information presented in this hour, try to answer the following questions without referring back to the text.

1. If the Cash in Bank account in the General Ledger has a credit balance, it indicates that the account is overdrawn.
   - **a.** True
   - **b.** False

2. When does an accrual basis bookkeeping system recognize income?
   - **a.** At the end of the month
   - **b.** When the sale occurs
   - **c.** When the customer pays the bill

3. The term "double-entry bookkeeping" is derived from posting what?
   - **a.** Two transactions at once
   - **b.** The same entry two times
   - **c.** The debit and credit sides of a transaction

Review

4. When all the account balances in the General Ledger are added up, the result should be …
   a. A debit balance.
   b. A credit balance.
   c. A zero balance.

5. The IRS only accepts the cash bookkeeping method on tax returns.
   a. True
   b. False

6. Why is Accumulated Deprecation listed after an asset?
   a. It modifies the value of the asset
   b. So it can be written off monthly
   c. It saves time

7. The accounts in the Profit & Loss section of the General Ledger do not offset each other.
   a. True
   b. False

8. The Balance Sheet accounts include …
   a. Income and Expenses.
   b. Cost of Sales and Accounts Payable.
   c. Assets, Liabilities, Equity.

9. The Chart of Accounts is a list of accounts that becomes …
   a. The Profit & Loss Statement.
   b. The General Ledger.
   c. The Net Worth of the Company.

10. Posting a cash sale should be done by …
    a. Debit to Sales, Credit to Cost of Sales.
    b. Credit to Sales, Debit Accounts Receivable.
    c. Credit to Sales, Debit to Cash in Bank.

Procedures for Keeping Accounts Updated and in Balance

Cash Receipts and Sales Tax

Chapter Summary

In this hour you will learn about …

- Handling cash sales
- Sales tax
- Balancing the cash register
- Posting the sales
- Adjustments to sales
- Depositing cash receipts

As the bookkeeper in a retail operation, you may not be the first person who handles the cash receipts. However, you may be the person who supervises the cashier and you will be the person responsible for recording the sales and making the bank deposits.

Depending on the size of the retail operation, the cash may flow through one simple cash drawer or multiple electronic cash registers. Regardless of how it is initially collected, there should be a system in place with checks and balances that minimize errors and discourage dishonesty.

The term "cash receipts" covers all forms of revenue. Cash, checks, and credit card purchases will flow from the initial *point of sale* to the bookkeeper.

STRICTLY DEFINED

 The **point of sale** is the place in the retail operation where customers actually pay for the merchandise they purchase.

Handling Cash Sales

Most large retail stores have electronic cash registers. These registers are actually computers programmed to categorize the merchandise as it is scanned or rung up. These modern-day marvels add up the cost of each item, calculate the sales tax, and may even deduct the item from the store's inventory classification.

At the end of the day, the cash register can print out a detailed report of every item sold and every cent that was collected. Obviously, this makes the bookkeeper's job much easier but does not lessen his or her responsibility to deposit and record the cash receipts properly.

The cash register also has the ability to process and get approval for any credit cards that have been presented for payment. Keep in mind that only purchases that are paid for with a credit card that was issued to customers by the retail store where the merchandise is purchased are considered credit sales. All other credit card sales are considered cash sales for the store. For example, if a customer is paying for merchandise with a Sears charge card in a Sears store, that is a credit sale to the store because Sears has not yet collected the money for that sale. If the customer is making a purchase in Sears with a bank-issued credit card, such as Visa or MasterCard, that is a cash sale to Sears because the register or cashier will process the credit card and the amount of the sale will be deposited directly into the Sears bank account.

JUST A MINUTE

 Credit card processing can be done in a number of different ways. Some smaller business entities do not have a credit card processing and deposit agreement with their banks. Instead the bookkeepers have computer software they use to process credit cards through a third party that verifies the cards, approves the amounts, and then sends the money for the sale to the merchants' bank accounts.

The report generated by the computerized register may total each type of sale separately or may give one grand total for all the cash sales processed through that register. Sales tax collected should be totaled in its respective categories as that is not income for the company, but money that belongs to the State or Local Department of Revenue.

The procedures for verifying the sales and the cash collected for them is the same whether you have one point of sale or twenty. The reports and cash from each point of sale must be reviewed and checked individually even if all the sales figures will eventually be added together to be posted on the books.

Remember that some retail stores are open in the evenings. Often the registers are closed out after the bookkeeper has left for the day. The reports are run and put into a safe or vault with the receipts from that register. This means that the bookkeeper may be reviewing and verifying the money on the next business day. Again, this does not alter the procedure for handling the cash receipts.

Because the size of the retail operation does not alter the procedure a bookkeeper should use to verify and handle the cash sales, we will use a small clothing store as a sample company. The following is a sales report generated by the cash register at On the Rack, a clothing store.

On the Rack
September 6, 2007

Item	# Sold	Total Cost	Sales Tax State	Local	Total
Dress	1	59.00	2.95	1.18	63.13
Skirt	3	44.85	2.25	.90	48.00
Skirt	1	16.50	.83	.33	17.66
Blouse	2	19.90	1.00	.39	21.29
Dress	2	78.00	3.90	1.56	83.46
Blouse	1	18.00	.90	.36	19.26
Blouse	1	12.95	.65	.26	13.86
Dress	1	21.95	1.10	.44	23.49
Skirt	1	8.95	.45	.18	9.58
Blouse	4	71.95	3.60	1.44	76.99
Dress	1	39.95	2.00	.80	42.75
Totals	18	392.00	19.63	7.84	419.47

The first thing the bookkeeper should do after viewing this report is count the cash, checks, and credit cards processed for that day and verify that the money collected matches the total sales shown on the report.

Once that is verified, the bookkeeper would go back over the report and categorize the sales to correspond with Sales accounts set up in the General Ledger. A more sophisticated cash register would provide that information, but you should be able to do it manually as well.

The recap figures should be noted on the register report. In this case, they would be as follows.

Posting Recap:

Dresses	198.90	
Skirts	70.30	
Blouses	122.80	
	392.00	
State Sales Tax		19.63
City Sales Tax		7.84
Total		27.47

Again, the sales tax amounts are shown separately from the sales' figures as sales tax will be posted to a liability account not an income account.

Sales Tax

All retail outlets are required to charge sales tax on the merchandise they sell. As mentioned earlier, the sales tax is not income to the company. Collecting and remitting sales taxes are obligations that companies and individuals must fulfill in order to be licensed to conduct business in their city and state.

Each state sets its own tax rates and cities within that state do the same. In the example we are using, the state sales tax rate is 5 percent and the city tax rate is 2 percent.

PROCEED WITH CAUTION

 Sales tax rates vary from state to state and from city to city. Always check with Revenue Departments of your state and city to make sure you have current rate information and are collecting the proper amount of tax. Fines and penalties are assessed for failure to pay the taxes correctly.

GO TO ▶
Hour 9 to learn how Sales Tax Reports are completed and how the tax is remitted.

Sales tax is accumulated on all retail sales from the first day of the month through the last day of the month. Taxes collected for one month are usually reported and paid around the 15th of the following month. It is also possible to report and pay sales taxes quarterly, semi-annually, or annually if the business entity is small or seasonal. Your state or local revenue departments will determine how your sales tax must be reported and paid based on the amount of sales processed by your company.

In some states, there are two tax reports that must be filed. One goes to the state with their share of the tax collected and the other goes to the city for the portion of the tax that belongs to them.

Balancing the Cash Drawer

The most efficient way to verify that the cash register or cash drawer is in balance is to have a balance sheet or cash verification sheet made up and used for each point of sale. In some instances, the cashier or the supervising cashier counts the money in the register and fills out the form that is then turned in to the bookkeeper. In other operations, where there is not a computerized register, all the daily receipts are turned over to the bookkeeper to review and balance.

The following is an example of the type of cash drawer balance sheet that could be used to balance the cash drawer for On the Rack clothing store.

Sales/Cash Verification	
Date: 9-6-07	
Beginning Balance:	
Change Fund	$100.00
Cash Sales	152.47
Checks Tendered	76.99
	23.49
Credit Cards Processed	166.52
Total in Register	519.47
Less Change Fund	−100.00
Total Receipts	419.47

This verification sheet shows that the amount in the cash drawer at the end of the day is correct because it includes the change fund and the total monies collected for the sales on that date.

Some cash verification sheets have a section where the currency and coins in the drawer at the end of the day can be listed by denomination.

Using the sample figures, that section of the verification sheet would be as follows:

Currency:	
3-20s	60.00
7-10s	70.00
10-5s	50.00
48-1s	48.00
60-quarters	15.00
51-dimes	5.10
66-nickels	3.30
107-pennies	1.07
Total Cash & Coin	252.47

Note that the cash and coins total is the change fund plus the cash collected for sales.

What has been presented here are very simple methods for verifying a cash drawer. Some companies have more detailed methods of balancing the cash drawer, but the results will be the same. The money in the drawer at the end of the day must equal the change fund plus the cash receipts of that business day.

TIME SAVER

Some companies save time by not counting the pennies in the cash drawer, which means the cash count will be short or over at the end of the day. However, the amounts should not fluctuate more than a dollar or so either way.

Change funds for a cash drawer or register vary in amounts depending on how many sales the retail operation expects to make during any given business day. Usually a certain amount of extra change is kept on hand to replenish the registers as needed.

Depositing Cash Receipts

Regardless of who has counted the cash drawer initially, the bookkeeper should always recount the money before making out a deposit slip and taking it to the bank. The frequency of bank deposits often depends on the amount of business activity an operation experiences on a daily basis. In large retail stores, the cash registers are balanced and cleared more than once a day and bank deposits are made up and transported to the bank as needed. Some companies use banks that provide armored cars to pick up deposits.

GO TO ◄
Hour 2 to review services provided by some banks for their business customers.

In smaller companies, the bookkeeper is the one responsible for taking the deposits to the bank. Sometimes there are already rules in place for how and when cash should be deposited. If not, it is up to the bookkeeper to set banking guidelines.

Deposit slips are pretty standard from bank to bank. They require a total for cash, a total for coins, and a total for checks.

Many banks refuse to take coins unless they are rolled and the customer's account number is noted on the roll. Some banks now have coin machines set up in their lobbies where coins of all denominations can be counted and sorted. The machine issues a receipt to the customer that can be taken to the teller who will credit the coin amount to the customer's account. However, be aware that there is usually a charge for this service.

The main thing to remember when doing a bank deposit is to count the cash and add up the checks more than once to verify the accuracy of the information entered on the deposit slip.

GO TO ►
Hour 10 for more information on entering deposits and keeping the checkbook balance current.

Once the deposit slip has been completed, the amount of the deposit must be entered in the checkbook.

Posting the Sales and Sales Tax

Once the deposit has been prepared and sent to the bank, the next task the bookkeeper needs to do is post the sales amounts to the General Ledger. Every time you record a transaction in the General Ledger you are making what is called a Journal Entry. The transactions you studied in Hour 5 were very basic entries that only affected two or three accounts. It was easy to see how the debits equaled the credits.

Posting the daily sales transactions often involves several accounts. Because you are just learning bookkeeping skills, it may help you to write out the entry before you actually enter the amounts into the General Ledger. This will also enable you to see that the entry is in

GO TO ▶
Hour 15 where
you will learn how
to correct post-
ing errors in the
General Ledger.

balance and allow you to make corrections if needed. Once the entry is entered into the General Ledger, the process to correct an error is more difficult.

Let's look at the sales figures that were recapped and categorized from On the Rack's cash receipts report and use them to write up the Journal Entry needed to post this day's sales to the General Ledger.

Posting Recap:

Dresses	198.90	
Skirts	70.30	
Blouses	122.80	
	392.00	
State Sales Tax		19.63
City Sales Tax		7.84
Total		27.47

The Journal Entry to post these figures would be as follows:

Date	Account	Description	Debit	Credit
9-6-07	4010	Sales-Dresses		198.90
	4020	Sales-Skirts		70.30
	4025	Sales-Blouses		122.80
	2190	Sales Tax Payable		27.47
	1000	Cash in Checking	419.47	
Totals			419.47	419.47

This is the way the entry would be posted to the General Ledger. In a computerized bookkeeping system you would only have to enter the Account Numbers and the descriptions would automatically appear. The entry screen in most computer programs looks just like the sample and the tab key moves the cursor to either the debit column or the credit column to enter the figures. The computer will also let you know whether or not your entry is in balance and will not continue the posting process until the debits equal the credits.

Note that each merchandise category will be recorded in its corresponding income account. The sales tax is recorded in the liability account, Sales Tax Payable, as a lump sum. The total in this account will be verified and split properly when it is time to issue the Sales Tax Reports and pay the tax. This procedure will be covered in Hour 9.

Once the entry is in balance, the computer will allow you to save it and the amounts will be automatically posted to the accounts you designate. In a manual system, the bookkeeper has to enter the figures as debits or credits on the ledger pages set up for the accounts. This entry could also be posted through the Cash Receipts Journal in a computerized program. However, that would allow the computer to automatically perform functions that a beginning bookkeeper needs to learn, practice, and understand in order to manage the accounts and system properly.

GO TO ▶

Hour 20 to learn about some of the automatic features and functions that provide additional information and reports with a minimum of time and effort.

PROCEED WITH CAUTION

 Remember that the basic fundamentals of bookkeeping originated in manual systems and taking the time to learn those basic principles and procedures allows you to enter financial data into a computer with confidence and accuracy.

Once the basic principles and procedures have been covered and explained fully, the shortcuts and extra reporting features of computerized programs will be presented.

Adjustments to Sales

Retail operations often run sales offering discounts on merchandise in order to attract more customers or to make room for new shipments. For example, clothing retailers offer discounts on bathing suits when the fall fashions arrive in their stores. Car dealers discount the current year's models when next year's models are introduced.

Stores often give refunds to customers who return merchandise for one reason or another and special price allowances are given on merchandise used for display or merchandise that is slightly damaged or soiled.

Discounts, refunds, and allowances are all common terms in the retail business. They are an expense or a cost of doing business that directly affects the sales income. As you may recall, accounts covering these costs were set up in the Income section of the Profit & Loss Statement.

While the Sales accounts are expected to maintain a credit balance, the accounts for Discounts and Returns & Allowances carry debit balances because they actually reduce the income posted in the Sales accounts.

Let's assume a car dealer has advertised that he will give you $3,000. for your trade-in, regardless of the condition it is in, when you buy a new car from him. A customer has an old wreck of a car that has to be towed onto the lot, but the car dealer gives him $3,000. for it, which has to be applied to the price of a new car. Because the old wreck of a car is going to go straight to the junk yard, the car dealer is actually just giving the customer a $3,000. discount on the new car he is buying.

The Journal Entry to write up this sales transaction would be as follows:

Date	Account	Description	Debit	Credit
9-6-07	4000	Sales-New Cars		28,000.00
	4280	Discounts	3,000.00	
	2190	Sales Tax Payable		1,250.00
	1000	Cash in Checking	26,250.00	
Totals			29,250.00	29,250.00

The full price of the car is posted to the sales account, but is reduced to $25,000. when the discount is posted to the adjustment account. The sales tax is then figured on the reduced sales price and the bank account receives the total of the reduced price plus the sales tax charged on the reduced price of the new car.

On the Rack clothing store gives a refund to a customer who has decided that the dress she bought doesn't fit properly. That entry would be written up as follows:

Date	Account	Description	Debit	Credit
9-25-07	4290	Returns & Allowances	59.00	
	2190	Sales Tax Payable	4.13	
	1000	Cash in Checking		63.13
Totals			63.13	63.13

In the case of a refund, it is posted just the opposite of a sale posting. The price of the dress and the sales tax are debited to cancel out the credits that were posted when the dress was originally sold. The bank account is credited because the money is being disbursed from the account rather than deposited into it.

On the same day, On the Rack gives a customer $2.00 off of a blouse that has a button missing. That entry would be posted as follows:

Date	Account	Description	Debit	Credit
9-25-07	4025	Sales-Blouses		18.00
	4290	Returns & Allowances	2.00	
	2190	Sales Tax Payable		1.12
	1000	Cash in Checking	17.12	
Totals			19.12	19.12

Note that in this entry, the sales tax is figured on the reduced price of the merchandise.

Adjustments to the Sales accounts are common transactions in any type of retail operation. Again, it is important for you to study how each transaction was written up and posted. Reviewing the sample entries in this hour will help you become familiar with the Sales accounts and understand how the debits and credits always offset each other to achieve a zero balance.

Review

Hour's Up!

The following questions are a review of the information presented in this chapter.

1. Which of the following is considered the point of sale?
   a. Display racks
   b. Cash register
   c. Helpful sales person

2. Sales tax is income to the merchant.
   a. True
   b. False

3. At the end of the day, the currency in the cash register should include ...
   a. Change fund plus cash sales.
   b. Cash and credit sales.
   c. Cash and checks.

4. Sales tax rates vary from state to state and city to city.
   a. True
   b. False

5. What information is required on bank deposit slips?
   a. Date
   b. Totals for currency and coins
   c. Total for checks
   d. All of the above

6. What is a Journal Entry?
   a. A note to the bookkeeper
   b. Recording a transaction in the General Ledger
   c. A list of General Ledger accounts

7. How many different sales' categories should be set up in the General Ledger?
   a. As many as needed
   b. Five
   c. No more than four

8. The basic fundamentals of bookkeeping originated in manual systems.
   a. True
   b. False

9. What accounts in the General Ledger modify the Sales accounts?
   a. Discounts
   b. Returns and Allowances
   c. Cash in Checking

10. Sales tax on discounted merchandise is figured on the original price.
    a. True
    b. False

Credit Sales and Customer Information

Chapter Summary

In this hour you will learn about …

- Credit sales
- Accounts Receivable
- Customer ledgers
- Posting credit sales

- Billing the customers
- Posting payments
- Beginning/Ending balances

Many retail operations issue credit cards to their customers allowing them to pay for their purchases over an extended period of time. Some stores even offer discounts and other incentives to coax customers into applying for their charge accounts. There's no doubt that offering credit to customers leads to higher sales figures. Buy now and pay later has become an accepted way to do business.

While other companies do not issue charge cards to their customers and clients, they do allow them to receive products and services on a credit basis.

As explained in the last hour, this does not include purchases paid for with bank-issued credit cards as those purchases are considered cash sales to the business. That's because the bank is the entity that is actually extending credit to the cardholders. In other words, the bank is paying the merchant or business for the purchase on behalf of the cardholder, and the cardholder will be expected to repay the bank according to the terms of her credit agreement.

Credit Sales

Once a company decides to allow its customers to pay for products and services on credit, a number of different tasks become necessary to process the purchases and collect the deferred payments.

In Hour 1, we discussed the necessity for large operations to have a separate department and personnel (clerks) to handle the work associated with credit sales. In this hour, we will look at smaller entities where the bookkeeper is the one who performs the additional tasks generated by credit sales. The process is the same regardless of the size of the business. It is the volume of credit sales that dictates the establishment of a separate department to handle it.

Assume you are the bookkeeper for a wholesale bakery that sells breads and pastries to a number of different restaurants in town. Every morning, the bakery delivers its products to various restaurants that have standing orders. Some of the bakery's customers pay cash when the goods are delivered; others are allowed to accept the goods and pay for them at a later date.

An important part of credit sales is checking on the creditworthiness of customers. Usually, determining whether credit should be extended to people is the responsibility of the sales staff or the owner of the company. The bookkeeper's responsibility at this fictional bakery begins when the delivery driver returns with the cash collected for sales and copies of the invoices issued to the customers that have a credit account with the bakery.

Accounts Receivable

A special account is set up on the books of any company that extends credit to its customers. As you may recall, Accounts Receivable is one of the accounts that can be found in the Balance Sheet section of the General Ledger.

Every credit sale is recorded in the proper Sales account and because no money has been collected for the bank account, the other side of the entry goes to Accounts Receivable.

Remember that recognizing income that has not yet been received means that the company's bookkeeping system is operating on an accrual basis. Also, remember that Accounts Receivable is an asset on the company's books because the amounts recorded there represent cash that will be collected in the future.

FYI   For more information on Accounts Receivable, its value, and how to manage it, read *Accounts Receivable Management* by John G. Salek (John Wiley & Sons, 2005).

Bookkeepers and clerks who work with Accounts Receivable have to monitor the potential cash flow it is expected to generate and, at the same time, make sure the customers are treated with courtesy.

Customer Ledgers

Good long-term customers provide financial stability for a company. The bakery we are using as a sample business has several flourishing restaurants that purchase baked goods every day.

The bookkeeper would set up ledger cards for all the existing credit customers and add ledger cards for any new credit customers that come along. This can be done a few different ways, depending on whether the bookkeeping system is computerized or manual. In a computerized system there will be a place in the Accounts Receivable section that allows the bookkeeper to input the customer's information. This would include the customer's name, address, phone number, and probably the customer's *credit limit* with the bakery.

STRICTLY DEFINED

 A **credit limit** is an amount agreed upon by the customer and the company extending credit. The credit limit is the maximum amount the creditor will allow the customer to charge to the account.

Most computer programs require that an identifying number be assigned to each customer. This avoids problems when there are customers with similar names (assigning numbers is not a bad idea even in a manual system). The computerized system automatically updates the customer's ledger whenever a sale to that customer is posted to Accounts Receivable.

For a manual bookkeeping system, ledger cards can be purchased at an office supply store to enter the customer information. There should be one card for each credit customer. Every time a purchase is recorded in the Accounts Receivable account, the same amount must be entered on the ledger card on file for that customer. Depending on the volume of credit sales a company does, alphabetical files for the unpaid and paid invoices may be set up to hold the company's copies.

File folders with the customers' names should also be set up to hold any open invoices to be billed to the customer. In a small operation, the file folders can take the place of the ledger cards as long as the sales' invoices are properly filed after they are recorded in the income accounts.

The following is an example of a customer ledger for a restaurant called The Egg Connection that could be used by the bakery.

The Egg Connection #125
3243 S. Park Ave.
Marquette, CA 92053
555-555-5555
Contact: George Egg
Credit Limit $5,000.
Resale # 200506

Date	Description	Invoice Amount	Payment	Balance
9-1-07	Inv.# 259	156.00		156.00
9-2-07	Inv.# 300	156.00		312.00
9-3-07	Inv.# 341	156.00		468.00

Note that all the information needed for billing is on the top of the card along with the contact name and phone number for the restaurant and the agreed-upon credit limit. The resale number on the card indicates that the restaurant does not have to pay sales tax on the bakery goods because the restaurant will resell the goods and the sales tax will be charged to the diners. This puts the responsibility for collecting and paying the sales tax on the restaurant owner rather than the bakery.

PROCEED WITH CAUTION

 There are standard forms that must be completed and kept on file at the wholesale business office to show why the company is not collecting sales tax from its customers. Fines and penalties may be assessed if the proper verifications are not on file.

The Egg Connection gets the same order every day and the bakery's deliveryman has Mr. Egg sign the invoice to show that he has received the baked goods. Again, those invoices are brought back to the bakery's bookkeeper and should be recorded and filed in the restaurant's file until the end of the month when the account is billed.

Posting Credit Sales

For a smaller business like our fictional bakery, the sales would be posted every day. All invoices for the day's sales should be reviewed by the bookkeeper and checked for accuracy.

The cash sales can be posted as explained in Hour 6. The credit sales would be posted for each customer. The entry for The Egg Connection for one day would be posted to the General Ledger as follows:

Date	Account	Description	Debit	Credit
9-1-07	4000	Sale to # 125		156.00
	1100	Accts. Receivable	156.00	

Remember that when this entry is posted in a computerized system, the customer's ledger card, which is also in the computer, will be automatically updated. In manual systems, the bookkeeper must find the ledger card and enter the amount of the invoice as in the sample ledger card previously shown for The Egg Connection.

GO TO ▶
Hour 20 where detailed information about Accounts Receivable postings and the reports that can be issued by the computer will be found.

Multiple credit sales can be posted in one Journal Entry. The entry would look like the following example.

Date	Account	Description	Debit	Credit
9-1-07	4000	Sales-#125	•	156.00
	4000	Sales-#130		89.00
	4000	Sales-#206		137.00
	4000	Sales-#208		100.00
	4000	Sales-#215		78.00
	4000	Sales-#234		210.00
	4000	Sales-#235		150.00
	4000	Sales-#236		217.00
	4000	Sales-#301		375.00
	4000	Sales-#313		129.00
	4000	Sales-#321		163.00
	4000	Sales-#337		90.00
	4000	Sales-#339		185.00
	4000	Sales-#343		350.00
	1100	Accts. Rec.	2,429.00	
Totals			2,429.00	2,429.00

The customer ledger cards stored in the computer system are not part of the General Ledger accounts and do not affect the balance of the General Ledger. They are there as a convenience to the bookkeeper who is using the computer program.

If you are working in a manual bookkeeping system, you can shortcut the posting process by only posting the total credit sales to the Income account (as a credit) and offsetting it by posting the same amount to Accounts Receivable (as a debit).

Even if you are using a computer to post credit sales, you must file the open invoices in a file that can be easily accessed when it is time to bill the credit accounts.

At end of the month, before the credit accounts are billed, the unpaid balances on the ledger cards should be totaled and compared to the balance shown in the Accounts Receivable account in the General Ledger. Be sure the totals match before you start issuing bills to the customers.

Billing the Customers

In companies other than financial institutions, customers are usually billed on the first of the month for the purchases made the previous month. There are a lot of different billing methods and formats that can be used and they may vary greatly from company to company. However, the important thing is the accuracy of the bill, not the format or design of the paper the bills are printed on.

Again, in a computerized system, the computer will print the bills and, if the information was input correctly, the bills will be accurate. The computer does not make mathematical errors, only people do that.

Some companies simply make a copy of the customer's ledger card and mail the copy off to them. Others use a word processor or a typewriter to produce a statement with a listing of all the invoices charged to the account and their amounts.

Most of the time, especially when businesses are billing other businesses, copies of the invoices are attached to the monthly statement. If the invoices have all been properly filed in the customers' folders they can be easily accessed for billing purposes. If you only have one copy of the invoice on file, make a photocopy of it to send to the customer. Never give anyone your only copy of an invoice or any other financial document.

TIME SAVER

Invoices that have multiple carbonized copies are available at most office supply stores. There is usually an original, a packing copy, and a billing copy. The billing copy can be sent with the monthly statement saving the time necessary to make photocopies.

Care should be taken when billing the credit accounts. Common mistakes like sending an invoice to the wrong customer or a mathematical error on a statement reflect poorly on the bookkeeper and the company he or she is employed by.

The bookkeeper or Accounts Receivable clerk must monitor the credit accounts a few times during the month to see if some of them are overdue. Reminders can be mailed out or phone calls can be made to try and collect the delinquent amounts. Before calling a customer or sending a reminder, double-check the account and make sure all payments and invoices have been properly posted.

Posting the Payments

Payments for purchases made on credit will probably come into the bookkeeper's office all month long. These checks should be posted to the customer's ledger card as soon as they are received. Because the bakery we are using as a sample company would continue to deliver baked goods to the credit customers, their ledger cards at the time the payment is received would look like the following.

The Egg Connection #125
3243 S. Park Ave.
Marquette, CA 92053
555-555-5555
Contact: George Egg
Credit Limit $5,000.
Resale # 200506

Date	Description	Invoice Amount	Payment	Balance
10-1-07	Balance Brought Forward			4,056.00
10-2-07	Inv.# 600	156.00		4,212.00
10-3-07	Inv.# 641	156.00		4,368.00
10-4-07	Inv.# 664	156.00		4,524.00
10-5-07	Inv.# 682	156.00		4,680.00
10-6-07	Check # 1501		4,056.00	624.00

There are several items for you to take note of in the sample ledger card. The first entry on the ledger card is the balance brought forward from the previous month. The new sales for the current month are added to the balance to keep it updated and current. Because The Egg Connection has a credit limit of $5,000. with the bakery, the bookkeeper needs to monitor the balance to make sure the credit limit is not exceeded. The owner of the restaurant pays his previous month's bill in a timely manner for the same reason. He does not want to exceed his credit limit and jeopardize the good relationship he enjoys with the bakery.

Once the payments are posted to the customer's ledger cards, they must also be posted to the General Ledger accounts. The Journal Entry to do that would be as follows:

Date	Account	Description	Debit	Credit
10-6-07	1100	Accts. Receivable		4,056.00
	1000	Cash in Checking	4,056.00	

Accounts Receivable is credited to record a reduction in the balance in that account and is offset by a debit to the bank account to record the fact that the money has now been collected and will be deposited into the checking account.

If the bookkeeper has received a number of checks that day for Accounts Receivable, they can be added together and the total for that day can be posted to Accounts Receivable and Cash in Checking.

Beginning/Ending Balances

You have just studied a ledger card with a Balance Brought Forward. The notation for the ending balance on the previous month's ledger would be Balance Carried Forward. Bringing a balance forward is only done on a ledger that is updated manually when the bookkeeper runs out of space on a page and must use an additional page to keep making entries on it. This is yet another task that the computer would do automatically.

Up to this point, we have been using sample entries that only showed the transaction to be posted. It is now time to talk about beginning and ending balances on General Ledger accounts.

At the beginning of the bookkeeping year all the Profit & Loss accounts will have a zero balance until the current year's transactions begin to be posted. Balance Sheet accounts will have their balances carried forward to the new year.

Once the new year's transactions begin to be posted, accounts will have a beginning balance and an ending balance. Because this hour deals with credit sales, we will use Accounts Receivable and the Sales accounts as samples of how the accounts will look in the General Ledger.

Remember that Accounts Receivable is a Balance Sheet account and that the Sales accounts belong to the Profit & Loss Statement accounts. Continuing to use the bakery as a sample company, let's look at how those two accounts would appear in the General Ledger after the first transaction in October was posted. They would be as follows:

GO TO ▶

Hour 17 where you will learn which General Ledger accounts retain their balances at the beginning of a year and which ones are zeroed out.

1100 Accounts Receivable

Date	Description	Debit	Credit
	Beginning Balance	10,354.00	
10-1-07	Record Sale #125	156.00	
	Payment #322		300.00
	Totals	10,510.00	300.00
	Ending Balance	10,210.00	

4000 Sales

Date	Description	Debit	Credit
	Beginning Balance		356,192.00
10-1-07	Record Sale #125		156.00
	Totals	0.00	356,348.00
	Ending Balance		356,348.00

Other types of bookkeeping systems may display these reports differently, but the information will be the same. Remember that the samples are for a specified time period so that only the posting and balances for that time period are displayed.

Note that on the Accounts Receivable report there are two postings, one for a new credit sale and one for a payment made on a credit account. The other side of the payment would be posted as a debit to Cash in Checking.

The ideal situation for a business that extends credit to its customers is to have all the prior month's credit sales paid in the current month. That would mean that the beginning balance of Accounts Receivable would be zeroed out by the payments received and the ending balance in Accounts Receivable would only reflect the charge sales made in the current month. Unfortunately, that rarely happens, so at the end of any given month the balance in Accounts Receivable includes accounts with outstanding balances that are more than 30 days old.

You may have heard the term Aged Receivables. This is a report that can be generated from a computerized system that lists all the outstanding balances in Accounts Receivable and shows how long the balance has been carried on the account. Some companies include this information on the statement when they bill their customers.

Usually, this report has columns for Current, 30 days, 60 days, and 90 days or more. If you are working in a manual system, you can produce an Aged Receivables report by reviewing the customer ledgers and listing the customers' names and how much time has lapsed since the invoices were posted.

TIME SAVER

There are ways to flag customer ledger cards that have overdue balances on them. Office supply stores sell colored clips that can be attached to the top of the ledger so the bookkeeper can quickly identify customers that have not paid their bills and, if necessary, have the owner suspend their credit privileges.

The financial stability of a business often is linked to the way their credit sales, customers, and collections are handled. Banks sometimes make loan decisions based on the value and collection rate of a company's Accounts Receivable. Therefore, managing and monitoring credit sales and Accounts Receivable is an important part of the bookkeeper's job.

Hour's Up!

Please answer the following questions on credit sales and Accounts Receivable.

1. Who is extending credit to a customer making a purchase with a Visa or MasterCard?
   a. The merchant
   b. The credit card processor
   c. The bank that issued the credit card

2. How is a credit sale recorded in the General Ledger?
   a. Credit Sales, Debit Accounts Receivable
   b. Credit Accounts Receivable, Debit Bank Account
   c. Debit Sales, Credit Accounts Receivable

3. How is a payment received on a customer's account posted?
   a. Debit Bank Account, Credit Sales
   b. Debit Sales, Credit Accounts Receivable
   c. Debit Bank Account, Credit Accounts Receivable

4. Who sets the credit limit for a customer?
   a. The customer
   b. The merchant and the customer
   c. The bookkeeper

5. Good long-term customers provide financial stability for a business.
   a. True
   b. False

6. What should be filed in the credit customer's folder?
   a. Paid invoices
   b. Personal information on customer
   c. Copies of open invoices for billing

7. When is a customer exempt for sales tax on purchased goods?
   a. When he or she asks nicely
   b. When the goods will be resold
   c. When he or she provides a resale tax number

8. Where does Accounts Receivable appear in the General Ledger?
   a. Balance Sheet Assets
   b. Balance Sheet Liabilities
   c. Profit & Loss Income

Review

9. An Aged Receivables report shows the amount of time a balance has been outstanding.
   a. True
   b. False

10. Loans are sometimes based on a company's …
    a. Goodwill.
    b. Employees.
    c. Accounts Receivable balance.

Inventory Control, Vendors, and Credit Terms

Chapter Summary

In this hour you will learn about ...

- Inventory
- Purchases and Accounts Payable
- Vendor ledgers

- Credit Terms
- Inventory adjustments

Manufacturing companies, retail and wholesale operations, and restaurants all depend on inventory to keep their businesses running and profitable. As you have learned, some companies are large enough to have a separate department that handles inventory and another that handles the purchases needed to replenish their inventory.

Inventory is often the most valuable item on a company's Balance Sheet. Like Accounts Receivable, banks have been known to accept inventory as *collateral* for loans.

STRICTLY DEFINED

 Collateral is property pledged to secure a debt. It must have value sufficient to protect the lender in the event the debtor fails to satisfy the obligation.

Because inventory is the backbone of many companies, it must be closely monitored and controlled. In smaller business operations, without separate departments for inventory and purchasing, the bookkeeper is usually expected to perform most of the tasks relegated to the clerks in those departments.

Inventory

Inventory can take various forms. The cost of an inventory item encompasses several things. First, there are the raw materials needed to produce the item for resale. Some of the industries that purchase raw materials to manufacture their products are ...

- Automobile manufacturers.
- Bakeries.
- Clothing manufacturers.
- Furniture companies.
- Restaurants.
- Toy manufacturers.

The list could go on and on, but the general idea is that most products on the market today were put together in a factory or a kitchen with a variety of materials that were purchased and assembled into the finished item offered to consumers.

Once the materials to make the product are in place, the cost to process those materials and the labor involved in the processing must be taken into consideration before a sales price can be set for the product.

The initial value of an inventory item is determined by the cost of the raw materials needed to produce that item. This and all the other data relating to the product eventually flow through the bookkeeping system, and recording the information accurately is a primary function of the bookkeeper. While other people may actually determine the final cost of a product, they will be relying on the bookkeeping system for most of the data they need to make that determination.

Understanding why and how financial data is used to establish the value of an inventory item, and the price a consumer will have to pay for it, will help you classify the necessary information and maintain the accounts and files used to process it in the bookkeeping system.

As usual, we'll start with a simple product because the process is the same no matter how many ingredients are involved in producing it. With that in mind, let's use the toy manufacturing company from the list and assume the inventory item is a yo-yo. The costs for the materials for this example are for demonstration purposes only.

The raw materials needed to manufacture these toys would be listed on invoices submitted to the bookkeeper for payment. Let's assume the following materials were obtained in a quantity sufficient to make 1,000 yo-yos.

Wood	$300.00
String	50.00
Paint	50.00
Wooden dowel rods	60.00
Total	460.00

Based on these figures, 1,000 yo-yos in the company's inventory would have a value of $460.00 or 46 cents per item. The company sells the yo-yos to retail outlets for $3.00 each. That translates to a Gross Profit of $2.54 per item or $2,540.00 for the entire batch.

This example gives you an idea of how an inventory item is valued. Remember that the value of an inventory item and the selling price of the item are two different things.

The company has set the selling price of the yo-yos at $3.00 each. If this were the only item the company manufactured, all the other expenses of the company would have to be covered by the Gross Profit on the yo-yos. For the retail stores that purchase these yo-yos and resell them to their customers, the inventory value of the yo-yos would be the price they paid for them, $3.00 each.

For a new retail business to post the inventory into the General Ledger the Inventory Account would be debited and either Cash in Checking or the Capital Account would be credited.

GO TO ◄

Hour 3 to review the opening entry for a new business operation that is posting Inventory for the first time.

If you are doing bookkeeping for an existing business there will already be an established inventory account that you will have to monitor and update each month.

Purchases and Accounts Payable

The balance in the Inventory Account is affected by both sales and purchases. In general, sales reduce the amount in the Inventory Account; purchases increase it. You have already studied cash and credit sales and know how to post them into the General Ledger. So, now it's on to purchases, which is the primary account in the Cost of Sales section of the Financial Statements.

In the sample you just studied for the fictional yo-yo manufacturer, you saw a list of the raw materials the company used to assemble its product. Each of the companies that provided the materials for the yo-yo would have sent an invoice along with the shipment.

Unless the company is very small, someone other than the bookkeeper will receive shipments and make sure the order is complete and correct. After that is done and the order is accepted, the invoices will be passed on to the bookkeeper.

It is the bookkeeper's responsibility to post the invoices into the General Ledger. Most companies have set times to pay their bills and the frequency of the payments depends on the volume of business and the number of bills received during the month. Many companies pay their bills once a month, usually on the first of the month following the receipt of the invoice. Therefore, when bills are received, they are posted into the account set up in the General Ledger to hold them until payment time. That is *Accounts Payable*.

Accounts Payable is an account that is used by companies that have their books set up on an accrual basis. Remember that allows the company to include the payment amounts in their Financial Statements even though the checks have not actually been written.

STRICTLY DEFINED

 Accounts Payable is used to record all bills received during one month that will not be paid until the first of the next month. This may include Cost of Sale invoices as well as general expenses.

The other side of the entry for the raw materials will be posted to Purchases. Although these purchases have been assembled into inventory items, unless you are working with a very large manufacturing company, the inventory is not adjusted until the end of the month.

Vendor Ledgers

All the businesses that extend credit to you or the company you keep books for are called vendors. In order to keep the companies and the amounts owed to each one separate and in order, a vendor ledger must be set up for each one. These ledger cards will be similar to the ones you set up for Accounts Receivable in Hour 7. Each vendor should be assigned a number which is required for a computerized system. Even if you are initially using a manual system, chances are you may switch to a computer program in the future.

When you are assigning numbers to vendors make them different than the numbers assigned to customers in Accounts Receivable. For example, if the customer numbers are three digits, make the vendor numbers four digits to avoid confusion.

The vendor cards should contain all the pertinent information needed to write and mail checks to that person or company. Using the list of raw materials displayed earlier for the yo-yo company, here is a sample of how a ledger card would look and be updated for one of the vendors supplying the materials.

Main Road Lumber Co. #1034
1222 Highway 5A
Crater City, CA 91940
555-555-5555
Contact: Sam Flowers

Date	Description	Invoice Amount	Payment	Balance
	Balance Brought Forward			918.00
9-1-07	Inv.# 32	360.00		1,278.00

Note that the balance from the prior month has been carried forward and the new invoice has been posted and added to it.

The vendor ledgers should be updated when the invoices are posted into the General Ledger. If you are using a computerized system, the computer will automatically post the ledgers when the invoice is posted to Accounts Payable and Purchases. Once again, using the materials purchased for the yo-yos, here's an example of how the entry would be written up for posting.

Date	Account	Description	Debit	Credit
9-1-07	4310	Vendor #1034	360.00	
	4310	Vendor #1035	50.00	
	4310	Vendor #1072	50.00	
	2000	Accounts Payable		460.00
Totals			460.00	460.00

If you are working in a manual bookkeeping system, you could post each ledger for that group of invoices and then add them together and post the totals to Purchases and Accounts Payable.

Note that the three debits posted to the Purchases account equal the credit posted to Accounts Payable. In a manual system you would be able to post an entry that is out of balance, so always go back and review your latest entry to make sure it is entered correctly. Of course, a computerized system does not allow you to post an entry that does not balance.

The same care that is taken to monitor and manage Accounts Receivable should be employed on the other side of the fence for Accounts Payable. Paying vendors correctly and in a timely manner protects your company's ability to borrow funds and finance new projects.

GO TO ▶

Hour 20 to learn how Accounts Payable and vendor ledgers are set up and posted.

Credit Terms

The one thing that is missing on the sample vendor ledger is a notation on the credit terms the vendor is offering to its customers. Many vendors that sell raw materials will allow a 2 percent discount on the invoice amount if the payment is made by the tenth of the month after the initial purchase. This term is noted on an invoice or statement as 2/10 and should be noted on the vendor ledger as well.

When taking this discount, the amount would be posted as a credit to Purchase Discounts. If merchandise or materials are returned to a vendor and special allowances are made for something like a damaged shipment of goods, those amounts would be posted as credits to Purchase Returns and Allowances.

Remember that discounts, returns, and allowances are amounts posted that reduce the amount that has been posted in the Purchase account and the vendor ledger cards should also be updated to reflect these special price reductions.

TIME SAVER

 When posting the invoice to Accounts Payable enter the total amount of the invoice and make a notation on the invoice of that amount and the discount that may be taken when the invoice is paid. This will avoid errors and extra work if the payment is made after the tenth of the month and the discount is lost.

The entry to update the ledger card would be made at the same time the check that was issued to pay the vendor was posted. It would appear on the ledger card as follows:

Main Road Lumber Co. #1034
1222 Highway 5A
Crater City, CA 91940
555-555-5555
Contact: Sam Flowers
Terms 2/10

Date	Description	Invoice Amount	Payment	Balance
	Balance Brought Forward			918.00
9-1-07	Inv.# 32	360.00		1,278.00
9-8-07	Check # 5204		899.64	378.36
	Discount		18.36	360.00

Note that the check was written and mailed on the eighth of the month and the discount is 2 percent of the balance that was brought forward from the previous month. Also be aware that after the check and discount are posted to the ledger, the updated balance is the amount of the only invoice posted to the ledger for the current month.

The entry to post the check and the discount to the General Ledger would be written up as follows:

Date	Account	Description	Debit	Credit
9-8-07	2000	A/P Check # 5204	918.00	
	4410	Discount # 5204		18.36
	1000	Cash in Checking		899.64
Totals			918.00	918.00

Once again study how the entry will be posted and be aware that the two credits offset the debit. This entry clears the original invoice amount from Accounts Payable, records the discount and the actual amount of the check that was written and deducted from the Cash in Checking account in the General Ledger.

Physical Inventories

On the last day of the month, a physical inventory should be taken. A physical inventory requires that everything that is in stock and can be sold to customers is counted. If there are multiple inventory items, each category should be counted separately and listed on the inventory sheet. There are forms that can be purchased to use to list the ending inventory count, but any format that works for your company can be used instead.

Once the inventory count has been done and verified, the information goes to the bookkeeper so that the Inventory account can be adjusted. Because sales and purchases are the two things that affect inventory, before an inventory adjustment is posted, all the sales and purchases for the current month should be posted.

Let's look at the yo-yo company once again and see how the sales, purchases, and physical inventory during the month all come together to adjust the balance in the account at the end of the month.

Beginning Inventory	51,000 @ .46 each = 23,460.00
Sales	-15,000
Purchases	10,000
Ending Inventory	46,000 @ .46 each = 21,160.00
Physical Inventory	46,000

Based on this example, it's clear that the yo-yo company is really good at keeping track of its products as the physical inventory matches the figure calculated by subtracting sales and adding the number of yo-yos that were assembled and added to the inventory in this month.

Unfortunately, that is not always the case. Inventory items are sometimes damaged or stolen causing the physical inventory count to be lower than the bookkeeping figures show. This is called inventory shrinkage.

PROCEED WITH CAUTION

 Inventory shrinkage should alert the owner and the bookkeeper that there is a problem within the company and measures should be taken to keep a closer watch to see why the inventory is disappearing. Lost inventory results in a reduction in profits.

In the case of the yo-yo company, the reduction in inventory is easy to understand. More yo-yos were sold in this month than were manufactured. This information provided by the bookkeeper would alert the owner to the fact that production on the product should be increased to keep up with the demand.

The reduction in the inventory value is $2,300. and an adjustment must now be made to the General Ledger so that the Inventory Account on the Balance Sheet reflects the correct amount. The Inventory Account carries a debit balance, so a credit of $2,300. will be posted to that account to reduce the balance.

The other side of the entry for inventory adjustments is always posted to the Purchases Account in Cost of Sales. That account will be debited for $2,300. This posting has the effect of reducing the company's overall profit as the $2,300. posted to Purchases increases the company's Cost of Sales. Keep in mind that any time the cost of raw materials used to produce inventory increases, the value of the inventory and selling price of the inventory should also increase.

The samples shown in this hour demonstrate the most common way of evaluating and adjusting inventory at the end of the month. There are two other methods that are used by companies to adjust and control inventory:

- FIFO (First In First Out) is a method of inventory control that requires that the oldest inventory be sold first.
- LIFO (Last In First Out) is a method of inventory control in which the most recently acquired inventory is sold first.

With both of these methods, the inventory value is determined by the cost of each item left in the company's stock.

The average cost method of inventory evaluation is another way that inventory can be evaluated. It is simpler than FIFO and LIFO because instead of trying to assign a value to individual items, an average cost is determined and then divided by the number of products remaining in stock at the end of the month.

FYI For more detailed and specific information on managing inventory within the bookkeeping system, read *Inventory Accounting* by Steven M. Bragg (John Wiley & Sons, 2005).

Many of the decisions regarding inventory control and evaluation will not be made by the bookkeeper. However, the bookkeeper will be responsible for making the proper adjustments to the accounts in the General Ledger so a basic understanding of the physical inventory process and the current value of inventory items is necessary.

Hour's Up!

Answering the following questions may help you retain the information that was presented in this chapter.

1. The value of an inventory item and the selling price are the same.
   a. True
   b. False

2. What is collateral?
   a. A computer program
   b. An inventory adjustment
   c. Property pledged for a loan

3. What affects the balance in the Inventory account?
   a. Sales and purchases
   b. Vendor terms
   c. Resale prices

4. What is LIFO?
   a. An insurance policy
   b. An inventory valuation method
   c. Inventory shrinkage

5. How is an invoice for raw materials posted to the General Ledger?
   a. Debit Accounts Payable, Credit Sales
   b. Debit Purchases, Credit Accounts Payable
   c. Debit Cash in Checking, Credit Accounts Payable

6. What does 2/10 mean on an invoice?
   a. Must be paid in ten days
   b. 10 percent discount
   c. 2 percent discount if paid by the 10th of the month

7. A physical inventory should be taken once a year.
   a. True
   b. False

Review

8. What does inventory shrinkage indicate?
   a. Extra sales
   b. Bigger discounts
   c. Lost or stolen inventory

9. What is the entry to post a reduction in inventory?
   a. Credit Inventory, Debit Purchases
   b. Credit Purchases, Debit Inventory
   c. Credit Bank, Debit Sales

10. Where does Accounts Payable appear in the General Ledger?
    a. Balance Sheet Assets
    b. Balance Sheet Capital
    c. Balance Sheet Liabilities

Paying the Bills

Chapter Summary

In this hour you will learn about …

- Managing Accounts Payable
- Sales tax reports
- Loans and accrued expenses
- Prepaid expenses
- Credit ratings

Paying the bills each month is not what most people look forward to doing. Receiving money is a lot more fun than paying it out. Still, in order to keep your household or business running smoothly, you must protect your assets by staying current on your liabilities and expenses.

You may have heard the term overhead in connection with a business but it also applies to households. Another term that is synonymous with overhead is operating costs. Operating costs for a household will include things like rent and utilities and any other expenses for things that are necessary to keep the household running smoothly.

The same is true for a business entity. The smallest home-based operation, a multibillion dollar corporation, and every company in between have overhead expenses that must be managed and kept current in order to stay in operation.

Other people in the household or business may have the job of bringing in revenue to cover the expenses, but the bookkeeper is the one who is always expected to administer the disbursements and record them into the bookkeeping system.

Managing Accounts Payable

In order to provide an accurate report of a company's financial condition in any given month, all the expenses that are incurred in the current month must be entered into the bookkeeping system. Because many of those expenses will not be paid in the same month that they are incurred, the bookkeeper posts the amounts to Accounts Payable.

You should recall from the last hour that the invoices for raw materials were posted into Accounts Payable allowing the company to recognize these purchases as a cost of sales that had not yet been disbursed out of the bank account. Most of the other monthly expenses are handled the same way. This includes overhead expenses and any other general business expenditures that will affect the company's *bottom line.*

STRICTLY DEFINED

 The **bottom line** so often referred to when discussing financial issues is the Net Profit or Loss of a business operation because it is reported on the last (bottom) line of the Financial Statements.

Most vendors send invoices with the shipments that are delivered and then at the beginning of the next month, send a statement with all the invoices listed and a total amount due for the purchases made the previous month. While it's a good idea to review the statement, you should not pay the vendor or base the amount set up in Accounts Payable on the statement total. Always work off of the invoices rather than a monthly statement. It avoids confusion and problems.

If there is ever a question about the payment of an invoice, it's a lot easier to look through the paid file and pull out the individual invoice than to try and locate the statement it was billed on. Also, errors on statements are common; for example, invoices may be left off the statement or invoices belonging to other companies may be included.

When the bills are being paid, note the invoice numbers you are paying on the check or include a remittance sheet listing them when you mail the check.

Let's look at another sample business. In a small town on the coast of Maine, there is an area of shops frequented by tourists. This port is a popular stop for cruise ships when the weather permits. One of the shops in this town sells nothing but clocks. This flourishing business has clocks for every subject and theme imaginable. Cartoon characters, sports, hobbies, and timepieces for every room in the house tick away the hours as customers crowd in to browse and buy. We'll call it the Clock Shop and use made-up figures to demonstrate how this business uses Accounts Payable each month to ensure that their bottom line is accurate.

The following is a list of purchases and other expenses incurred by the Clock Shop in the month of September.

Football clocks	70.00
Kitchen clocks	152.00
Teddy bear clocks	85.00
Fishing clocks	63.00
Weekly ad in cruise ship newsletter	350.00
Wrapping paper	35.00
Electric	102.00
Gas/Heat	78.00
Telephone	56.00
Sales invoices	37.00
Repair glass in display case	76.00
Total Expenses	1,104.00

JUST A MINUTE

 Whenever you are adding up a column of figures always check your answer by adding it twice. This extra step will save you time by ensuring that you have the correct total to work with.

Let's look at the same list again. This time we will note what General Ledger Accounts will be used for posting.

Football clocks	70.00 (Purchases)
Kitchen clocks	152.00 (Purchases)
Teddy bear clocks	85.00 (Purchases)
Fishing clocks	63.00 (Purchases)
Weekly ad in cruise ship newsletter	350.00 (Advertising)
Wrapping paper	35.00 (Supplies)
Electric	102.00 (Utilities)
Gas/Heat	78.00 (Utilities)
Telephone	56.00 (Telephone)
Sales invoices	37.00 (Office Expense)
Repair glass in display case	76.00 (Repairs & Mtn.)
Total Expenses	1,104.00 (Accts. Payable)

Note that there is no expense listed for Rent Expense because rent is usually paid a month in advance, so the rent for the current month would have already been paid on the first of the month and the amount posted to that account when the check was posted.

Also, the absence of any salary and wages on the Clock Shop's list of expenses tells us that this business is run by the owner and his wife, who also does the bookkeeping for the business. They are *sole proprietors* and have no employees.

<u>STRICTLY DEFINED</u>

 A **sole proprietor** is a term used by the IRS to identify taxpayers who run businesses on their own. These business owners do not draw regular salaries from the business. Their income is the amount of profit the business earns. Therefore, this type of business is not a separate legal entity.

The following is an example of how the Journal Entry to record the expenses for the Clock Shop would be written up and posted.

Date	Account	Description	Debit	Credit
9-30-07	4310	Vendor # 23	70.00	
	4310	Vendor # 4	152.00	
	4310	Vendor # 12	85.00	
	4310	Vendor # 16	63.00	
	5100	Vendor # 45	350.00	
	6440	Vendor # 2	35.00	
	6220	Vendor # 1	102.00	
	6220	Vendor # 7	78.00	
	6520	Vendor # 3	56.00	
	6300	Vendor # 18	37.00	
	6380	ABC Glass Co.	76.00	
	2000	Accounts Payable		1,104.00

Here are the points to study in this example. The Clock Shop has a number of regular vendors that provide their inventory. They have also set up vendor accounts for other expenses that they use on a monthly basis, like the cruise line where they spend the bulk of their advertising dollars, utility companies, and other local businesses where they have accounts to buy supplies. ABC Glass Company was called in to repair a display case, and because they do not plan on using this company again, they did not set up a vendor ledger for it.

If the Clock Shop is using a computerized program the vendor ledgers will be updated when this entry is posted. When this entry is posted to the General Ledger all the expenses incurred during the month of September will be in the General Ledger and will show up on the September Financial Statements.

Because we're using pretend figures to demonstrate how the Clock Shop sets up Accounts Payable each month, let's also use pretend sales figures and look at how all this information comes together on the company's Profit & Loss Statement for the month of September.

Clock Shop
Income Statement for the Period
September 1, 2007 to September 30, 2007

Sales:		
Sports clocks	$2,500.00	
Household clocks	1,220.00	
Hobby clocks	825.00	
Cartoon clocks	3,400.00	
Total Sales	7,945.00	(Credit)
Cost of Sales:		
Purchases	370.00	
Total Cost of Sales	370.00	(Debit)
Gross Profit:	7,575.00	(Credit)
Expenses:		
Advertising	350.00	
Rent	1,200.00	
Repairs & Maintenance	76.00	

continues

(continued)

Office Expense	37.00
Supplies	35.00
Telephone	56.00
Utilities	180.00
Total Expenses	1,934.00 (Debit)
Net Profit or (Loss)	5,641.00 (Credit)

Take some time to review this sample statement and see how the Accounts Payable entry is evident in the Profit & Loss Statement. The notations for debits and credits would not normally be printed on the statement. They are there just to help you remember that income accounts carry credit balances and expense accounts carry debit balance.

Remember, the formula to calculate Net Profit is Income minus Cost of Sales minus Expenses. A Net Profit is a credit because income accounts are credits and they should exceed the expenses to result in a profit. A Net Loss would be a debit because the Cost of Sales and Expense accounts are debits and if they exceed the income it results in a loss.

Sales Tax Reports

Any liability payments made in the month of September do not appear on the Profit & Loss Statement. Those payments are posted to the Balance Sheet Liability accounts set up for loans and other accrued expenses, like sales tax.

GO TO ◄
Hour 3 where the Liability accounts set up on the Balance Sheet are explained.

Sales tax is not an expense to the business as it is money collected from customers that is posted to the Sales Tax Payable account and held there until it is remitted to the taxing entity.

Sales Tax Payable is a liability to the business and is a task that must be handled by the bookkeeper. As explained in Hour 6, sales tax rates vary from state to state and often the city where you conduct business imposes a sales tax in addition to the state tax.

In Maine the sales tax rate is 5 percent, so based on the imaginary sales of $7,945.00 for the Clock Shop, at the end of the month, the shop would have $397.25 posted as a credit in the Sales Tax Payable account. That is the amount that would be paid when the sales tax report is filed.

Every state and locality has its own tax rates and forms that must be completed and filed. If you are doing bookkeeping for an existing business, all the information and forms you need should already be on file. A new business must apply for a Sales Tax License through the state and maybe the city where it is located as well.

When the check is written to pay the sales tax and posted to the Sales Tax Payable account, it should clear the tax collected on the prior month's sales and leave only the tax collected on the current month's sales.

Loans and Accrued Expenses

Any outstanding loans and other accrued expenses must also be paid at the beginning of each month or on the due date set forth in the loan agreement. Only the interest charged on these debts by the lender will be posted to the Interest Expense account in the General Ledger. The payment on the *principle of the loan* will be posted to the Liability account set up for it in the Balance Sheet accounts.

<u>STRICTLY DEFINED</u>

 The **principle of the loan** is the amount received by the borrower from the lender. It does not include interest charges or any other loan fees.

Before a loan is funded, the borrower receives a statement showing all the interest and other fees that the lender is charging for the loan. The interest rate and the term of the loan should have already been agreed upon.

In Hour 3 you learned about the liability accounts that should be set up for any long term debts incurred by the business. Now that we are talking about making payments on those loans, we will learn how to calculate the interest that is a part of the payment and post it to an expense account in the General Ledger.

Let's assume the company you are doing bookkeeping for has a simple interest loan with Silver Savings Bank for $3,000. The loan is for three years, making it a Long-Term Liability and the interest rate is 10 percent per year.

Only the principle amount of $3,000. is recorded as Loan Payable-Silver Savings in the Liability section of the Balance Sheet. However, when the monthly payment is made on the loan, the interest charged on the loan for that month is recorded in the Interest Expense account in the General Ledger.

The following worksheet shows how the interest on the loan would be calculated and broken down into a monthly figure. Because this is a simple interest loan the process is easy.

Principle	$3,000.00
Times Interest Rate	× .10
Annual Interest	$300.00
Times Term of Loan	× 3 years
Total Interest	$900.00
Divided by Number of Payments	36
Equals Interest Expense per Month	$25.00

The principle payment is $83.34 per month and the interest is $25.00 per month resulting in a total payment each month of $108.34.

Every month when the check is written for the loan payment it is posted as follows:

Date	Account	Description	Debit	Credit
9-15-07	2800	Silver Savings	83.34	
	6260	S.S. Interest	25.00	
	1000	Cash in Checking		108.34
Totals			108.34	108.34

A mortgage is set up the same way, with only the principle amounts recorded in the payable account. However, interest on mortgages is compounded and fluctuates from month to month. The lender can provide the bookkeeper with a principle/interest schedule that will show how much of the payment goes to principle and how much should be expensed as interest each month.

Payroll taxes and other deductions for insurance and retirement funds are also posted in special accrual accounts, but they are posted whenever paychecks are issued. The taxes are paid out according to the rules and regulations set by the IRS based on the frequency and amount of a company's payroll.

GO TO ▶

Hour 12 for detailed instructions on calculating taxes and other deductions and posting the amounts to the designated accrual accounts.

Prepaid Expenses

Insurance premiums and equipment leases are two items that usually have to be paid in advance. However, expensing an annual insurance premium or a 12-month equipment lease in the month it was paid would have an adverse effect on the profit for that month. Even though the full amount of the premium or lease has been paid up front, the expense should be written off on a monthly basis to more accurately reflect the true financial status of the company throughout the entire year.

Let's assume the annual liability insurance premium for a company is $6,000. That amount divided by 12 months means that the company is paying $500. per month for the insurance coverage. The following is how the initial entry to set up the Prepaid Expense is done when the annual premium is paid.

Date	Account	Description	Debit	Credit
1-10-08	1350	Liability Ins.	6,000.00	
	1000	Check # 512		6,000.00
	1350	January Expense		500.00
	6240	January Expense	500.00	
Totals			6,500.00	6,500.00

Based on this entry, this is what has taken place in the company's General Ledger:

- The annual insurance premium has been paid and the full amount has been posted to the Prepaid Expense account set up for it in the Balance Sheet.
- The check amount has been posted as a credit to the bank account because it is a disbursement.
- The expense for the month of January has been recorded as a credit to Prepaid Expenses reducing that account to 11 months of premium instead of 12.
- The expense for the month of January has only been posted to the Insurance Expense account.

In the month of February the entry to expense that month's liability insurance premium would be as follows:

Date	Account	Description	Debit	Credit
2-1-08	1350	February Expense		500.00
	6240	February Expense	500.00	

Remember that a Prepaid Expense is an Asset and therefore carries a debit balance because it reflects something of value that the company has paid for in advance.

JUST A MINUTE

 If an account in the General Ledger carries a debit balance, it is increased by posting another debit to it; it is reduced by posting a credit to it. If the account carries a credit balance, it is increased when another credit is posted to it and decreased when a debit is posted.

There can be any number of Prepaid Expense accounts set up in the Balance Sheet as Assets. You have just seen an example for liability insurance, and it is a good idea to set up one account for each type of expense the company has paid for in advance. Writing off the Prepaid Expenses one month at a time is what is known as a recurring Journal Entry.

Credit Ratings

Paying bills on time has advantages for an individual and a business. It enables both to establish and maintain a good credit rating. A good credit rating makes it possible to borrow money, have credit card privileges, and finance personal or business purchases. People with high credit ratings receive preferential treatment from lenders in the form of lower interest rates and better terms on debts.

Currently there are three major credit bureaus that provide reports on individuals and businesses to lenders:

- Equifax
- TransUnion
- Experian

Contact information for these credit bureaus can be found in Appendix D.

Consumer credit and credit bureaus come under the jurisdiction of the Federal Trade Commission (FTC). Based on legislation enacted by the FTC, all three credit bureaus are required to supply free credit reports once a year to businesses or consumers who ask for them. To receive your free credit report or to access more information on these subjects, visit the Federal Trade Commissions website: www.ftc.gov. More information on contacting the FTC can also be found in Appendix D.

The FTC has rules regarding the following subjects that may be of interest to individuals and businesses:

- Equal Credit Opportunity
- Fair Credit Billing
- Fair Credit Reporting
- Fair Debt Collection Practices

Whether you are performing bookkeeping duties for yourself and your family or working for a business entity, keep in mind that credit history depends largely on how existing debts are handled and paid. Having a good bookkeeping system in place to organize your financial data and schedule the payment of bills allows individuals and companies to build financial stability and a good credit history.

Review

Hour's Up!

Answering the following questions may help you retain the information that was presented in this chapter.

1. How is the entry to post the telephone bill to Accounts Payable done?
   a. Debit Purchases, Credit Accounts Payable
   b. Debit Accounts Payable, Credit Telephone Expense
   c. Credit Accounts Payable, Debit Telephone Expense

2. Vendors should be paid on a monthly statement rather than invoices.
   a. True
   b. False

3. What is the IRS classification for an unincorporated small business owner with no employees?
   a. Sole Proprietor
   b. Company Owner
   c. Corporate Officer

4. What is the formula to calculate Net Profit?
   a. Assets minus Liabilities
   b. Assets plus Equity
   c. Income minus Cost of Sales minus Expenses

5. Sales Tax is usually reported and paid monthly.
   a. True
   b. False

6. What part of a loan payment is posted to an Expense account?
   a. Total payment
   b. Interest
   c. Principle

7. What is the formula to calculate the total interest on a simple interest loan?
   a. Principle × rate × term
   b. Principle × rate
   c. Principle × term

8. Annual insurance premiums are a good example of Prepaid Expenses.
    a. True
    b. False

9. Where is the Prepaid Expense account found in the General Ledger?
    a. Balance Sheet Liabilities
    b. Balance Sheet Capital
    c. Balance Sheet Assets

10. What is the title of the government agency that regulates consumer credit?
    a. The IRS
    b. Federal Trade Commission
    c. Transamerica Credit Bureau

Updating and Balancing the Checkbook

Chapter Summary

In this hour you will learn about ...

- Entering deposits
- Writing checks
- Work papers
- Canceled checks

- Audits
- Balancing business bank accounts
- Balancing your personal bank accounts

You have learned that the General Ledger must be kept in balance and that this is accomplished by posting entries where the debits equal the credits.

It is equally important to make sure that the checkbook is in balance. For bookkeepers this is a twofold responsibility. The balance shown in the checkbook should match the balance in the Cash in Checking Account in the General Ledger at the end of the month. The balance in the checkbook must also match the balance reported by the bank on the monthly statement. If your cash account doesn't balance, your bookkeeping system is in trouble. This applies to business bookkeepers and to individuals as well.

In this hour, we'll cover the proper procedures for handling a checkbook. Following these procedures will make balancing your checkbook to the bank and/or the General Ledger simple and painless.

Entering Deposits

For the business bookkeeper, part of keeping the checkbook updated is entering the deposits into the check register as soon as the deposit slip has been completed. The deposit receipts issued by the bank when the deposit is accepted should be filed in a safe place so that they are easily accessed when the bank statement is received.

This is a good habit for individuals to adopt, too. Although many people have their paychecks automatically deposited into their personal checking accounts, they will still receive a paycheck stub from their employer that should be kept on file until their annual W-2 statement is received.

GO TO ▶
Hour 16 where you will find samples of business check vouchers.

While individuals usually use the small check registers supplied by the bank, businesses of any size should use business checks that are larger and come three to a page. The checks detach from the voucher that allows the bookkeeper to write information and notations regarding each check issued.

The vouchers also have sufficient room to enter deposit information. Brief notations next to the deposit amount are invaluable reference aids. The date should always be entered next to the deposit amount. Specific information about the deposit could also be noted in the check register or on the deposit slip itself.

TIME SAVER

 If you are in the type of business that may have to verify the receipt of a payment, such as rent or dues, make a photocopy of the checks before they are deposited into the bank account. Keep them on file for easy access.

Self-employed individuals should always make copies of checks for fees or royalties collected from clients to have on hand for tax time. All deposits, manual or electronic, should be entered into the checkbook promptly and added into the current balance, so you always have an idea of how much you have on hand.

Writing Checks

GO TO ▶
Hour 20 where detailed information on how the computer prints checks and posts them to the appropriate accounts can be found.

Checks written from a bookkeeping system are called Cash Disbursements. In a computerized system these checks can be issued by the computer and automatically posted to the accounts in the General Ledger where the disbursement is supposed to be posted.

Remember if the bills were set up in Accounts Payable, that is the General Ledger account that will receive a debit posting as the Cost of Sales or Expense accounts were debited when the bill was set up to be paid through Accounts Payable.

Even if you use a computerized bookkeeping program, it is still likely that some checks will have to be hand written so you will still be using a business checkbook. Also the checks written by the computer will be posted to the Cash in Checking General Ledger account, but the total of the disbursements will have to be entered manually into the checkbook.

Today, many individuals pay their bills electronically online. This results in an electronic transfer being made from the payer's account to the vendor or creditor's account. Again, even if the bills are paid online without the use of paper checks, the amounts of these disbursements must still be entered into the check register to update the bank account.

Large corporations and other business entities that have many monthly disbursements use computers to print the checks. However, the information that the computer needs to issue the checks has to be input by the bookkeeper or clerk.

With this in mind, let's go over the basics of check writing, because learning the proper procedures will prepare you to handle disbursements for any size business. With the business checkbook in hand, begin by filling out the voucher that will stay with the checkbook. It will look similar to the following sample.

Check No. 1226

Balance _____
(Brought Forward)

Date _____   Deposits

To _____

For _____   Amount of this check _____

_____

_____   Balance _____

The check number is preprinted for each voucher on the page.

The checking account balance brought forward from the previous page should be entered. Then, the bookkeeper enters the date and the name of the person or company the check is to be written to. Note that there are three lines to enter other information on the check. In those lines you can record things like the invoice number(s) being paid, the account number in the General Ledger or the name of the account where the payment is to be posted. To the side of that enter the amount of the check.

After this information is entered on the voucher, write the check and detach it for mailing. If you train yourself to fill out the voucher every time a check is written, you will have all the information needed to trace the check or post it into the General Ledger.

The invoice you are paying with the check should also be marked paid, and the check number you are writing for it noted on the invoice as well.

Although it is not necessary to deduct every check individually, the three checks on the same voucher page should be subtracted from the balance and the deposits added so that the balance on the third voucher can be carried forward to the next page.

PROCEED WITH CAUTION

 Don't take shortcuts and neglect to subtract the checks you have written from the current balance. With electronic banking, checks clear the banks very quickly and you need to know if your bank balance is low before you write another check.

Some bookkeepers or Accounts Payable clerks have the authority to sign checks for the companies that employ them. Take that responsibility very seriously. Even if you are not the person who signs checks, remember you are still the person who is responsible for making sure that there is enough money in the bank account to cover every check written regardless of who signs it. When not in use, checkbooks and checks should be kept in a secure location to avoid theft or misuse.

Work Papers

This is an area where organization and neatness are the most essential qualities a bookkeeper can possess. You have just reviewed the procedure for writing checks and were told to mark the invoice being paid with the check number that paid it. Writing that information on the invoice will do you no good if you can't find the invoice when you need it. Even if you have a ledger card for each vendor where some information is recorded on the invoices and payments, the invoice itself should still be kept on file. It may provide much needed information on the purchases, such as item numbers and the prices of each item shipped and billed on it.

It is not necessary to have a paid bill file for every vendor; one file that holds all the paid bills is sufficient, especially in a smaller business operation. Some bookkeepers use the expandable alphabetical files that can be found at most office supply stores to hold the paid bills.

If you have made partial payments on any bills, those should be kept in a separate file until the total amount due on the bill has been satisfied. This applies to revolving credit card bills for individuals. Always keep the prior month's statement with a notation of the payment amount so you can check it against the next month's bill to make sure you got proper credit for the payment.

When credit cards are used by company employees, the employees should turn in the receipts for all purchases to the bookkeeper so that the receipts can be matched to the credit card bill when it arrives. These receipts should be kept in a separate file and then attached to the credit card statement when it is checked and paid. Often the receipts are also needed to break down the charges on the credit card so that they get posted to the proper expense accounts in the General Ledger.

Any work papers supporting calculations for payroll, taxes, or other financial data should be attached to the report or bill they apply to and filed properly. For example, the calculations made to allot sales tax collected to the state and city should be retained for future reference.

Depreciation schedules, Prepaid Expenses, and other adjustments that are made on a monthly basis should have their own files where work papers and calculations can be easily accessed when and if needed.

GO TO ▶

Hour 15 to see how Depreciation Schedules are created and how the deductions are posted in the General Ledger.

Audits are yearly events for some businesses and work papers are always requested by auditors. For example, an auditor will look at the cash disbursements recorded on the books and will then want to match the disbursements with the actual invoices those disbursements paid.

Businesses are required by the IRS to keep records for the current year and three past years. Much of the bookkeeping data can be stored on computer disks, but there is still a need to keep some of the paperwork that backs it up.

Canceled Checks

Mentioned in Hour 2, a canceled check is one that has been processed by the banks and contains the dates and endorsements from the banks that processed it. Only a canceled check can satisfactorily settle a dispute over whether a bill has been paid or not. The canceled check proves that the vendor received payment and processed it through its bank.

If the IRS disputes any deductions on a tax return, the burden is on the taxpayer to verify that the deduction is legitimate and canceled checks are the easiest way to do that.

Canceled checks were once included with the monthly statement for the checking account, but that is no longer the case. Very few banks continue to send canceled checks with bank statements. Some banks photocopy the checks that have cleared the account during the month and the photocopies appear on the statement.

JUST A MINUTE

 If there is a dispute over whether a bill has been paid, the first thing the bookkeeper should do is find the invoice and get the check number. With this information, the bank statements can be checked to see if that check is still outstanding or if it actually cleared the bank account.

Even though banks no longer automatically send canceled checks with the bank statement, they are still available to you. The banks keep canceled checks on microfilm and will send you a copy of a specific check upon request. Be aware that some banks charge a fee for this service.

Audits

Many businesses hire professional accountants to audit their books once a year. Sometimes the IRS sends in auditors to review payroll records or the books in general. Sales tax audits are often conducted by the State Department of Revenue.

Certain businesses are required by law to have their books audited once a year. Property Management companies often have audits of their books to make sure their Trust accounts are accurate.

If you are a bookkeeper at a company that is being audited you will be expected to assist the person or company that is conducting the audit. That means you will have to provide access to all financial data and files the auditor wants to examine.

GO TO ▶
Hour 11 to learn about the forms that must be completed and kept on file for employees.

Sometimes IRS agents come into a business and do a payroll audit. They check to see that payroll taxes are being deducted and paid properly and that the legal forms required for each employee are in order and on file.

While audits usually mean extra work for the bookkeeper, they can be beneficial for the company and the bookkeeper. Auditors often suggest new ways to work within the bookkeeping system that save the company time and money.

Balancing the Business Bank Accounts

For the most part, the bank statements arrive the first week of the month. They report the bank account activity for the previous month. Sometimes the Financial Statements for that month have already been issued.

Years ago, Financial Statements were seldom issued until the bank statements had arrived and the balances in the bank accounts had been reconciled and verified. That was before computerized bookkeeping programs were widely used and before online banking became popular. Today, everyone is accustomed to receiving instant information and that includes Financial Statements.

Issuing the Financial Statements before the bank statements have arrived should not be a problem if the checkbook has been kept updated all month. After all the entries are posted in the General Ledger, the bookkeeper will be able to verify that the balance shown in the checkbook is the same as the balance for the Cash in Checking account in the General Ledger. If they are the same, the Financial Statements can be issued. If the checkbook balance does not agree with the General Ledger account, the difference must be found and corrected before the financial reports are issued.

PROCEED WITH CAUTION

 Do not assume that because the checkbook balance agrees with the balance in the Cash in Checking account in the General Ledger that there is no need to reconcile the bank statement when it arrives. The bank statement may reveal errors or report fees and adjustments that the bookkeeper did not record in the checkbook or the General Ledger.

Online banking makes it possible for the bookkeeper to view the bank account at the end of the month without waiting for a hard copy of the bank statement to arrive in the mail. The bank reconciliation could be done from the information viewed online. However, it can be more difficult to do it directly from the computer, especially if the books you manage are for a company with a lot of daily business activity.

You should become adept at balancing the bank statement the old-fashioned way with a hard copy of the bank statement and a work sheet. Once you have mastered the skill, transferring that knowledge to an electronic version of the bank statement or the bank reconciliation process built into some computerized bookkeeping systems may work well for you.

Before we discuss the steps that you will take to reconcile the bank's balance to your checkbook and General Ledger balance, you need to understand how the information on the bank statement is reported. The following is a sample bank statement with made-up figures. The one you receive may be presented a little differently, but the information in general is standard for most banks.

Checking Summary:

Beginning Balance	6,165.91
Deposits and Additions	5,147.00
Checks Paid	-3,493.57
Electronic Withdrawals	-2,212.00
Fees and Charges	-24.99
Ending Balance	5,582.35

Deposits and Additions:

Date	Description	Amount
09/04	Deposit	1,245.00
09/04	Deposit Adjustment	16.00
09/15	Deposit	2,610.00
09/20	Deposit	1,000.00
09/27	Deposit	276.00
Total Deposits and Additions		5,147.00

Checks Paid:

Check Number	Date	Amount
1460	9/02	10.00
1464	9/01	10.00
1465	9/17	200.00

1466	9/02	809.00
1468	9/03	200.00
1469	9/08	47.07
1472	9/10	1,104.76
1473	9/19	300.00
1476	9/22	150.00
1478	9/24	41.65
1479	9/28	390.00
1485	9/29	231.09

Total Checks Paid   3,493.57

Electronic Withdrawals:

Chase Card services, Check 1474	452.00
FTD 9-15-07	825.00
ABC Mortgage, Check 1467	935.00

Total Electronic Withdrawals   2,212.00

Fees and Charges:

Date	Description	Amount
9/01	Credit Card Discount	16.99
9/30	Service Fee	8.00
Total Fees and Charges		24.99

Notice that the statement begins by reporting the beginning balance from the prior month. In our sample, that would be the month of August. The statement then lists the different transactions and the total amounts of each category that were processed in the month of September. Then each transaction type has its own section, where the items that fall under each category are listed individually. Each of these sections is totaled and you can see that the amounts agree with the totals shown in the summary.

There will also be a section on the bank statement that shows the balance on the account for each day that a transaction was processed by the bank. Because that section and information will not help you reconcile the account, it is not shown on the sample statement.

On the back of the bank statement, most financial institutions provide a worksheet that the customer can use to reconcile the bank balance to the customer's checkbook and General Ledger account. You can use that if it provides enough space for your particular needs. Otherwise, make up your own worksheet according to the following directions.

The first thing you should do when the bank statement is received is to review it for any new charges or adjustments that you did not enter into the checkbook or the General Ledger and highlight those items on the statement. If they are small amounts, you can post them in the current month and they can be reported on the next Financial Statement. As the bookkeeper, you will have to decide when an adjustment is large enough to warrant reissuing the prior month's Financial Statements to include the change. With computerized programs you can go back and forth between the current month and the prior month with no problem and reprint the reports if necessary.

GO TO ▶

Hour 20 to learn how corrections and adjustments can be posted to prior months.

The sample shows a correction to a deposit made on September 4. However, banks usually notify customers immediately when there is an adjustment made to a deposit, so you would have known about this adjustment and recorded it in the checkbook and the General Ledger.

Next review the deposits listed on the bank statement and make sure all the deposits you made and entered in the checkbook are on the statement. Sometimes a deposit made at the end of the month, especially through a bank drop box, may not have been counted and verified by the bank in time to be included on your bank statement. That type of deposit is called a Deposit in Transit.

A Deposit in Transit must be noted on your worksheet in order to balance your checkbook to the bank's balance. You also need the notation so that you can check and make sure the deposit is credited to your account on the next bank statement. Again, if your banking information is available online, you can access the activity for the current month and check on the Deposit in Transit. For this example, let's assume there was a Deposit in Transit of $500.

Once you have verified that a deposit has been credited to the bank account, you may dispose of the receipt for that deposit. Because the deposit for $500. has not yet been verified, that deposit receipt should be retained.

The bank statement lists in numerical order checks that have cleared your account in the month you are reconciling. However, this list does not usually include any checks that were processed electronically. On the worksheet that was used to reconcile the bank statement the month before, there will be a list of outstanding checks that did not clear the bank in August. Check the August list against the September list of checks and mark off all the checks that have now cleared the bank.

There were only two outstanding checks from August and they were as follows:

1460	10.00
1464	10.00

Looking at the September statement you can see that both of those checks cleared, so you are done with the August worksheet and can return it to the folder.

Now go through the rest of the checks listed on the bank statement and on your worksheet. Write down every check number written from your checkbook in the month of September that is not included on the bank's list. You are making up a new list of *outstanding checks* for September.

STRICTLY DEFINED

 Outstanding checks are checks that have been written and posted to the General Ledger that have not yet been processed by your bank.

Refer to your checkbook and see if the last check written for the month of September agrees with the last check number that cleared the bank account. Usually checks written at the end of the month are not processed in time to be reported on the bank statement. On the sample statement the last check number listed is 1485. Let's assume the last check you wrote for September is check number 1486, so that check number gets added to your list of outstanding checks.

Based on the missing checks on the bank statement and the last check you wrote that didn't clear, the list of outstanding checks you would have for the month of September would be 1467, 1470, 1471, 1474, 1475, 1477, 1480, 1481, 1482, 1483, 1484, and 1486. These check numbers and the amounts the checks were written for will be listed as part of your worksheet. However, before you fill in the amounts of the checks, you must review the section on the bank statement for checks that may have been processed electronically.

Reviewing the electronic withdrawals reveals that check number 1467 for the mortgage payment and 1474 for the credit card payment were both processed electronically. So those numbers can be eliminated from your list of outstanding checks. While you're at it, look at the other item deducted electronically from the bank account. On the sample statement, it is listed as FTD, an acronym for Federal Tax Deposit. This amount should already be entered in your checkbook and posted to the General Ledger because your bank has a program that allows you to enter the amount of the deposit for payroll taxes into their program and the bank automatically deducts that amount from your company's checking account and transmits it to the IRS.

GO TO ▶

Hour 13 to find instructions for making tax payments electronically through the bank where your company has its bank accounts.

With check numbers 1467 and 1474 accounted for on the bank statement, you would list the rest of the outstanding checks and the amount of each on your worksheet. Let's assume when it's completed it looks like the following.

Outstanding Checks:

1470	53.39
1471	29.00
1475	18.00
1477	176.02
1480	81.00
1481	10.00
1482	16.34
1483	100.00
1484	32.25
1486	12.17
Total	528.17

You have already reviewed the section of the bank statement that lists fees and charges. The bank service charge is the same every month, so that was already deducted from the checkbook balance and posted as a debit to the expense account, Bank Service Charges.

However, we'll assume that the discount for the credit cards processed in August was not posted. When the bookkeeper processes credit cards using a software program, the total amount of the credit cards is initially deposited into the bank account just like a regular cash deposit. However, depending on the volume of credit cards processed each month by the company, fees are assessed by the bank for the processing service.

The fees are usually called Discount fees because they reduce the amount of the initial credit card deposit. In this sample, the fee was $16.99. Because this is not a large amount, it will not make a significant reduction in the bottom line of the Financial Statements already issued, so it can just be included on the worksheet and an entry for it will be posted into the General Ledger for the current month.

GO TO ▶

Hour 15 to read about adjustments, including credit card fees, that are made to the General Ledger before closing the books at the end of the month.

Ordinarily, a notice for the credit card fees is sent to the company before the end of the month, and the bookkeeper makes the adjustment. In this case, we'll assume this was an especially hectic month and the additional charge was simply overlooked.

The discovery of fees or other adjustments that have been overlooked and have not been posted to the checkbook or the General Ledger is a common occurrence. It is the reason that the bank statement has to be reconciled even though the checkbook and the cash account in the General Ledger are in agreement.

With the fictional information used in the sample, the following worksheet can be completed to reconcile the bank's balance with the checkbook and the General Ledger account for Cash in Checking.

Bank Reconciliation
September 2007

Balance per Bank Stmt.		$5,582.35
Deposit in Transit		500.00
Outstanding Checks:		
1470	53.39	
1471	29.00	
1475	18.00	
1477	176.02	
1480	81.00	
1481	10.00	

continues

(continued)

1482	16.34	
1483	100.00	
1484	32.25	
1486	12.17	
	────	
Total	528.17	-528.17
		────
Ending Balance		5,554.18
Checkbook Balance:		5,571.17
		-16.99 Credit Card Fee
		────
		5,554.18

This worksheet should be attached to the bank statement and filed in the folder set up to hold the bank statements. An entry should be made in the checkbook and posted to the General Ledger for the credit card fee not previously posted.

When the bank statement arrives for the current month, the worksheet for September will be taken out and the list of outstanding checks in September will be checked against the October statement to make sure they have now cleared the bank. Once in a while, you have a check that still hasn't cleared so it will be carried over to the list of outstanding checks for the month of October.

You will also look at the October deposits and make sure the Deposit in Transit for the month of September has been credited to the account. If it has been credited, you can destroy the deposit receipt. If it has not been credited, you bring the receipt to the bank and ask them to correct their error. The deposit receipt is your proof that you brought that money to the bank. Although it is very unusual for a bank to make an error on your account, it can happen. A check may have been encoded for an incorrect amount that was deducted from your account. Any errors you find on your bank statement should be reported to the bank immediately.

Balancing Your Personal Bank Account

The step-by-step procedure outlined for balancing a business account should also be used to balance your personal bank account.

The only thing that can make balancing a checking account more complicated is the use of a debit card. As you learned in Hour 2, every time you use a debit card to make a purchase, the amount of the purchase is withdrawn from your account. All debit card purchases should be recorded in the check register. When the bank statement is received, you can simply compare the debit card entries in your register to the ones listed on the bank statement. There should be no outstanding debit card transactions as those purchases are electronic transactions and are instantly deducted from your account.

Remember that your personal checkbook and check register should be kept organized and updated. Doing so helps you protect your assets and your credit rating.

Balancing your checkbook every month will alert you to any problems or discrepancies. Today identity fraud is a growing problem and people who do not keep a close watch on their financial data may become easy targets.

Hour's Up!

See how many of the following questions you can answer without looking back on the text.

1. Deposit receipts can be discarded at any time.
   a. True
   b. False

2. How should you handle checks received for rents or dues?
   a. Deposit within 10 days
   b. Make a list of them
   c. Photocopy them

3. What information should be noted on each invoice you pay?
   a. Date and # of the payment check
   b. Your name
   c. Date received

Review

4. When would work papers be needed?
   a. To complete your file
   b. Audits
   c. Both of the above

5. Only a canceled check can settle a dispute over whether a bill has been paid or not.
   a. True
   b. False

6. What company records are sometimes audited by IRS agents?
   a. Sales
   b. Payroll
   c. Liabilities

7. Corrections found on the bank statement always require that the Financial Statements be reissued.
   a. True
   b. False

8. What is an outstanding check?
   a. One for a large amount
   b. The final payment on a loan
   c. One that has not yet cleared the bank account

9. When is a debit card purchase deducted from your bank account?
   a. The next business day
   b. Within three days
   c. Immediately

10. Employees using company credit cards should turn the receipts over to the bookkeeper for review.
    a. True
    b. False

Earnings and Taxes for Employees, Employers, and the Self-Employed

Part III

Employees, Wages, and Taxes

Chapter Summary

- Payroll taxes
- Expense accounts

...ies with many employees usually ...dle hiring and all the paperwork ...t complete for everyone hired by ..., all those extra duties are normally ...per.

...regulations imposed on employers ...cifically trained to handle the ...data into the bookkeeping system. ...ea of bookkeeping requires more than ...is hour and expanded on and com-

...nd taxes are more complex than other ...ow to handle payroll and taxes will ...nt potential.

...es for the first time, it will have ...on Number (EIN) from the IRS. ...ion, the tax number assigned to it by ...e EIN.

...EIN as an employer's account number ...hey receive, and all the federal taxes associated with those wages. The EIN can be obtained instantly by phoning the IRS Monday through Friday at 1-800-829-4933 or by applying online at the IRS website, www.irs.gov.

If you do business in a state that has an income tax, that state will assign its own employer number but will also reference all reports with your federal EIN. Most state revenue departments have websites where you can apply for tax identification numbers.

GO TO ▶
Hour 13 to find instructions on reporting and paying state and federal unemployment taxes.

The federal government also has an unemployment tax that is imposed on employers and most states have their own unemployment tax fund as well.

Once a company receives its EIN and state numbers, it will also receive publications outlining its duties as an employer and stating what qualifies a person as your employee. In short, an employee is defined as someone who performs services for you, providing that you can control what will be done and how it will be done.

In general, self-employed professionals such as doctors, lawyers, contractors, and others who offer their services to the public are not considered employees. However, if their companies are incorporated, corporate officers who work in the business can be employees as well as employers.

Required Forms

In the United States, an employee must provide the employer with a valid Social Security number. The employer is also required by law to verify that the employee is a citizen of the United States. Therefore, the employee must also supply a valid drivers license or a certified copy of his or her birth certificate.

These documents support Form I-9, a form for the federal Immigration and Naturalization Service (INS) that verifies that the employee is legally eligible to work in the United States. The bookkeeper should make a copy of the employee's documents, and keep them in the employee's file along with a copy of the employee's application and copies of the other government forms that are required.

The official employer publications from the IRS contain information on ordering the following forms that must also be kept on file:

- Form W-4 is the form that a new employee fills out for tax deductions. The completed W-4 will indicate the marital status of the employee and how many dependents he or she is claiming for tax purposes. The information on the W-4 determines the amount of Federal Withholding Tax that will be deducted from the employee's pay. If the company employs part-time high school or college students they may claim that they are *tax exempt* on the W-4.

STRICTLY DEFINED

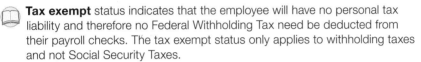

Tax exempt status indicates that the employee will have no personal tax liability and therefore no Federal Withholding Tax need be deducted from their payroll checks. The tax exempt status only applies to withholding taxes and not Social Security Taxes.

- Form W-5 is the Earned Income Credit Advance Payment Certificate. It is used for an employee with a qualifying child who is eligible to receive an Earned Income Credit. When properly completed, this form requires the employer to make advance payments on the Earned Income Credit that the employee is entitled to receive on his or her federal tax return.

Copies of Form W-4 and the Form W-5 can be viewed and downloaded at www.irs.gov or ordered from IRS by calling 1-800-829-3676.

The hours an employee is expected to work and the wages received for the work are negotiable items between the employer and the potential employee. However, there are minimum-wage requirements under federal and state labor laws that must be followed by employers. Tipped workers do not fall under the full minimum wage requirements, but other regulations apply to them, especially if the employees are under 18 years of age.

Although the owner of the company is ultimately responsible for wages and working conditions, the bookkeeper is usually the first person employees go to with questions. Therefore, it is a good idea to become familiar with the federal laws that apply to workers.

FYI The Department of Labor maintains a website where an abundance of information can be found pertaining to workers, wages, and the rights of employees. Go to www.dol.gov/elaws to find answers to any questions you may have.

Wages and Salaries

The most common way to pay wages to an employee is by using an hourly rate that is multiplied by the number of hours the employee has worked. Paychecks are issued weekly or biweekly.

Often time clocks are used to track the exact number of hours employees put in at a company. When the employee reports for work, a time card is inserted into the clock, and the time is recorded on the card. At quitting time, the time card is inserted into the clock again, and the time the employee left for the day is recorded. Some companies also have their employees use the time clock to record the times that they start and end their lunch breaks.

At the end of the pay period, the time cards used for that pay period are given to the bookkeeper to calculate the exact number of hours each employee worked.

Time clocks usually run on 24-hour military time. For those who have never been in the military or punched a time clock, take a moment to study the following chart that converts conventional time to the military time that would be printed on a time card.

0100 = 1:00 A.M.	1300 = 1:00 P.M.
0200 = 2:00 A.M.	1400 = 2:00 P.M.
0300 = 3:00 A.M.	1500 = 3:00 P.M.
0400 = 4:00 A.M.	1600 = 4:00 P.M.
0500 = 5:00 A.M.	1700 = 5:00 P.M.
0600 = 6:00 A.M.	1800 = 6:00 P.M.
0700 = 7:00 A.M.	1900 = 7:00 P.M.
0800 = 8:00 A.M.	2000 = 8:00 P.M.
0900 = 9:00 A.M.	2100 = 9:00 P.M.
1000 = 10:00 A.M.	2200 = 10:00 P.M.
1100 = 11:00 A.M.	2300 = 11:00 P.M.
1200 = Noon	2400 = Midnight

If an employee works from 8 A.M. to 5 P.M. with one hour for lunch, here's an example of what the employee's time card might look like after two days:

Date	Time In	Time Out
9-1-07	0800	1200
9-1-07	1300	1700
9-2-07	0730	1200
9-2-07	1300	1730

When the time card goes to the bookkeeper, the hours are calculated by subtracting the time-in numbers from the time-out numbers as follows:

9-1-07	1200 minus 0800 = 4
	1700 minus 1300 = 4
9-2-07	1200 minus 0730 = 4.5
	1730 minus 1300 = 4.5

Using a time clock with military time makes it easy to calculate the number of hours the employee has worked each day. Note that on the second day the employee worked an extra hour. At the end of the week, if the employee's total is over 40 hours, the law requires that overtime wages be paid for the hours exceeding 40 for that week.

Salaried employees usually do not punch a time clock. Their paycheck is based on a set amount for a month or a week. Salaried employees are still entitled to overtime unless they are in a supervisory position responsible for at least two employees. In that case, the supervisor is exempt from overtime wages. The reasoning behind this is that a supervisor has a higher salary to begin with and is usually able to set his or her own hours.

As mentioned earlier, working owners in a business that has been incorporated are considered employees of the corporation. They are paid a salary that is subject to payroll taxes.

Some employees, especially sales staff, work on a commission basis and earn a percentage of the total sales they complete for the company. Commissions can be paid daily, weekly, biweekly, semimonthly, or monthly. Workers in the manufacturing industry are sometimes paid by the number of items they produce for the company in a specific time period. Regardless of whether an employee earns hourly wages, a set salary, or is paid on commission, the company can regulate how often the employee is paid.

The following list shows the most common pay periods used to compensate employees:

- Weekly: 52 pay periods per year
- Biweekly: 26 pay periods per year
- Semimonthly: 24 pay periods per year
- Monthly: 12 pay periods per year

GO TO ▶
Hour 12 to learn
how to compute
gross wages and
salaries for various
types of employees.

The type of wages and the payroll schedule are determined by several factors. The size of the company, the number of employees, and whether the payroll is done in-house or is sent out to a payroll service may affect the decision of how and when to pay employees.

Issuing payroll checks is a big responsibility for a bookkeeper, and obviously in a company where employees are paid weekly, it generates a lot of work. While some of the work, like calculating the employees' hours from the time cards, can be assigned to an assistant bookkeeper, many companies employ payroll services to do the bulk of the work.

Keep in mind, even if a payroll service is used to cut down on the bookkeeper's workload, he or she must still possess all the knowledge and skills needed to oversee the payroll service and manage this area of the bookkeeping system.

Payroll Taxes

There are several taxes associated with the wages and salaries paid to employees by employers. Some of the payroll taxes are paid by the employee, some of them are paid by the employer, and some are shared equally by the two.

The burden of collecting and paying the taxes is the employer's responsibility and failure to do so properly results in fines and penalties for the employer. So, the bookkeeper handling the payroll for a company has to make sure the taxes are calculated and paid correctly.

At the beginning of each tax year, the IRS sends out booklets to employers containing tax rate schedules and other information on payroll taxes pertaining to employees and employers. If a copy of Circular E, Employer's Tax Guide, is not received by mail, the bookkeeper can access the same information online at the IRS website (www.irs.gov) or call 1-800-829-3676 to order a copy.

When Circular E is received, the bookkeeper should review it to see if there are any changes that will affect the payroll taxes being deducted from the employees' paychecks. The guide contains a number of different tax rate tables and instructions for computing taxes using a percentage method. The rate tables are also categorized by the various pay periods commonly used. There are tables for weekly, biweekly, and monthly payroll periods.

As you have just learned that the purpose of a Form W-4 is to provide the employer with the marital status and the number of deductions an employee is claiming, we will begin with the tax the W-4 modifies. That is Federal Withholding Tax.

Federal Withholding Tax is a tax imposed on all gainfully employed citizens of the United States. It is based on the amount of the employee's wages and is adjusted to reflect the marital status and the number of deductions the employee has listed on the W-4 on file with the employer. This tax is actually an advance payment against the employee's tax liability on his or her personal income tax return. Therefore, many people choose to report fewer deductions than they actually have on their W-4 so more tax will be taken from their wages and they will not have any tax due on their annual tax return.

A married person may also opt to claim a single status on the W-4 to increase the amount of tax deducted. Others may indicate a flat amount to be deducted that is higher than what would be calculated from the tax rate schedules used to figure deductions. Choosing to have more taxes deducted than the IRS withholding rate schedules indicate is not a problem for the bookkeeper. It's simply a matter of noting the payroll file for the tax that should be deducted from a particular employee.

In general, some employees want to overpay their income tax so that they will receive a refund from the IRS when they file their annual return. On the other hand, some employees claim more dependents on their W-4 than they can legally claim on their tax return in an attempt to reduce the amount of withholding tax subtracted from their *Gross Wages*.

STRICTLY DEFINED

 Gross Wages is the amount an employee would be paid if no taxes or other items were deducted from his or her paycheck. Regardless of how the Gross Wages are computed, all taxes are based on this amount.

This gives the employees more cash with which to run their household during the year and is permissible to a point. W-4 forms normally stay on file at the employer's office. However, when an employee claims 8 or more dependents on the W-4 a copy of the W-4 is supposed to be transmitted to IRS.

In addition to Federal Withholding Tax, the state where the company is located may require that State Withholding Tax be deducted from Gross Wages. Once an employer is registered with the state, the tax department will supply forms and all the information needed to compute the tax, and deduct it from paychecks. Reporting forms and instructions for remitting the tax will also be provided. Some state income tax is a percentage of the Federal Withholding Tax. In Arizona, for example, employees fill out a form indicating whether they want 10, 15, or 20 percent of their Federal Withholding Tax deducted for the State Withholding Tax.

Social Security Tax and Medicare Tax come under the Federal Insurance Contributions Act (FICA), a government program that provides retirement and disability benefits. Funding for these programs comes from another payroll tax. Social Security Tax is a percentage of Gross Wages, currently 6.2 percent. This is one of the taxes that is paid by both employees and employers. The amount of tax that is deducted from the employee's paycheck must be matched by the employer.

Medicare Tax works the same way. Both the employee and the employer must contribute 1.45 percent of the employee's Gross Wages to this fund that provides health insurance benefits to retired and disabled Americans.

GO TO ▶
Hour 12 where you will find instructions for computing payroll checks and tax deductions.

Before issuing paychecks, bookkeepers should double-check and make sure they have the latest information on the FICA tax rates and a current copy of Circular E with the most up-to-date withholding schedules.

Expense Accounts

Many companies reimburse their sales people and executives for expenses incurred while conducting company business. Some employees also have the use of a company car. The employee is usually required to fill out a report weekly or monthly that itemizes the expenses incurred and turn in receipts that verify the reported expenses. The employees have what is commonly known as Expense Accounts and the bookkeeper is responsible for overseeing these accounts and issuing checks to the employees.

Expense Accounts are administered in a few different ways. Some simply reimburse the employee for the total expenses on the expense report. That means that the employees are initially paying the expenses out of their own pockets.

Other companies give the employee an advance against expenses at the beginning of the month. This advance is sometimes called a draw. This is usually a set amount each month. When the expense report is completed, the total expenses are compared to the draw amount and the difference is calculated. If the expenses exceed the draw amount, the difference is added to the next draw check. If the expenses are less than the beginning of the month draw amount, the difference is subtracted from the next draw.

PROCEED WITH CAUTION

 Expense Accounts should not be confused with Expense Allowances, where a set amount is paid to the employee to defray the use of a personal auto or other business expenses. An Expense Allowance may be considered taxable income to the employee and may need to be reported to the IRS as such.

After the Expense Reports are checked by the bookkeeper, the expenses are categorized and posted to the General Ledger. The following is an example of a Journal Entry to post the figures from an Expense Account report. For this sample, we will assume that the employee is receiving a draw of $200. at the beginning of the month.

Date	Account	Description	Debit	Credit
10-3-07	5100	Sales Flyers	22.00	
	6100	Auto Expenses	135.00	
	6540	Hotel Charge	65.00	
	6300	Order Pad	6.95	
	1000	Draw Check # 560		228.95
Totals			228.95	228.95

Note that the expenses for September exceeded the draw amount so the new draw check was increased by the difference. From the entry, you can see that the expenses reported by the employee are now recorded on the books as expenses for the company.

Although no taxes are deducted from the draw amount, Expense Accounts may be considered to be part of the payroll department's work because the checks are often issued at the same time the payroll checks are being distributed.

Hour's Up!

See how many of the following questions you can answer without looking back on the text.

1. What is an EIN?
   a. Employee Identification Number
   b. Employer Identification Number
   c. Employee Retirement Plan

2. Corporate officers are not considered employees of the corporation.
   a. True
   b. False

3. What is Form I-9?
   a. A Federal Tax Withholding form
   b. State tax form
   c. Form verifying U.S. employment eligibility

4. Information on a W-4 determines how much Federal Withholding Tax will be deducted from an employee's wages.
   a. True
   b. False

5. What is a requirement for receiving an Earned Income Credit?
   a. Must be married
   b. Must be single
   c. A qualifying child

6. What government agency regulates how and when overtime wages will be paid?
   a. Department of Labor
   b. The IRS
   c. Social Security Administration

7. What type of time do most time clocks operate on?
    a. Eastern Standard Time
    b. Mountain Time
    c. Military time

8. How many times per year are biweekly paychecks issued?
    a. 24 times
    b. 26 times
    c. 22 time

9. Bookkeepers can eliminate their responsibilities by using a payroll service.
    a. True
    b. False

10. What are FICA taxes?
    a. Social Security and Medicare
    b. Federal and State Withholding Taxes
    c. Unemployment Taxes

Gross Payroll and Deductions

Chapter Summary

In this hour you will learn about …

- Computing wages
- Federal and state tax deductions
- Other deductions
- Employer taxes
- Posting payroll checks

Processing payroll begins with correctly calculating the Gross Wages of the employees and it doesn't end when checks for the net amount due each employee are issued and distributed. Issuing the paychecks brings the bookkeeper to the next step in the process, which involves reviewing the tax deductions subtracted from the paychecks and determining what the employer's costs will be for that particular pay period.

There are payroll services and computer programs that can process payroll and tax reports in a matter of minutes, but the bookkeeper still needs to understand how it is done manually. The bookkeeper also needs to know the rules and regulations for reporting and remitting the accrued taxes. As mentioned earlier, in a small company, the bookkeeper is the manager of the payroll department and ultimately responsible for the accuracy of the paychecks and payroll reports.

Computing Wages

The computation of Gross Wages only requires basic mathematical skills. In the last hour, you learned about time clocks and how time cards are used to verify the number of hours actually worked by employees. For a company that pays wages based on an hourly rate, the bookkeeper only has to multiply the hourly rate by the number of hours worked regardless of whether the company pays weekly, biweekly, twice a month, or monthly.

To demonstrate, let's assume the employee makes $12. per hour and works 40 hours every week. The computations would be 40 × $12. = $480. Gross Wages for one week; 80 × $12. = $960 for two weeks.

If nonexempt employees work more than 40 hours, they are entitled to overtime pay, which is generally one and one half times the hourly rate. The following is an example of how the Gross Wages would be determined if there were 5 hours per week of overtime involved.

Regular Hours	40 × 12. =	480.00
Overtime Hours	5 × 12. × 1.5 =	90.00
Gross Wages		570.00

Any nonexempt employee who works overtime is entitled to overtime pay regardless of the way the paycheck or pay period is structured. For workers who are paid twice a month based on a monthly salary, the bookkeeper would have to break down the monthly salary into an hourly rate. Assume the employee has worked 10 hours of overtime in one of the pay periods and his or her regular wage is $3,000. a month, or $1,500. paid twice a month. Calculating the pay rate for one hour and then the overtime wages for the first paycheck in the month is done as follows:

40 hours per week for 52 weeks = 2,080 hours per year
3,000 per month × 12 months = $36,000 per year

$$\frac{36,000}{2,080} = \$17.31 \text{ per hour}$$

Regular Wages	$1,500.00
Overtime Wages 10 × 17.31 × 1.5 =	259.65
Gross Wages	1,759.65

Some retail employees earn an hourly rate and then receive commission on the sales they have handled for the company. Others, like car salespeople, work strictly on commission.

Assume that a retail employee earns $7. per hour plus 5 percent commission on sales. The following is how such an employee's Gross Wages would be computed:

Regular Wages	40 × 7. =	$280.00
Commission	$4,235 (sales) × .05 =	211.75
Gross Wages		$491.75

In the restaurant business, the wait staff usually earns a very small hourly wage and depends on tips to supplement their income. Tips must be reported to the employer so that taxes can be calculated on that income. The employer adds the tip amount into the employee's hourly wages, calculates the taxes on the total, and then subtracts the tip amount from the net amount of the paycheck because the employee has already received the tip income.

GO TO ▶

Hour 21 for more information on the bookkeeping procedures for employees that receive tips.

Once you have calculated the Gross Wages of the employees, you are ready to move on to the next step: figuring the deductions and the net amount each employee will take home.

Federal and State Tax Deductions

The Gross Wages of all employees are subject to the taxes you were introduced to in the last hour. Tax-exempt employees may not have Federal and State Withholding Taxes deducted from their paychecks, but they are not exempt from the two FICA taxes: Social Security and Medicare.

There is however a wage limit on deductions for Social Security taxes. Effective in 2007, the wage limit is $97,500. Once an employee's earnings reach that limit in a calendar year, that employee no longer has Social Security taxes withheld from his or her wages. There is no such limit for Medicare taxes. Be aware that this wage limit may change from year to year and the changes will be reported in the employer's Circular E for the current year.

JUST A MINUTE

 Payroll records and payroll taxes are always on the calendar year. Even if the company's books are kept on a fiscal year, the ending date for payroll is December 31st and the dates for filing and remitting payroll information and taxes are based on the calendar year.

As you know, Social Security tax is 6.2 percent of the employee's Gross Wages and Medicare tax is 1.45 percent of the employee's Gross Wages. Federal Withholding tax can also be a percentage of the Gross Wages, especially for workers who earn high salaries. However, for most workers, the Federal Withholding tax is determined by the tax rate schedules supplied by the IRS.

The Federal Withholding Tax is usually taken from the tax rate schedules provided in Circular E. The tax rates in the tables are based on the Gross Wages, but modified by the employee's marital status and the number of dependents claimed on the W-4 completed upon hiring. There are different tables depending on whether the payroll is issued, weekly, biweekly, or monthly.

The following is a portion of the Federal Withholding Tax rate table for a weekly payroll schedule.

Married Persons-Weekly Payroll Period (for Wages Paid in 2007)

If Wages Are		Number of Withholding Exemptions					
At Least	But Less Than	0	1	2	3	4	5
490	500	36	28	21	15	8	1
500	510	38	29	22	16	9	2
510	520	39	30	23	17	10	3
520	530	41	31	24	18	11	4
530	540	42	33	25	19	12	5
540	550	44	34	26	20	13	6
550	560	45	36	27	21	14	7
560	570	47	37	28	22	15	8
570	580	48	39	29	23	16	9
580	590	50	40	30	24	17	10

590	600	51	42	32	25	18	11
600	610	53	43	33	26	19	12
610	620	54	45	35	27	20	13
620	630	56	46	36	28	21	14
630	640	57	48	38	29	22	15
640	650	59	49	39	30	23	16

As you can see, the withholding tax increases as the Gross Wages increase and decreases as the number of exemptions claimed gets higher.

PROCEED WITH CAUTION

 The tax rates and percentages provided in this book are for demonstration purposes only. Before calculating tax deductions be sure you have the most current tax schedules and rate information from the IRS.

Remember that some states will have their own State Withholding Tax table to be used to calculate the state deduction. Others require that a percentage of the Federal Withholding Tax be deducted to satisfy the state deduction.

Let's assume three people work in the office at the yo-yo manufacturing company and we'll make up a worksheet for their weekly paychecks. We'll also assume that the state they reside in has an income tax and the deduction rate is 20 percent of the Federal Withholding Tax each payday.

- David Fine is the bookkeeper. He is married and claims three exemptions on his W-4. His weekly wage is $645.
- Jane Mars is the receptionist. She is married but claims no exemptions on her W-4. Her weekly wage is $530.
- Susan Warren is the secretary. She is married and claims five exemptions on her W-4. Her weekly wage is $565.

The following is a sample of how the payroll worksheet would be completed for these three employees. Note that the marital status and the number of exemptions claimed on their respective W-4 forms is abbreviated and entered on the worksheet after each employee's name.

Office Payroll Week Ending 9-7-07						
Name	Gross	SS (.062)	MC (.0145)	FWH	SWH (.20)	Net Pay
D. Fine M-3	645.00	39.99	9.36	30.00	6.00	559.65
J. Mars M-0	530.00	32.86	7.69	42.00	8.40	439.05
S. Warren M-5	565.00	35.03	8.20	8.00	1.60	512.17
Totals	1,740.00	107.88	25.25	80.00	16.00	1,510.87

<u>TIME SAVER</u>

 Worksheets can be set up with all the headings and the employee's names and deduction codes and then photocopied and filed. On payday the book-keeper only has to pull out the worksheet and fill in the numbers for each employee.

All the information the bookkeeper needs can be taken from the work-sheet when the payroll check is written. Some companies have separate bank accounts used only for payroll and payroll taxes, while others simply run the payroll checks through their regular checking account. If a special payroll account is used, the checks usually have a stub attached to them that allows the bookkeeper to list the Gross Wages, all the deductions, and the Net Paycheck amount. Otherwise, a separate slip should be attached to each paycheck containing that information.

Other Deductions

If the employees pay into a hospitalization plan or a retirement plan through the company, there would be additional columns on the work-sheet to record those deductions.

Let's assume the three employees we are using as examples all pay a portion of the premium each week to be included in the company's Group Hospitalization Insurance Plan. The worksheet would then look as follows:

Office Payroll Week Ending 9-7-07

Name	Gross	SS (.062)	MC (.0145)	FWH	SWH (.20)	Ins. Prem.	Net Pay
D. Fine M-3	645.00	39.99	9.36	30.00	6.00	20.00	539.65
J. Mars M-0	530.00	32.86	7.69	42.00	8.40	10.00	429.05
S. Warren M-5	565.00	35.03	8.20	8.00	1.60	20.00	492.17
Totals	1,740.00	107.88	25.25	80.00	16.00	50.00	1,460.87

With other deductions like hospitalization insurance, the employees pay different amounts each payday, depending on the type of coverage they have opted to take. The same would be true for employees who pay into retirement plans as their contributions are often based on a percentage of their wages and the employee can usually choose to contribute more or less into the plan.

Each employee should have a ledger card or sheet that is set up like the worksheet. The employee's wages for each pay period are entered onto the ledger and totaled for each month and each quarter. This information is used for other tax reports and to issue *W-2s* to the employees at the end of the year.

STRICTLY DEFINED

 A **W-2** is a statement showing the wages received by an employee during the preceding tax year and the amount of Federal and State taxes paid by the employee on those wages. The information on the W-2 is used to complete the employee's personal tax return.

Employer Taxes

Every time payroll checks are issued, the bookkeeper must also calculate how much tax the employer owes for that particular pay period. Remember that the employer must match the Social Security and Medicare taxes that the employees have had deducted from their paychecks.

The employer is also liable for Federal and State Unemployment Taxes but those taxes are paid quarterly or annually depending on the number of employees a company has and the dollar amount of the gross payroll. So, for now we will just calculate the employers portion of the FICA taxes.

GO TO ▶

Hour 13 to find instructions for calculating and reporting Federal and State Unemployment Taxes.

The computation of the employer's taxes should be done on the same worksheet that was used for the payroll checks. Some bookkeepers may just take the employee deductions for FICA taxes and set the same amount up for the employer portion. However, there is another way of doing it that is more accepted because it is how the Federal Tax Deposit amount is determined and it provides the exact information needed for the quarterly payroll tax report.

The following sample worksheet shows how the Federal Tax Deposit should be computed.

Office Payroll Week Ending 9-7-07

Name	Gross	SS (.062)	MC (.0145)	FWH	SWH (.20)	Ins. Prem.	Net Pay
D. Fine M-3	645.00	39.99	9.36	30.00	6.00	20.00	539.65
J. Mars M-0	530.00	32.86	7.69	42.00	8.40	10.00	429.05
S. Warren M-5	565.00	35.03	8.20	8.00	1.60	20.00	492.17
Totals	1,740.00	107.88	25.25	80.00	16.00	50.00	1,460.87

Payroll Taxes Employer and Employee:

Gross Wages	1,740.00 × .124 =	215.76	Social Security Tax
	1,740.00 × .029 =	50.46	Medicare Tax
		80.00	Federal Withholding Tax
		————	
		346.22	Federal Tax Deposit
		16.00	State Withholding Tax

The percentage for Social Security Tax (06.2) has been doubled and multiplied by the Gross Wages because the employer's percentage of Gross Wages is the same as the employees (6.2 + 6.2 = 12.4). The same function is performed to obtain the Medicare Tax amount. Then these two figures and the total of the Federal Withholding Tax from this payroll are added together. This gives the bookkeeper the amount that has to be included in the Federal Tax Deposit for this particular payroll.

GO TO ▶

Hour 13 for instructions on completing payroll reports and the rules and regulations for depositing and paying the payroll taxes.

When a company issues paychecks weekly, it is prudent to post each payroll into the General Ledger as soon as it is completed to make sure all the payroll taxes that are supposed to be accrued are included.

Using the same sample worksheet, the Journal Entry to post the payroll for that week would be as follows:

Date	Account	Description	Debit	Credit
9-7	6000	Gross Wages	1,740.00	
	2200	FWH Tax		80.00
	2210	SS Tax		215.76
	2212	Med. Tax		50.46
	2220	SWH		16.00
	2100	Health Ins.		50.00
	1000	Cash in Bank		1,460.87
	6490	Taxes-Payroll	133.09	
	Totals		1,873.09	1,873.09

The Gross Wages and the employer's portion of the payroll taxes are both posted as debits to expense accounts in the General Ledger. The taxes and health insurance amounts are posted as credits to the corresponding liability accounts because the company will have to pay out these amounts in the near future.

The amount of the net payroll checks is of course posted as a credit to the bank account as that is the amount paid out to the three office workers.

Note that using the method shown on the worksheet reduces the employer's tax by four cents. However, if the difference is more than a dollar either way, it indicates an error in the calculations, and they will have to be redone.

After the payroll has been posted, the worksheet should be filed where it can be easily accessed. This is the first payroll of the month, and the worksheet may be needed for reference at the end of the month to make sure the monthly totals are accurate.

Whether the payroll worksheet covers one employee or a hundred employees, the procedures to calculate the employer's portion of the tax and post the payroll to the General Ledger are the same.

Hour's Up!

There are a number of rules for processing payroll and payroll taxes. See how much of the information you remember by answering the following questions.

1. How many hours do most employees work in a year?
   a. 3,600
   b. 2,080
   c. 2,440

2. What is the normal rate for hourly overtime wages?
   a. 1.5
   b. 2.0
   c. 1.45

3. The wait staff at restaurants must report tips to their employer to be taxed.
   a. True
   b. False

4. What is the annual wage limit on Social Security tax?
   a. $87,500
   b. No limit
   c. $97,500

5. What is the wage limit on Medicare tax?
   a. $97,500
   b. No limit
   c. $50,000

6. Federal Withholding Tax increases as an employee's exemptions increase.
   a. True
   b. False

7. What is the percentage rate for Social Security tax in 2007?
   a. 6.2 percent
   b. 5.4 percent
   c. 1.45 percent

8. All payroll taxes are based on Gross Wages.
   a. True
   b. False

9. Gross Wages are posted to what type of account in the General Ledger?
   a. Liability
   b. Expense
   c. Cost of Sales

10. Where are net paycheck amounts posted in the General Ledger?
    a. Cash in Checking
    b. Salaries & Wages
    c. Miscellaneous Expenses

Payroll Tax Reports and Payments

Chapter Summary

In this hour you will learn about ...

- Federal Tax Deposits
- Employer's Federal Tax Returns
- State reports and payments
- Unemployment taxes
- Payroll services

Regardless of the number of people a company employs, the book-keeper will find that the tasks associated with issuing the paychecks become routine. This is especially true in a company that has steady long-term workers on the payroll, because their paychecks tend to be close to the same amounts each pay period.

It is the payroll tax reports associated with the paychecks and pay periods that are more difficult to manage. This is because tax rates may change from year to year; wage limitations on taxes may change from year to year, and reporting forms and remittance requirements are also subject to change. That is the reason the IRS sends out Circular E to all employers at the beginning of each calendar year, and the reason that the bookkeeper should take the time to read Circular E and make the necessary adjustments to the payroll ledgers and worksheets.

The only thing that does not and should not change is the bookkeeping method that tracks and records the taxes. If the information from each payroll is handled and posted correctly, completing and filing the reports and paying the taxes on time will never be a problem.

In this hour, you will learn about the rules and regulations that are imposed on employers by federal and state taxing authorities regarding reports and payments of payroll taxes.

Federal Tax Deposits

Employers that accrue payroll taxes of $2,500. or more in a quarter must make Federal Tax Deposits (FTDs). These tax deposits include the employee and employer portions of the FICA taxes plus the Federal Withholding Taxes deducted from the employees' paychecks. These taxes are reported on Federal Form 941 Employer's Quarterly Federal Tax Return and the deposits are also referred to as Form 941 Deposits. The deposits are actually advance payments of the taxes reported on Form 941.

The frequency of the FTDs depends on the total amount of tax accrued each pay period. New employers with no prior tax history become Monthly Schedule Depositors for their first year in business.

After the first year, employers must determine whether they qualify to be Monthly Schedule Depositors or Semiweekly Schedule Depositors. This is determined by looking back at the last four tax quarters and adding up the total taxes reported for that period. If the taxes reported were $50,000. or less, the company is a Monthly Schedule Depositor. If the taxes reported exceeded $50,000., the business must adhere to the Semiweekly Schedule.

Monthly Schedule Depositors must deposit each month's taxes by the 15th of the following month. That is, taxes accrued in the month of June, must be deposited by July 15th. Semiweekly Schedule Depositors that pay wages on Saturday, Sunday, Monday, or Tuesday must deposit the payroll taxes by the following Friday. For wages paid on Wednesday, Thursday, or Friday of the week, payroll taxes must be deposited by the following Wednesday.

The exception to these rules applies to any employer who has $100,000. in accrued tax liability during any pay period. Those employers are required to make a deposit on the next banking day. Obviously, this rule would apply mainly to large corporations with many employees.

Deposit rules are based on when the wages are actually paid to the employees. Also, if the due date of the FTD falls on a weekend or banking holiday, the deposit can be made the next banking day.

FYI　The ABCs of FTDs, Quick Reference Guide for Understanding Federal Tax Deposits, can be found online at the IRS website (www.irs.gov).

The IRS prefers that Federal Tax Deposits be made electronically and there is a free service called Electronic Federal Tax Payment System (EFTPS) that is available 24 hours a day.

Employers are assigned a Personal Identification Number (PIN) that is used to make electronic tax deposits. New employers that apply for an Employee Identification Number are automatically assigned a PIN and enrolled in EFTPS. For employers and bookkeepers that have never used the system, it is best to call the customer service line at 1-800-555-4477 for information and instructions.

Federal Tax Deposits can also be made electronically through an employer's bank or the old fashioned way by a manual bank deposit using Form 8109 Federal Tax Deposit Coupons. All methods of deposits can be used for 941 Deposits and also for 940 Deposits. Federal Tax Deposits may also be required for Federal Unemployment Taxes that are reported on Form 940, which will be covered later in this hour.

Bookkeepers for companies that are Monthly Schedule Depositors should post every payroll as soon as the checks are issued. At the end of the month, the balances in the accrual accounts can be added together to obtain the amount of the FTD due on the 15th of the next month.

If possible make the tax deposit at the beginning of the month or before the first paychecks of the current month are issued and posted. That way, the accrual accounts will be cleared and ready for the current month's tax accruals. If this is not possible and other payrolls are issued and posted, go back to the Balance Sheet issued for the prior month or to the payroll worksheets to obtain the correct amounts for the FTDs.

Let's assume the payroll for the yo-yo company's office staff is the same for the four weekly payrolls in September. The following is an example of how the check or electronic transfer for the Federal Tax Deposits for the September payrolls would be posted to the General Ledger.

Date	Account	Description	Debit	Credit
10-5	2200	FWH-September	320.00	_____
	2210	SS-September	863.04	_____
	2212	Medicare-September	201.84	_____
	1000	Check # 5106, FTD		1,384.88
Totals			1,384.88	1,384.88

Remember that the accrual accounts are liabilities and carry a credit balance. The debits posted when the FTD is made clear the amounts accrued for the September payroll periods. The employer's expense was posted at the time the payroll was posted and those expenses remain on the books in the Profit & Loss Section of the Financial Statements.

Also, note that the payroll taxes for one month of the quarter equal $1,384.88 and that means the total for all three months in the quarter will be well over the $2,500. limit that would allow the employer to omit the FTDs and pay the taxes with the 941 report.

Whether the Federal Tax Deposit is made manually at the bank with a coupon or electronically through EFTPS, the amount is instantly deducted from the company's bank account. Failure to make accurate Federal Tax Deposits on time will trigger penalties and interest charges from the IRS. So, bookkeepers and business owners need to be diligent in making the FTDs in full and on time.

Employer's Federal Tax Return

Most employers are required to file Form 941, Employer's Quarterly Federal Tax Return, to report wages and taxes for each of the four periods during the calendar year. The four quarterly reports are due as follows:

> 1st Quarter (January, February, March) is due April 30th.
> 2nd Quarter (April, May, June) is due July 31st.
> 3rd Quarter (July, August, September) is due October 31st.
> 4th Quarter (October, November, December) is due January 31st of the following year.

Please take a few minutes to review Form 941. All IRS forms come with detailed line-by-line instructions for completing them. If you don't have the instructions for the form you are working on, they can be obtained online at www.irs.gov or by calling 1-800-829-4933.

The 941 Form asks for the same information that bookkeepers should have compiled on the payroll worksheets and posted to the General Ledger with a few exceptions. Let's look at the questions on the form that would apply to all employers.

Form **941 for 2007:** **Employer's QUARTERLY Federal Tax Return**

(Rev. January 2007)   Department of the Treasury — Internal Revenue Service

990107

OMB No. 1545-0029

(EIN)
Employer identification number   ☐☐ – ☐☐☐☐☐☐☐

Name *(not your trade name)*

Trade name *(if any)*

Address
Number   Street   Suite or room number

City   State   ZIP code

Report for this Quarter of 2007
(Check one.)

☐ **1:** January, February, March

☐ **2:** April, May, June

☐ **3:** July, August, September

☐ **4:** October, November, December

Read the separate instructions before you fill out this form. Please type or print within the boxes.

Part 1: Answer these questions for this quarter.

1 Number of employees who received wages, tips, or other compensation for the pay period
   including: *Mar. 12* (Quarter 1), *June 12* (Quarter 2), *Sept. 12* (Quarter 3), *Dec. 12* (Quarter 4) **1**

2 Wages, tips, and other compensation **2**

3 Total income tax withheld from wages, tips, and other compensation **3**

4 If no wages, tips, and other compensation are subject to social security or Medicare tax . ☐ Check and go to line 6.

5 Taxable social security and Medicare wages and tips:

    Column 1   Column 2

   5a Taxable social security wages   ☐ × .124 = ☐

   5b Taxable social security tips   ☐ × .124 = ☐

   5c Taxable Medicare wages & tips   ☐ × .029 = ☐

   5d Total social security and Medicare taxes *(Column 2, lines 5a + 5b + 5c = line 5d)* . **5d**

6 Total taxes before adjustments (lines 3 + 5d = line 6) **6**

7 **TAX ADJUSTMENTS** (Read the instructions for line 7 before completing lines 7a through 7h.):

   7a Current quarter's fractions of cents . . . .

   7b Current quarter's sick pay . . . .

   7c Current quarter's adjustments for tips and group-term life insurance

   7d Current year's income tax withholding (attach Form 941c) . . .

   7e Prior quarters' social security and Medicare taxes (attach Form 941c)

   7f Special additions to federal income tax (attach Form 941c) . . .

   7g Special additions to social security and Medicare (attach Form 941c)

   7h **TOTAL ADJUSTMENTS** (Combine all amounts: lines 7a through 7g.) **7h**

8 Total taxes after adjustments (Combine lines 6 and 7h.) **8**

9 Advance earned income credit (EIC) payments made to employees **9**

10 Total taxes after adjustment for advance EIC (line 8 – line 9 = line 10) **10**

11 Total deposits for this quarter, including overpayment applied from a prior quarter . . . **11**

12 **Balance due** (If line 10 is more than line 11, write the difference here.) **12**
    Follow the Instructions for Form 941-V, Payment Voucher.

13 **Overpayment** (If line 11 is more than line 10, write the difference here.)   ☐ Check one ☐ Apply to next return.
    ☐ Send a refund.

▶ You **MUST** fill out both pages of this form and **SIGN** it.

Next ➡

For Privacy Act and Paperwork Reduction Act Notice, see the back of the Payment Voucher.   Cat. No. 17001Z   Form **941** (Rev. 1-2007)

941 (2007) Employer's QUARTERLY Federal Tax Return.

990207

Name *(not your trade name)*	Employer identification number (EIN)

Part 2: Tell us about your deposit schedule and tax liability for this quarter.

If you are unsure about whether you are a monthly schedule depositor or a semiweekly schedule depositor, see *Pub. 15 (Circular E)*, section 11.

14 ☐☐ Write the state abbreviation for the state where you made your deposits OR write "MU" if you made your deposits in *multiple* states.

15 Check one: ☐ Line 10 is less than $2,500. Go to Part 3.

☐ You were a monthly schedule depositor for the entire quarter. Fill out your tax liability for each month. Then go to Part 3.

Tax liability: Month 1 ☐.

Month 2 ☐.

Month 3 ☐.

Total liability for quarter ☐. Total must equal line 10.

☐ You were a semiweekly schedule depositor for any part of this quarter. Fill out *Schedule B (Form 941): Report of Tax Liability for Semiweekly Schedule Depositors*, and attach it to this form.

Part 3: Tell us about your business. If a question does NOT apply to your business, leave it blank.

16 If your business has closed or you stopped paying wages . . . . ☐ Check here, and

enter the final date you paid wages ☐ / /

17 If you are a seasonal employer and you do not have to file a return for every quarter of the year . . . ☐ Check here.

Part 4: May we speak with your third-party designee?

Do you want to allow an employee, a paid tax preparer, or another person to discuss this return with the IRS? (See the instructions for details.)

☐ Yes. Designee's name

Select a 5-digit Personal Identification Number (PIN) to use when talking to IRS. ☐☐☐☐☐

☐ No.

Part 5: Sign here. You MUST fill out both pages of this form and SIGN it.

Under penalties of perjury, I declare that I have examined this return, including accompanying schedules and statements, and to the best of my knowledge and belief, it is true, correct, and complete.

X **Sign your name here**

Print your name here

Print your title here

Date / /

Best daytime phone ( ) –

Part 6: For paid preparers only *(optional)*

Paid Preparer's Signature	
Firm's name	
Address	EIN
	ZIP code
Date / / Phone ( ) –	SSN/PTIN

☐ Check if you are self-employed.

Form **941** (Rev. 1-2007)

Adjacent to the employer's EIN and mailing information is a box where the person that completes the 941 would check the quarter that the report covers.

The next section of the report asks about the wages paid for that quarter and the taxes associated with those wages. The first question in this section asks for the number of employees that received wages, tips, or other compensation on the 12th of the last month of the quarter. Unless your company increases and reduces its number of employees regularly, that number will remain basically the same on every quarterly report.

Line 2 of the report asks for the total wages paid to employees during the quarter.

Line 3 asks for the total income tax withheld for the wages reported on Line 2. This only refers to the Federal Withholding Taxes, not the FICA taxes.

We'll skip Line 4 as it does not apply to most employers.

The next section, Lines 5a, 5b, and 5c, is used to report the Gross Wages and the FICA taxes that apply to them. Note that the information on these three lines is calculated the way you were instructed to calculate the Social Security and Medicare taxes on the sample worksheet for the yo-yo company employees in the last chapter.

GO TO ▶

Hour 21 for more information on tip income and how it is reported and taxed.

This brings us to Line 5d where the total of all FICA taxes is reported. On Line 6, the total of Federal Withholding Taxes (Line 3) plus the FICA taxes on Line 5d are reported.

Bookkeepers should take care not to make errors on the 941 report that would make it necessary to complete Lines 7a through 7h on the next report. If adjustments are necessary refer to the 941 instructions and keep in mind that IRS Form 941c, Supporting Statement to Correct Information, may also have to be completed.

Moving ahead to Line 8, enter the total of all taxes for this quarter.

We will skip Line 9 because it only applies to employers that have workers that qualify for the Earned Income Credit. This credit is normally taken on the employee's personal tax return, because the employer is limited as to the amount of credit that can be paid out in advance.

FYI Earned Income Credit is for low-income taxpayers with a qualifying child. For more information on the credit itself and how to obtain advance payments visit www.irs.gov where you will find documents explaining the credit and advance payment process. If you don't have access to a computer, call the IRS at 1-800-829-1040.

In the absence of Earned Income Credit payments, Line 10 will be the same as Line 8.

Line 11 asks for the total Federal Tax Deposits made for the quarter.

Although Lines 12 and 13 are provided to report underpayments and overpayments of the taxes, it is prudent for employers to have paid the correct amount of tax in advance, so there is no underpayment or overpayment. If there is an underpayment for a prior month in the quarter, penalties and interest will be charged on that amount. Overpayments will be refunded or applied to the next quarter's tax liability, but they can lead to confusion and other errors.

On the reverse side of the form, the breakdown of Federal Tax Deposits are listed. Pay attention to the line for the total of the deposits where there is a note that says *Total Must Equal Line 10*. This is another indication that the IRS doesn't like overpayments or underpayments.

Semiweekly Schedule Depositors have an additional form to fill out and attach to the 941. It is Form 941b,Report of Tax Liability for Semiweekly Schedule Depositors. Again, this form can be viewed on the IRS website or ordered by telephone.

In the event an employer has less than $2,500. in tax liability on a quarterly report, the tax can be remitted with the report. In this event, the employer must complete Form 941-V, Payment Voucher for QUARTERLY Tax Return, which will be included with Form 941 and its instructions.

The IRS recently recognized the fact there are some very small businesses with employees. Their tax liabilities for a quarter are well under the limit of $2,500. so to reduce paperwork, these employers are allowed to file an annual report, rather than four quarterly reports. This annual report is Form 944, Employer's ANNUAL Federal Tax Return.

PROCEED WITH CAUTION

 Do not file Form 944 Employer's Annual Federal Tax Return unless the IRS has sent you a notice telling you to file it. If employers believe they qualify to file Form 944, they should call the IRS at 1-800-829-0115 to verify that they may do so.

The key to completing Form 941 accurately is to take each line one at a time and supply only the information asked for on that line. If the company uses a payroll service, Form 941 will be completed by the service and sent to the bookkeeper for review and filing.

There are also computerized payroll programs that can be used for all payroll reports.

State Reports and Payments

As discussed in Hour 11, workers in many states must also pay state income tax. Employers in most of those states are required to withhold state income tax in addition to the federal taxes.

Because this is usually a single tax that is only imposed on the employee, there are generally no deposits required. However, there may be a State Quarterly Report that has to be filed. The state taxing authority where the employer is located will supply the reports and instructions for completing the forms and paying the tax.

Unemployment Taxes

Unemployment programs are a joint effort between the federal government and the states. Employers are first subject to the State Unemployment Taxes, but will usually have to pay into the Federal Unemployment Fund as well.

State Unemployment Taxes (SUTA) are deposited in a fund that is used to pay benefits to people who have lost their jobs. While unemployment benefits are usually a fraction of what the worker earned at his or her job, they help sustain the worker until new employment is acquired. Benefits that are paid to a worker that was laid off or fired are usually charged against the unemployment tax account of the employer that dismissed the worker.

Each state has its own rules and regulations regarding this tax. Each state sets its own tax rates and also determines what the wage limit will be for the tax. Employers only have to pay tax on the Gross Wages of employees up to a certain limit. For example, if the wage limit for the state is set at $7,000., once an employee's wages exceed that amount within a calendar year, the excess wages are exempt from unemployment tax for the remainder of that year.

The tax rate the state imposes on employers is based on the employer's experience record with the state. The experience record is based on the number of unemployment claims filed by workers that were laid off or fired by the company. Claims filed against a company's account may increase the unemployment tax rate for that employer.

State Unemployment Taxes are usually reported and paid quarterly. For forms, reporting, and payment instructions, contact the state unemployment department in your area.

Most State Unemployment Tax reports require the following information:

- The name and Social Security Number of each employee
- The Gross Wages of each employee for the quarter
- The Exempt Wages for the quarter
- The Taxable Wages for the quarter

The Taxable Wages for the quarter are multiplied by the employer's assigned rate to obtain the amount of the tax liability that has to be remitted with the completed report. The information for the state reports would be taken from the employees' payroll ledgers, as discussed in Hour 12.

Employers are also required to pay the Federal Unemployment Tax if they have had one or more employees within a 20-week period and have paid $1,500. or more in wages in any quarter. The account number for Federal Unemployment Tax is the same Employer Identification Number used for the other federal taxes. Federal Unemployment Tax (FUTA) has its own set of rules and regulations.

FUTA tax is reported annually on Form 940. However, the tax liability for FUTA should be computed at the end of each quarter. If the tax liability at the end of any quarter is close to $500., a Federal Tax Deposit should be made for the FUTA tax. However, the federal unemployment program allows the employer to claim credit for the taxes being paid into the State Unemployment Fund, and that reduces the federal tax rate to .008 of the taxable wages. The wage limit on FUTA tax is $7,000. regardless of the limit set by the state where the employer is located.

As you review Form 940, you will see that the formula to compute the FUTA tax liability is as follows for employers that are paying unemployment taxes into their state funds:

Gross Wages less Exempt Wages = Taxable Wages × .008 = Tax Liability

Also, take note of the instructions on Line 14 of the 940 report that say that for a tax liability of $500. or more a Federal Tax Deposit must be made. Tax liabilities under that amount may be remitted with the report.

Form **940 for 2006:** Employer's Annual Federal Unemployment (FUTA) Tax Return

850106

Department of the Treasury — Internal Revenue Service

OMB No. 1545-0028

(EIN)
Employer identification number ☐ ☐ – ☐ ☐ ☐ ☐ ☐ ☐ ☐

Name *(not your trade name)*

Trade name *(if any)*

Address

Number   Street   Suite or room number

City   State   ZIP code

Type of Return
(Check all that apply.)

☐ **a.** Amended

☐ **b.** Successor employer

☐ **c.** No payments to employees in 2006
☐ **d.** Final: Business closed or stopped paying wages

Read the separate instructions before you fill out this form. Please type or print within the boxes.

Part 1: Tell us about your return. If any line does NOT apply, leave it blank.

1   If you were required to pay your state unemployment tax in ...

    1a One state only, write the state abbreviation . . . . **1a** ☐ ☐

    - OR -

    1b More than one state (You are a multi-state employer) . . . . **1b** ☐ Check here. Fill out Schedule A.

2

Part 2: Determine your FUTA tax before adjustments for 2006. If any line does NOT apply, leave it blank.

3   Total payments to all employees **3**

4   Payments exempt from FUTA tax **4**

    Check all that apply: **4a** ☐ Fringe benefits   **4c** ☐ Retirement/Pension   **4e** ☐ Other
                   4b ☐ Group term life insurance   **4d** ☐ Dependent care

5   Total of payments made to each employee in excess of $7,000 . . . . **5**

6   **Subtotal** (line 4 + line 5 = line 6) **6**

7   Total taxable FUTA wages (line 3 – line 6 = line 7) **7**

8   FUTA tax before adjustments (line 7 × .008 = line 8) **8**

Part 3: Determine your adjustments. If any line does NOT apply, leave it blank.

9   If ALL of the taxable FUTA wages you paid were excluded from state unemployment tax, multiply line 7 by .054 (line 7 × .054 = line 9). Then go to line 12   **9**

10   If SOME of the taxable FUTA wages you paid were excluded from state unemployment tax, OR you paid ANY state unemployment tax late (after the due date for filing Form 940), fill out the worksheet in the instructions. Enter the amount from line 7 of the worksheet onto line 10 . . . **10**

11

Part 4: Determine your FUTA tax and balance due or overpayment for 2006. If any line does NOT apply, leave it blank.

12   Total FUTA tax after adjustments (lines 8 + 9 + 10 = line 12) **12**

13   FUTA tax deposited for the year, including any payment applied from a prior year **13**

14   **Balance due** (If line 12 is more than line 13, enter the difference on line 14.)
    ● If line 14 is more than $500, you must deposit your tax.
    ● If line 14 is $500 or less and you pay by check, make your check payable to the United States Treasury and write your EIN, *Form 940,* and *2006* on the check **14**

15   **Overpayment** (If line 13 is more than line 12, enter the difference on line 15 and check a box below.) **15**

                                    Check one ☐ Apply to next return.
                                               ☐ Send a refund.

▶ You **MUST** fill out both pages of this form and **SIGN** it.

Next ➡

For Privacy Act and Paperwork Reduction Act Notice, see the back of Form 940-V, Payment Voucher.   Cat. No. 11234O   Form **940** (2006)

940 (2006) Employer's Annual Federal Unemployment Tax (FUTA) Return.

850206

Name *(not your trade name)*	Employer identification number (EIN)

Part 5: Report your FUTA tax liability by quarter only if line 12 is more than $500. If not, go to Part 6.

16   Report the amount of your FUTA tax liability for each quarter; do NOT enter the amount you deposited. If you had no liability for a quarter, leave the line blank.

16a   1st quarter (January 1 – March 31) . . . . **16a**   [.   ]

16b   2nd quarter (April 1 – June 30) . . . . **16b**   [.   ]

16c   3rd quarter (July 1 – September 30) . . . . **16c**   [.   ]

16d   4th quarter (October 1 – December 31) . . . . **16d**   [.   ]

17   Total tax liability for the year (lines 16a + 16b + 16c + 16d = line 17) **17**   [.   ]   Total must equal line 12.

Part 6: May we speak with your third-party designee?

Do you want to allow an employee, a paid tax preparer, or another person to discuss this return with the IRS? See the instructions for details.

☐   **Yes.**   Designee's name   [   ]

Select a 5-digit Personal Identification Number (PIN) to use when talking to IRS   [   ][   ][   ][   ][   ]

☐   **No.**

Part 7: Sign here.

You MUST fill out both pages of this form and SIGN it.

Under penalties of perjury, I declare that I have examined this return, including accompanying schedules and statements, and to the best of my knowledge and belief, it is true, correct, and complete, and that no part of any payment made to a state unemployment fund claimed as a credit was, or is to be, deducted from the payments made to employees.

✗ Sign your name here   [   ]   Print your name here   [   ]

Print your title here   [   ]

Date   [/   /   ]   Best daytime phone   [(   )   –   ]

Part 8: For PAID preparers only (optional)

If you were paid to prepare this return and are not an employee of the business that is filing this return, you may choose to fill out Part 8.

Paid Preparer's name	[ ]	Preparer's SSN/PTIN	[ ]
Paid Preparer's signature	[ ]	Date	[/ /]
	☐ Check if you are self-employed.		
Firm's name	[ ]	Firm's EIN	[ ]
Street address	[ ]		
City	[ ] State [ ]	ZIP code	[ ]

Form **940** (2006)

The second page of Form 940 requires the employer to list the FUTA liability for each quarter of the calendar year. It does not ask for the FTDs made for the year, but the IRS has that information on file and will check it against the quarterly liabilities and assess penalties and interest if the FTDs were not sufficient and timely.

If the tax due on Form 940 is under $500. and will be paid with the report, the employer also has to complete Form 940-V, the payment voucher to go along with the report and the check.

Remember that except for the state of Alaska, unemployment taxes, both state and federal, are the sole responsibility of the employer. Also, even if an employer is exempt from FUTA, the broader rules of individual states will require the employer to pay SUTA.

Payroll Services

Now that you have learned the basic procedures and duties associated with payroll and payroll taxes, you can see the advantages for bookkeepers or employers to engage a professional payroll service to handle it all. Many banks provide payroll services for their business customers, and there are also a number of privately owned services as well.

Be sure to check out any service you are thinking of using. Get references from their existing customers. Payroll processing and tax payments and reports must be handled efficiently and accurately. The information entrusted to a payroll service must also be held in the strictest confidence.

Here are some of the tasks a payroll service should provide:

- Computations of Gross Wages and deductions
- Issuing paychecks and supporting information for employees
- Calculating the payroll taxes for each payroll period
- Providing the bookkeeper with the amounts of Federal Tax Deposits
- All payroll tax reports
- Printed reports that the bookkeeper can use to post the payroll into the General Ledger

If a separate payroll account is used for issuing the paychecks, the payroll service should advise the bookkeeper of the amount needed to cover the net payroll checks and taxes.

Remember that the bookkeeper is still the person who is ultimately responsible for errors or omissions in the payroll, FTDs, and reports, so always review the data returned to you by the service and remember that the service is working for you.

Review

Hour's Up!

See if you can answer the following questions about payroll reports and payments without referring back to the text.

1. What are FTDs?
   a. Federal Tax Deductions
   b. Final Tax Dates
   c. Federal Tax Deposits

2. What is the form number for the Employer's Quarterly Tax Return?
   a. 941
   b. 940
   c. 941-V

3. Employers can choose to file an annual tax report instead of the quarterly report.
   a. True
   b. False

4. FTDs for monthly depositors must be made on what day of the month?
   a. 1st
   b. 15th
   c. 25th

5. What is the method of making FTDs preferred by IRS?
   a. Through the employer's bank
   b. With 8109 coupons
   c. Through EFTPS

6. FTD rules are based on when the wages are actually paid to employees.
   a. True
   b. False

7. What federal form number is used to report FUTA?
   a. 941
   b. 940
   c. 944

8. What dollar amount can be paid with the 941 report?
   a. $5,000. or less
   b. $3,000. or less
   c. Less than $2,500.

9. What dollar amount can be remitted with the 940 report?
   a. Less than $500.
   b. Less than $1,000.
   c. Less than $2,500.

10. What is the 2007 wage limit on FUTA?
    a. $5,000.
    b. $7,000.
    c. No limit

Wage Earners and the Self-Employed

Chapter Summary

In this hour you will learn about ...

- Net paychecks
- Issuing W-2s
- The self-employed
- Issuing and receiving 1099s
- Self-employment taxes

At the end of every calendar year, bookkeepers are faced with one final payroll task. Every employee who has been on the company's payroll during the past year, even if only for a short time, must receive a W-2 from the company.

The bookkeepers who manage the payroll system and issue the paychecks are also employees. Knowing how to compute wages and calculate tax deductions for others may be all in a day's work but, when the office closes, the bookkeeper has to deal with his or her own finances. This includes reviewing his or her own wages and taxes at the end of the year when the W-2s are issued.

For every taxpayer and business that operates on a calendar year, December 31st is not just New Year's Eve. December 31st is the end of the tax year and a time for reviewing the prior year's income.

Net Paychecks

Think back to the first paycheck you ever received. Did you think it was a grand amount of money or were you surprised by the amount of money the government took from your Gross Wages?

There's no way to control the amount of FICA taxes deducted from your paycheck. It's a percentage of your Gross Wages. When you are old and gray you will collect Social Security checks and be glad you have the health benefits associated with Medicare.

Federal Withholding Taxes are different. This is an area you can control up to a point. As you've learned, the tax amount withheld from your Gross Wages are based on the information you provided on the W-4 form you filled out for your employer.

No one is happy about owing the IRS money at the end of the tax year, so many wage earners claim fewer dependents on their W-4 so more withholding taxes will be taken from their paychecks. Others have taxes deducted at the single rate although they actually qualify for the lower rate of the married status.

While a large tax refund at the beginning of the year may help you pay off Christmas bills, consider that the IRS does not pay interest on the money you let them keep all year long. Banks do pay interest, and even if interest rates are low, the money you earn on a savings account is still extra money in your pocket at the end of the tax year. If you're the type of person who has trouble saving money, see if your employer can arrange an automatic deduction that goes directly into your savings account.

Some mortgage brokers advise new home buyers to reduce their withholding allowances, which will increase their take-home pay and help them make the mortgage payment. This is based on the belief that the interest on a new mortgage loan will provide a large tax deduction at the end of the year and offset the amount by which the withholding tax was lowered.

PROCEED WITH CAUTION

 While lowering your Federal Withholding Tax deduction will increase your net pay, don't claim exemptions you don't have. Seek the advice of a tax professional who can estimate your tax liability to make sure you still pay enough in withholding taxes to avoid owing money at the end of the year.

If your employer offers a form of 401k program, by all means take advantage of the program. Increase your contribution each time you receive a wage increase. That way, your retirement income increases and you still take home more in your paycheck.

Employees who work for a company that does not have a retirement program should consider opening an IRA. You already know that IRA stands for Individual Retirement Account and is a savings account you can open at your local bank.

Most senior citizens will tell you that retirement came along much faster than they ever thought it would. The money you put into an IRA may also be tax deductible, but there are limitations based on your income. Consult your tax advisor and talk to your banker for more information on the benefits of an IRA savings account.

Making your paycheck go farther and saving for your future are just two aspects of financial planning that individuals should consider.

Issuing W-2s

At the end of the calendar year, W-2s must be prepared and issued by the company's bookkeeper, a professional accounting firm, or the payroll service. The information for the W-2s comes directly from the Employee Ledgers. All payroll checks should have been posted to the individual ledger sheets and totaled monthly and quarterly so that at the end of the year, the four quarterly amounts can be totaled and transferred to the W-2 statement for each employee.

After the W-2 forms are completed, Form W-3 must be completed to go along with them. Samples of these forms may be viewed on the IRS website (www.irs.gov), but cannot be downloaded. Employer tax products such as these can be ordered by calling the IRS at 1-800-829-3676.

Unlike all other tax forms, the W-2s are not transmitted to the IRS. They are sent to the Social Security Administration, Data Operations Center, Wilkes-Barre, PA 18700.

The Social Security Administration has a website where employers can file W-2s electronically (www.socialsecurity.gov/employer). The best thing about it is that you are able to create and file "fill-in" versions of the W-2 Forms at the site and then print out the completed copies for filing with state and local governments, distribution to your employees, and your company records. Form W-3 will be automatically created based on the W-2s you completed.

Several copies of each W-2 are needed and should be distributed as follows:

- The first copy is filed electronically or mailed to the Social Security Administration

- Employees receive four copies:
  a. Copy to be filed with the Federal Tax Return
  b. Copy to be filed with the State Tax Return
  c. Copy to be filed with the Local Tax Return
  d. Copy for the employee's records
- Employer copy to be filed with the State Income Tax Bureau if needed
- Employer copy to be filed with the Local Income Tax Bureau if needed
- Employer copy for company records

If your company uses a payroll service, the service will issue the W-2s and may transmit them to Social Security and distribute them to the employees depending on your agreement with the service. Professional accounting firms often do the same for their clients.

TIME SAVER

 If you are the person completing and mailing the W-2s to the employees, keep a few blank W-2s in your office as extras. If there is an error, and sometimes the error is not caught until several months later, you will have blank forms to complete for the corrections.

Employers are required to supply W-2s to their employees and the various government agencies by January 31st of each year.

The Self-Employed

In the last hour, you learned about unemployment taxes and how those taxes are used to help people who find themselves out of work. Today, many of the jobs people once did have been taken over or made obsolete by technology. Computers can accomplish the tasks of several people with a few simple keystrokes. The career path people have followed can end abruptly, forcing them to look elsewhere for a way to earn a living. This has caused scores of people to become entrepreneurs. While there is a certain comfort zone that exists for employees with steady paychecks, the ingenuity and challenge of striking out in a new business venture is very appealing.

Entrepreneur is a term embraced by many and has become a popular label for people establishing a new business venture. This is because some of these entrepreneurs have become very successful. The thing to remember about entrepreneurs is that they are no longer employees receiving a paycheck for the work they perform. The entrepreneur is self-employed.

Self-employed individuals no longer have to answer to a boss or punch a time clock. Many of them work out of their homes, so there's no need to dress up or put gas in the car to commute to work. However, they do have to assume all the responsibilities that go with running a business. That includes financial planning and bookkeeping. In fact, a bookkeeping system and a financial plan should be the first things a self-employed person establishes.

The bookkeeping system need not be computerized or complex, but like the small companies used as samples earlier in this book, accounts and files should be set up to record and store the financial data. A business checking account should also be established so that the business operations are kept separate from the household activities.

GO TO ▶
Hour 19 to find detailed information on self-employed individuals and how they report their income and expenses to the IRS.

The IRS allows owners of home-based businesses to deduct expenses for the business use of their home. This works best if there is a designated area of the home that is strictly used for business purposes. If the basic income from the business comes from sales, a separate phone line to handle the sales calls is also a good idea.

The financial plan must include an estimate of how much capital the business will need to operate for at least one year. There are new businesses that become overnight successes, but those are few and far between. You read about them in the newspaper, because it is an unusual occurrence.

If the business is the owner's only means of support, additional funds will be needed to keep the household running. Loans and lines of credit can be established to raise the necessary cash. A good financial plan evolves from research and sensible goals that will allow the business to grow slowly and steadily.

There are many people who work from their homes or offices and supply services to individuals and companies, including freelance writers, editors, accountants, lawyers, and counselors to name a few. The IRS has specific rules for reporting the income these people receive for their services.

On the sample Chart of Accounts we reviewed in Hour 4, there is an account in the expense section for Outside Services. As you may recall that account is used to record payments to individuals or companies that provide various services to the company but cannot be classified as employees.

This is, of course, income to the service provider and an expense to the company that has received the service. If the service provider has a business that is incorporated, the company simply pays the service provider's fee and posts it as an expense in the General Ledger. However, to find out if the provider is part of a corporate entity or self-employed individual, there is a form that must be completed by the service person and kept on file by the company paying for his or her help. This is especially important if the company pays more than $600. per year to the service person.

A completed Form W-9, Request for Taxpayer Identification Number and Certification, should be on file for any outside service providers that the company uses. A sample of this form can be viewed on the IRS website (www.irs.gov).

In the event the service provider is not part of a corporation, the bookkeepers on both sides of the transaction will have additional tasks to perform.

Several years ago, the IRS suspected that self-employed people might not be reporting all of the income they earned. Regardless of whether this is accurate or not, the government came up with a way to check on the veracity of the tax returns filed by the self-employed. So, a brand new reporting form was created and the businesses using outside service people were assigned the responsibility of completing and issuing the new form, called a 1099. 1099s do not have to be issued for outside services performed by corporations but are required for all other individuals and business entities that have received $600. or more in payments.

The original of these reporting forms go directly to the IRS and must be issued and filed by February 28th of each year. A sample of a 1099 Form along with the transmittal Form 1096, Annual Summary and Transmittal of U.S. Information Returns can be viewed on the IRS website (www.irs.gov).

Issuing 1099s

In most cases, the bookkeeper is already keeping ledger cards on vendors, so the simplest thing to do is to add a ledger card for any outside service people. This ledger card should include their mailing address and tax identification number. An individual's tax identification number is his or her Social Security Number.

All payments to the service provider are posted to the card. At the end of the calendar year, the payments are totaled. If the provider is not part of a corporation and has received more than $600. in revenue from the company, a 1099 must be issued.

The 1099 is also used for reporting income other than outside services. Individuals receive 1099s for gambling winnings and casinos and lottery offices are required to deduct and report Federal Withholding Taxes on winnings over a certain amount.

Property Management companies issue 1099s to the owners of the properties they collect rents for. Book publishers and agents issue 1099s for advances and royalties paid to authors.

The following information must also be included on the 1099 when it is issued:

- Payer's Tax Identification Number
- Payer's Name and Mailing Address
- Recipient's Tax Identification Number
- Recipient's Name and Mailing Address

The 1099 is another multiple-copy carbonized form that is distributed as follows:

- The first copy is transmitted to the IRS with Form 1096
- The second copy goes to the recipient
- The third copy is for the payer's records

The taxpayer who receives the 1099 must make sure that all the incomes on all the 1099s for that particular calendar year are included on his or her personal tax return.

With electronic processing, the IRS has the capability of checking an individual's tax return against the 1099s issued. Taxpayers are quickly notified and asked to explain any discrepancies between their returns and the 1099s on file with the IRS.

Self-Employment Taxes

GO TO ▶

Hour 19 to learn how individuals report and pay Federal Income Taxes on their business enterprises.

Employees benefit from the fact that the taxes they pay into Social Security and Medicare funds are matched by their employers. A self-employed person has no one to share the tax burden with and must therefore pay both portions of the tax. This is in addition to the Federal Income Tax resulting from the net profit of the business.

Schedule SE, Self-Employment Tax, must be filed as a part of the business owner's personal tax return. When you review this form, you will see that it is divided into two parts, Short SE and Long SE. The form itself contains instructions for its general use and also indicates which part of the form the taxpayer is required to complete.

Exceptions apply to ministers and farmers, but most small business owners will have to complete the long section of SE and will pay 15.3 percent in self-employment taxes on the net profit generated by their business endeavors. That includes 12.4 percent for Social Security taxes and 2.9 percent for Medicare taxes.

The IRS does allow the self-employed taxpayer to deduct one half of the tax amount from Schedule SE on the Adjusted Gross Income section of his or her personal tax return, but the total of the self-employment tax is added into the amount due for taxable income on the return.

Self-employed individuals need to keep their books updated month to month so they know how much profit is being accumulated. To avoid penalties and interest for underpaid taxes at the end of the calendar year, the self-employed should estimate their tax liability for the year and make advance payments to the IRS.

Of course, the IRS has yet another form to estimate net business income or any income that is not subject to tax deductions by an employer or other payer. This is Form 1040-ES. Anyone who has self-employment income or income from sources other than wages subject to Federal Withholding Tax deductions and expects to owe $1,000. or more by the end of the calendar year should file Form 1040-ES.

FYI For detailed instructions on computing your estimated tax, completing and filing Form 1040-ES, and making payments visit the IRS website at www. irs.gov. In addition, individuals may call the IRS for assistance at 1-800-829-1040. Businesses needing more information and assistance can call the IRS at 1-800-829-4933.

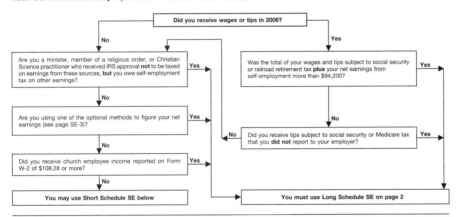

SCHEDULE SE
(Form 1040)

Department of the Treasury
Internal Revenue Service (99)

Self-Employment Tax

▶ Attach to Form 1040. ▶ See Instructions for Schedule SE (Form 1040).

OMB No. 1545-0074

2006

Attachment
Sequence No. **17**

Name of person with **self-employment** income (as shown on Form 1040)

Social security number of person
with **self-employment** income ▶

Who Must File Schedule SE

You must file Schedule SE if:

- You had net earnings from self-employment from **other than** church employee income (line 4 of Short Schedule SE or line 4c of Long Schedule SE) of $400 or more, **or**
- You had church employee income of $108.28 or more. Income from services you performed as a minister or a member of a religious order **is not** church employee income (see page SE-1).

Note. Even if you had a loss or a small amount of income from self-employment, it may be to your benefit to file Schedule SE and use either "optional method" in Part II of Long Schedule SE (see page SE-3).

Exception. If your only self-employment income was from earnings as a minister, member of a religious order, or Christian Science practitioner **and** you filed Form 4361 and received IRS approval not to be taxed on those earnings, **do not** file Schedule SE. Instead, write "Exempt–Form 4361" on Form 1040, line 58.

May I Use Short Schedule SE or Must I Use Long Schedule SE?

Note. Use this flowchart **only if** you must file Schedule SE. If unsure, see Who Must File Schedule SE, above.

Section A—Short Schedule SE. Caution. Read above to see if you can use Short Schedule SE.

1	Net farm profit or (loss) from Schedule F, line 36, and farm partnerships, Schedule K-1 (Form 1065), box 14, code A	**1**
2	Net profit or (loss) from Schedule C, line 31; Schedule C-EZ, line 3; Schedule K-1 (Form 1065), box 14, code A (other than farming); and Schedule K-1 (Form 1065-B), box 9, code J1. Ministers and members of religious orders, see page SE-1 for amounts to report on this line. See page SE-3 for other income to report	**2**
3	Combine lines 1 and 2	**3**
4	**Net earnings from self-employment.** Multiply line 3 by 92.35% (.9235). If less than $400, **do not** file this schedule; you do not owe self-employment tax . . . . ▶	**4**
5	**Self-employment tax.** If the amount on line 4 is:	
	• $94,200 or less, multiply line 4 by 15.3% (.153). Enter the result here and on **Form 1040, line 58.**	**5**
	• More than $94,200, multiply line 4 by 2.9% (.029). Then, add $11,680.80 to the result. Enter the total here and on **Form 1040, line 58.**	
6	**Deduction for one-half of self-employment tax.** Multiply line 5 by 50% (.5). Enter the result here and on **Form 1040, line 27** . . .	**6**

For Paperwork Reduction Act Notice, see Form 1040 instructions.　　Cat. No. 11358Z　　**Schedule SE (Form 1040) 2006**

Schedule SE 1040 (2006) Self-Employment Tax.

Schedule SE (Form 1040) 2006 | Attachment Sequence No. **17** | Page **2**

Name of person with **self-employment** income (as shown on Form 1040)	Social security number of person with **self-employment** income ▶		

Section B—Long Schedule SE

Part I   Self-Employment Tax

Note. If your only income subject to self-employment tax is **church employee income,** skip lines 1 through 4b. Enter -0- on line 4c and go to line 5a. Income from services you performed as a minister or a member of a religious order **is not** church employee income. See page SE-1.

A   If you are a minister, member of a religious order, or Christian Science practitioner **and** you filed Form 4361, but you had $400 or more of **other** net earnings from self-employment, check here and continue with Part I . . . . . . ▶ ☐

1	Net farm profit or (loss) from Schedule F, line 36, and farm partnerships, Schedule K-1 (Form 1065), box 14, code A. **Note.** Skip this line if you use the farm optional method (see page SE-4)	**1**		
2	Net profit or (loss) from Schedule C, line 31; Schedule C-EZ, line 3; Schedule K-1 (Form 1065), box 14, code A (other than farming); and Schedule K-1 (Form 1065-B), box 9, code J1. Ministers and members of religious orders, see page SE-1 for amounts to report on this line. See page SE-3 for other income to report. **Note.** Skip this line if you use the nonfarm optional method (see page SE-4)	**2**		
3	Combine lines 1 and 2	**3**		
4a	If line 3 is more than zero, multiply line 3 by 92.35% (.9235). Otherwise, enter amount from line 3	**4a**		
b	If you elect one or both of the optional methods, enter the total of lines 15 and 17 here . . .	**4b**		
c	Combine lines 4a and 4b. If less than $400, **stop;** you do not owe self-employment tax. **Exception.** If less than $400 and you had **church employee income,** enter -0- and continue. . . . . . ▶	**4c**		
5a	Enter your **church employee income** from Form W-2. See page SE-1 for definition of church employee income . . . . `5a`			
b	Multiply line 5a by 92.35% (.9235). If less than $100, enter -0-	**5b**		
6	**Net earnings from self-employment.** Add lines 4c and 5b	**6**		
7	Maximum amount of combined wages and self-employment earnings subject to social security tax or the 6.2% portion of the 7.65% railroad retirement (tier 1) tax for 2006	**7**	94,200	00
8a	Total social security wages and tips (total of boxes 3 and 7 on Form(s) W-2) and railroad retirement (tier 1) compensation. If $94,200 or more, skip lines 8b through 10, and go to line 11 . . . . `8a`			
b	Unreported tips subject to social security tax (from Form 4137, line 9) `8b`			
c	Add lines 8a and 8b	**8c**		
9	Subtract line 8c from line 7. If zero or less, enter -0- here and on line 10 and go to line 11 . ▶	**9**		
10	Multiply the **smaller** of line 6 or line 9 by 12.4% (.124)	**10**		
11	Multiply line 6 by 2.9% (.029)	**11**		
12	**Self-employment tax.** Add lines 10 and 11. Enter here and on **Form 1040, line 58**	**12**		
13	**Deduction for one-half of self-employment tax.** Multiply line 12 by 50% (.5). Enter the result here and on **Form 1040, line 27** . . . . `13`			

Part II   Optional Methods To Figure Net Earnings (see page SE-3)

Farm Optional Method. You may use this method only if **(a)** your gross farm income[1] was not more than $2,400, **or (b)** your net farm profits[2] were less than $1,733.

14	Maximum income for optional methods	**14**	1,600	00
15	Enter the **smaller** of: two-thirds (⅔) of gross farm income[1] (not less than zero) **or** $1,600. Also include this amount on line 4b above	**15**		

Nonfarm Optional Method. You may use this method **only** if **(a)** your net nonfarm profits[3] were less than $1,733 and also less than 72.189% of your gross nonfarm income,[4] **and (b)** you had net earnings from self-employment of at least $400 in 2 of the prior 3 years.

Caution. You may use this method no more than five times.

16	Subtract line 15 from line 14	**16**		
17	Enter the **smaller** of: two-thirds (⅔) of gross nonfarm income[4] (not less than zero) **or** the amount on line 16. Also include this amount on line 4b above	**17**		

[1] From Sch. F, line 11, and Sch. K-1 (Form 1065), box 14, code B.

[2] From Sch. F, line 36, and Sch. K-1 (Form 1065), box 14, code A.

[3] From Sch. C, line 31; Sch. C-EZ, line 3; Sch. K-1 (Form 1065), box 14, code A; and Sch. K-1 (Form 1065-B), box 9, code J1.

[4] From Sch. C, line 7; Sch. C-EZ, line 1; Sch. K-1 (Form 1065), box 14, code C; and Sch. K-1 (Form 1065-B), box 9, code J2.

Schedule SE (Form 1040) 2006

Estimated tax payments can be divided into four equal payments and paid quarterly or made as one lump-sum payment. The IRS accepts estimated tax payments by mail, through the Electronic Federal Tax

Payment System (EFTPS) or by electronic withdrawals from your bank account. For a fee, you can even make your payments with your credit card by calling 1-877-754-4413.

Whether you are an employee or a self-employed individual, remember that keeping your own books in order and up to date is the best way to avoid money problems. It also helps you to assess your economic situation and make choices that protect your assets and improve your financial condition.

Hour's Up!

Please try to answer the following questions about wage earners and the self-employed.

1. What payroll tax deduction can be modified by an individual?
    a. Social Security
    b. Medicare
    c. Federal Withholding

2. The interest on a new mortgage may provide a large tax deduction at the end of the year.
    a. True
    b. False

3. What is an IRA?
    a. A savings account
    b. A retirement plan
    c. Both a and b

4. Which government agency receives the original copies of W-2 forms?
    a. The IRS
    b. State Department of Revenue
    c. Social Security Administration

5. What date are W-2s supposed to be provided to employees?
    a. January 15th
    b. February 29th
    c. January 31st

Review

6. 1099s are issued to people who provide services to a company, but are not employees.
   a. True
   b. False

7. What form number is titled Taxpayer Identification Number and Certification?
   a. W-4
   b. W-2
   c. W-9

8. Corporations must receive 1099s for services rendered.
   a. True
   b. False

9. What is the 2007 rate for Self-Employment Taxes?
   a. 12.4 percent
   b. 15.3 percent
   c. 2.9 percent

10. How much of Self-Employment Tax can be taken as a deduction on the taxpayer's personal return?
    a. 50 percent
    b. 25 percent
    c. 33 percent

Closing the Books, Issuing Financial Reports, and Gathering Tax Data

Part IV

Closing the Books at the End of the Month

Chapter Summary

In this hour you will learn about …

- Adjusting entries
- Depreciation Schedules
- Amortization Schedules
- Petty Cash
- Balancing customer ledgers
- Bad Debts
- Balancing vendor ledgers

The end of the month is one of the busiest times for bookkeepers. As one month is closed out so that the Financial Statements can be issued, a new month is about to begin. The business activity does not come to a halt while the bookkeeper makes adjustments and makes sure everything is posted to the General Ledger. The business operation continues to generate transactions that also have to be reconciled and posted.

As you have already learned, a computerized bookkeeping system allows the bookkeeper to go back and forth between the current month and the prior month, so that all the new transactions and all the adjustments for the prior month can be dealt with easily.

Because manual bookkeeping systems are generally for small business operations without a large number of accounts, a new set of ledger sheets can be set up for each month of the business year. Leave a blank line at the beginning of the new monthly sheet to record the balance that will be carried forward from the prior month when it is closed out.

Adjusting Entries

Most of the adjusting entries that are posted to the General Ledger at the end of the month have been introduced in prior chapters. In this hour, we will review them again, and then provide more information on the ones that may need additional attention at the end of the month.

The adjusting entries that are made by the majority of companies at the end of every month include the following:

GO TO ▶

Hour 17 where samples and instructions on correcting posting errors can be found.

- **Corrections**—some posting errors can be corrected in the General Ledger by reversing the original entry and reposting it correctly.
- **Inventory**—a physical inventory is taken and the inventory account is adjusted to the actual amount of inventory on hand.
- **Accounts Payable**—bills to be paid after the first of the new month are posted to Accounts Payable so that the expenses can be included in the Financial Statement for the month they were incurred. Vendor ledgers should be updated so the balances are current.
- **Prepaid Expenses**—adjustments are made for items like insurance premiums that were paid in advance for the year, so that the expense can be written off month by month to provide a more accurate financial picture.
- **Payroll and Payroll Taxes**—all payroll and payroll taxes should be posted when the paychecks are issued so no further adjustments should be necessary. Employee payroll ledgers should be updated at the same time and Gross Wages, Taxes, and other deductions totaled and reviewed after the last paycheck of the month has been issued and posted.
- **Accounts Receivable**—all invoices and all payments should be posted and the ledger cards updated so that the balances on the customers' accounts are ready to be billed.
- **Bank Accounts**—as soon as the bank statements are received they should be reconciled with the checkbook and the General Ledger accounts. Adjustments for discrepancies between the bank and the company books should be made in the month the error occurred.
- **Liability Accounts**—accounts for loans payable should be reconciled each month to make sure the balance on the books agrees with the balance on the lender's books.
- **Interest**—interest expense should be posted when the loan payments are made each month.

Other adjustments like Depreciation and Amortization follow a specific schedule depending on the rate and time period assigned to them.

Depreciation Schedules

While most assets depreciate in value as they are used, for bookkeeping purposes, Accumulated Depreciation and Depreciation Expense accounts in the General Ledger are there for another important reason.

These accounts are used to record the tax deductions the IRS allows the business to claim on its tax return. This deduction reduces the Net Profit and therefore reduces the amount of income tax the business has to pay.

The tax regulations state that property that is acquired for business use that is expected to last more than one year can be depreciated. This means that the cost of the property can be recovered as a tax deduction over the useful life of the asset.

In order to be depreciated the asset must qualify as follows:

- The taxpayer must own the property.
- The property must be used in the taxpayer's business or income-producing activities.
- The property must have a useful life longer than one year.

Property that cannot be depreciated includes the following:

- Land
- Property acquired and disposed of in the same tax year
- Intangible assets, such as the costs of franchises and goodwill.

There are many other rules that apply to this tax deduction and several methods that are used to calculate the depreciation depending on the asset and its useful life. In years past, the Straight Line method of depreciation was the one most commonly used. This simple method divided the cost of the asset by the number of years it was expected to be used. For example, if an automobile was used for business and cost $15,000. and was expected to last three years, the Depreciation Expense was $5,000. per year or approximately $416. per month.

While the Straight Line method is still used, today there are many more complex methods and even more rules associated with them. MACRS stands for Modified Accelerated Cost Recovery System and is a popular method that allows quicker, larger depreciation deductions.

Today's bookkeeper should have some basic knowledge of the depreciation process and methods of calculating the deduction, but the Depreciation Schedules and the methods should be handled by a professional accountant who can advise the business owner on the best way to depreciate the company's assets.

Whenever a new property is acquired by a business the accountant should be notified so that a Depreciation Schedule that will give the owner the maximum tax benefit can be discussed and structured. Also, as you learned earlier, some companies do not record the depreciation until the end of the tax year when the accountant prepares their return. For other companies, once the accountant has written up the Depreciation Schedule, it is given to the bookkeeper so that the adjustments can be posted into the General Ledger on a monthly basis.

Regardless of the method of depreciation that is used, the monthly entry to post the expense into the General Ledger is the same. Let's look at a sample of a Depreciation Schedule and then review how the expenses will be posted.

Depreciable Assets

Acquired	Description	Cost	Months	Depreciation Amount
Real Property:				
2000	Building	250,000.00	480	$520.84
Totals		250,000.00		520.84
Office Equipment:				
2006	Computer	6,000.00	60	100.00
2000	Furniture & Fixtures	12,000.00	84	142.86
Totals		18,000.00		242.86
Vehicles:				
2004	Ford Truck	23,000.00	60	383.34
Totals		23,000.00	—	383.34

PROCEED WITH CAUTION

The sample Depreciation Schedule is for demonstration purposes only and should not be used to estimate costs, terms, or Depreciation Expenses on actual business property.

The end of the month adjustment to record the Depreciation Expense laid out on the sample schedule would be written up as follows:

Date	Account	Description	Debit	Credit
9-30-07	1511	Acc. Depr. Building		520.84
	1581	Acc. Depr. F & F		242.86
	1651	Acc. Depr. Vehicles		383.34
	6160	Sept. Expense	1,147.04	
Totals			1,147.04	1,147.04

Note that each category of assets receives a credit to its Accumulated Depreciation Account and then the total of all the depreciation is posted to Depreciation Expense.

Depreciating costly assets provides a good tax break for companies. However, keep in mind that when an asset that has been depreciated is sold, the depreciation amounts may be charged back to the owner as taxable income by the IRS. The advice of a professional accountant or tax advisor should be sought before disposing of any asset that has been depreciated.

Amortization Schedules

Intangible assets such as franchise fees and goodwill are not eligible for depreciation. However, these costs can be substantial and are often written off over time through the process called Amortization.

There are, of course, IRS rules and procedures for taking this tax deduction. Again, the bookkeeper would not be the person setting up the Amortization Schedules associated with these costs. The company's professional accountant will set up the schedules and then turn them over to the bookkeeper for posting.

The bookkeeper will post the expense monthly or yearly as indicated by the CPA. For example, a Franchise Fee of $150,000. could be written off over a period of ten years. This would result in an annual expense of $15,000. or a monthly write-off of $1,250.

The monthly entry to post this expense would be done as follows:

Date	Account	Description	Debit	Credit
9-30	1851	Acc. Amort.-Org		1,250.00
	6150	Sept. Amort	1,250.00	

FYI For more information on Amortization and the costs that can be written off through this process, read IRS Publication 535, which can be accessed on the IRS website (www.irs.gov) or ordered by calling 1-800-829-3676.

Petty Cash

Many offices keep cash on hand for incidental expenses, like delivery fees or small supplies. This is called the Petty Cash fund because the word petty means little or insignificant. The Petty Cash fund is usually between $50. and $100. It is not necessary to review and post the expenses paid out of the Petty Cash every month. Petty Cash should be reconciled and the expenses posted only when it is close to depletion and needs to be replenished.

The bookkeeper usually has custody and control of the Petty Cash fund and any time money is taken out of this fund, a notation of the expense or a receipt for the amount spent should be put into the box or envelope where the cash is kept.

Let's assume the following receipts are in the Petty Cash box to explain why the fund has dwindled from $50. to $2.00 and needs to be replenished.

2 rolls of adding machine tape	3.75
1 dozen donuts	5.50
Postage due	1.50
Paper clips	2.25
Coffee	8.00
Paper cups	5.00
2 books of stamps	15.60
Sugar and creamer	6.40
	48.00

To replenish the Petty Cash fund a check for $48. would be written and cashed and the check would be posted as follows:

Date	Account	Description	Debit	Credit
9-30	1000	Check # 143		48.00
	6340	P.C. Postage	17.10	
	6300	P.C. Office Exp.	30.90	
Totals			48.00	48.00

If there is not an account on the Balance Sheet titled Petty Cash that shows a balance of $50., the amount is posted to Cash on Hand. However, it is not necessary to post to that account unless the amount in the Petty Cash fund is going to be increased or decreased. In this case, there was $2. remaining in Petty Cash and the $48. added to it brought the fund back to the $50. shown on the Balance Sheet.

It is necessary to post the check that replenished the Petty Cash fund as a credit to the Cash in Checking (Account 1000) and to post the expenses that were paid out of Petty Cash to the proper accounts.

If the bookkeeper decided that the Petty Cash Fund should be increased to $75., the entry to post the expenses and increase the fund would be as follows:

Date	Account	Description	Debit	Credit
9-30	1000	Check # 143		73.00
	6340	P.C. Postage	17.10	
	6300	P.C. Office Exp.	30.90	
	1020	Cash on Hand	25.00	
Totals			73.00	73.00

Now the Cash on Hand account has been changed on the Balance Sheet to the new amount of $75. to reflect the increase in the office's Petty Cash fund.

This is a minor bookkeeping procedure, but it should help you understand a little more about how small transactions are categorized and posted on the books. You should have noted that there are two amounts added together to obtain the amount for Postage Expense and the other expenditures were simply added together and charged to Office Expense.

Balancing Customer Ledgers

At the end of the month, the customer ledger cards should be reviewed and the balances on the cards totaled and compared with the balance in the Accounts Receivable account. If the two amounts match, it indicates that all the credit sales and all the customer payments received during the month were posted to the customer ledger cards and to Accounts Receivable.

If the ledger cards add up to more than the Accounts Receivable balance in the General Ledger, it probably means that a customer's payment was posted to Accounts Receivable but not to the customer's ledger card. Because the payment was a cash receipt, the amount posted as a deposit (debit) to the bank account would have to match the amount posted as a payment (credit) to Accounts Receivable. So, it is most likely the ledger card that is incorrect.

 Payments received for credit sales should be posted to the customers' ledger cards first. Then, make a separate deposit for the payments and post the deposit total to the Cash in Checking account and Accounts Receivable. It will be easier to go back and compare the deposits by dates.

If the ledger cards' total is less than that recorded in Accounts Receivable, there may be a credit sale that was not posted to the ledger card. Remember that the daily sales total should add up to the bank deposit made for cash sales and the total of credit sales posted to Accounts Receivable. The month should not be closed out until the customer ledger cards and the total in Accounts Receivable are in agreement.

In a computerized system, the ledger cards are automatically posted when the credit sale or payment is posted to Accounts Receivable eliminating the errors that can occur in a manual system.

Bad Debts

As discussed in Hour 4 when the Bad Debts Account was added to the General Ledger, not all customers pay their bills in full. In some businesses, trying to collect delinquent accounts may be the bookkeeper's job.

When all of the company's efforts to collect a delinquent account have failed, the account could be turned over to a professional bill collector.

However, professional collectors keep a percentage of all they collect, so the company that extended credit to the customer is still going to come out short even if the bill collector is successful.

Accounts Receivable is part of the accrual bookkeeping method, so the income for the uncollected sale amount has already been recognized on the company's books. To offset the income that is on the books, but in reality never materialized, the delinquent amount is removed from Accounts Receivable and recorded in the Bad Debt Account.

In large operations, moving the accounts that cannot be collected to Bad Debts may happen at the end of every month. In smaller companies, these accounts may only be purged once a year. However, bookkeepers need to be aware of the process and be able to make the entry.

GO TO ◄

Hour 7 for a review of the posting process that occurs when a customer buys merchandise or services on credit.

Remember that when the sale was originally made, it was posted as a credit to Income and a debit to Accounts Receivable.

The entry to offset the unrealized income would be as follows:

Date	Account	Description	Debit	Credit
9-30-07	1100	A.R. Customer # 606		375.00
	6550	Bad Debts	375.00	

Once the customer's balance has been posted to the Bad Debt Account, remove the customer's ledger card from the file and refile it in the Bad Debt file folder. This is because the customer may have a change of heart and pay the bill and if that happens in the same year it was written off, the above entry can be easily reversed, the ledger card put back in Accounts Receivable, and then posted for the payment. If the customer pays the bill after the current year, it is simpler to just accept the payment and credit it to Income and debit it to Cash in Checking.

If a bill collector is working on the delinquent accounts, you would simply leave them in Accounts Receivable in the event the collector is successful. Then, the bookkeeper would post the partial payment to the ledger card and write off the rest as a bad debt. On the other side of the fence, remember that delinquent accounts are reported to the Credit Bureau and have an adverse affect on the payer's credit history and rating.

Balancing Vendor Ledgers

The end of the month is a good time to review the vendor ledgers and make sure that all the amounts have been posted to Accounts Payable.

The Accounts Payable balance should agree with the total due on the vendor ledgers. Accounts Payable should also be zeroed out when the payments are made. Remember that if the bill was posted in Accounts Payable, the check that pays the bill should also be posted to Accounts Payable and to the vendor ledger to clear that as well.

TIME SAVER

 In companies where the business activity never slows down, the bookkeepers may have to put in some overtime at the end of the month to get everything done. A list of tasks that have to be done at the end of the month can be created and checked off as they are completed. As you become more adept at the procedures your particular company requires, you will find that some of the tasks on your list may be able to be done before the end of the month, making the last days of the month less hectic.

The main thing to remember about issuing Financial Statements is not to rush. Bookkeeping is a systematic process and needs to be done one step at a time to avoid errors.

Hour's Up!

Answering the following questions about closing the books at the end of the month will help you remember the main points covered in this chapter.

1. Which of the following adjusting entries is made by most companies at the end of the month?
   a. Sales
   b. Inventory
   c. Accounts Payable

2. Bank accounts should be reconciled as soon as the bank statements are received.
   a. True
   b. False

3. What qualifies a property to be depreciated?
   a. Used for income-producing activities
   b. Cost of property
   c. Location of property

4. What property cannot be depreciated?
    a. Vehicles
    b. Equipment
    c. Land

5. What is an example of an intangible asset?
    a. Insurance premiums
    b. Organizational costs
    c. Rents

6. What is Amortization?
    a. A liability
    b. Capital expenditure
    c. The write-off of intangible assets

7. What IRS publication explains Amortization?
    a. 451
    b. 535
    c. 329

8. The Petty Cash fund should be reconciled and reimbursed every week.
    a. True
    b. False

9. What account in the General Ledger often holds the Petty Cash fund amount?
    a. Cash in Checking
    b. Cash in Savings
    c. Cash on Hand

10. What is posted to the Bad Debts Account?
    a. Delinquent Accounts Receivable
    b. Delinquent Accounts Payable
    c. Errors in Accounts Receivable

Issuing Financial Statements

Chapter Summary

In this hour you will learn about …

- Posting from the checkbook
- Profit & Loss Statement
- Current month and year-to-date
- Balance Sheet
- Notes to Financial Statements

Issuing the Financial Statements for an employing company or your own small business is what a bookkeeper works toward all month long. It's a little like crossing the finish line after a race. All the steps, large and small, taken during the preceding month have led up to this point.

In smaller business operations the checkbook balance is a good indication of whether the month has been profitable or not. However, the Financial Statements are what make it possible to study the overall picture.

Every account where data was recorded will have a debit or credit balance that consolidates every transaction that has been posted to the General Ledger. This enables the owners and bookkeepers to see the strengths and weaknesses of the business and it gives them an opportunity to make adjustments in the operating activities if needed.

Posting from the Checkbook

As you learned in Hour 10, the checkbook itself is a mini-financial report. It is the heart of the bookkeeping system, especially for businesses that operate on a cash basis.

While all business operations should have accounts set up in a General Ledger, small cash basis bookkeeping systems, such as those used by a home-based one person business, may choose to record all transactions in the checkbook and only post to the General Ledger when it's time to issue the Financial Statements. This is an acceptable way to operate a bookkeeping system as long as the owner is diligent about extracting the information from the checkbook to issue Financial Statements on a regular basis.

Using Cakes by Claire, the home-based business you looked at in Hour 2, as a sample company, we will review her checkbook and see how it is posted into the General Ledger at the end of each month so that Financial Statements can be issued.

Here are the accounts that were set up in the General Ledger for Cakes by Claire:

> 1000-Cash in Checking
> 1010-Cash in Savings
> **Sales:**
> 4000-Birthday Cakes
> 4010-Wedding Cakes
> 4020-Anniversary Cakes
> 4030-Miscellaneous Cakes
> **Cost of Sales:**
> 4310-Baking Ingredients
> 4315-Decorating Supplies
> 4320-Boxes and Platters
> **Expenses:**
> 6000-Advertising
> 6010-Delivery Expense
> 6020-Equipment
> 6300-Office Expense
> 6350-Miscellaneous Supplies
> 6400-Telephone Expense
> 6450-Website
> 3210-Capital
> 3040-Retained Earnings

Cakes by Claire operates on a cash basis, and the following figure shows a portion of her checkbook vouchers detailing deposits and disbursements for the month of September. A worksheet, shown after the checkbook vouchers, is then created and used to recap all the deposits and disbursements from the checkbook.

	1502	bal. brought forward 9-1 >	1,042	00
			350	00
			Wedding	
Date 9-1-07			45	00
To Yahoo		DEPOSITS	BD Cake	
For Website	total		1,437	00
	this check		14	95
	other			
tax deductible	balance		1,422	05

	1503	bal. brought forward 9-5 >	300	00
			Wedding	
Date 9-7-07			125	00
		DEPOSITS	Misc	
To Alltel			45	00
			BD	
For Cell Phones	total		1,892	05
	this check		29	35
	other			
tax deductible	balance		1,862	70

	1504	bal. 9-10 > brought forward		
			100	00
			BD	
Date 9-15-07			400	00
To Bakers Wholesale		DEPOSITS	Wedding	
Products				
For Flour and Sugar	total		2,362	70
	this check		152	35
	other			
tax deductible	balance		2210	35

1505

bal. brought forward

9-20 ▷

Date _____ 9-22-07 _____

To _____ Grover's Market _____

For _____ Eggs and Milk _____

DEPOSITS

	2,210	35
	75	00
	Misc	
	100	00
	BD	
total	2,385	35
this check	23	56
other		
balance	2,361	79

tax deductible

1506

bal. brought forward

9-21 ▷

Date _____ 9-30-07 _____

To _____ Daily Star _____

For _____ Display Ad _____

DEPOSITS

	100	00
	BD	
	350	00
	Anniv.	
total	2,811	79
this check	525	00
other		
balance	2,286	79

tax deductible

1507

bal. brought forward

9-28 ▷

Date _____ 9-30-07 _____

To _____ Party Store _____

For _____ Decorating _____
_____ Supplies _____

DEPOSITS

	80	00
	Misc	
	40	00
	BD	
total	2,406	79
this check	72	34
other		
balance	2334	45

tax deductible

1508   bal. brought forward   2,334 | 45

Date _____ 9-30-07

To _____ Paper Warehouse

DEPOSITS

For _____ Boxes

total	2,334	45
this check	110	00
other		

tax deductible

| balance | 2,224 | 45 |

1509   bal. brought forward

Date _____ 9-30-07

To _____ Buy the Book

DEPOSITS

For _____ Cake Decorating

Book

total	2,224	45
this check	25	93
other		

tax deductible

| balance | 2,198 | 52 |

1510   bal. brought forward

Date _____

To _____

DEPOSITS

For _____

total		
this check		
other		

tax deductible

| balance | | |

Cakes by Claire

September, 2007

			4000	4010	4020	4030			
			Birthday Cakes	Wedding Cakes	Anniversary Cakes	Misc. Cakes			
1			45.00	350.00	350.00	125.00			
2			45.00	300.00		75.00			
3			100.00	400.00		80.00			
4			100.00						
5			100.00						
6			40.00						
7									
8			430.00	1050.00	350.00	280.00	Income		
9									
10			4310	4315	4320				
11			Baking	Decorating	Boxes and				
12			Ingredients	Supplies	Platters				
13			152.35	72.34	110.00				
14			23.56						
15									
16			175.91	72.34	110.00		Cost of Sales		
17									
18									
19									
20			6000	6010	6020	6300			
21			Advertising	Delivery	Equipment	Office			
22			Expense	Expense	Expense	Expenses			
23			525.00	—0—	—0—	—0—			
24									
25			525.00	—0—	—0—	—0—	Expenses		
26									
27			6350	6400	6450				
28			Misc.	Telephone	Website				
29			Supplies	Expense	Expense				
30			25.93	29.35	14.95				
31									
32			25.93	29.35	14.95		Expenses		
33									
34									
35									
36									
37									
38									
39									
40									

Based on the recap figures, the entry to post the September activity to the General Ledger is as follows:

Date	Account	Description	Debit	Credit
9-30-07	4000	Sept. Sales		430.00
	4010	Sept. Sales		1,050.00
	4020	Sept. Sales		350.00
	4030	Sept. Sales		280.00
	4310	Sept. COS	175.91	
	4315	Sept. COS	72.34	
	4320	Sept. COS	110.00	
	6000	Sept. Exp.	525.00	
	6350	Sept. Exp.	25.93	
	6400	Sept. Exp.	29.35	
	6450	Sept. Exp.	14.95	
	1000	Checking Acct.	1,156.52	
Totals			2,110.00	2,110.00

As you can see, the debits equal the credits because the difference between the income and expenses taken from the checkbook has been posted as a debit to the bank account.

A simple calculation verifying that the offset posted to the bank account is correct is as follows:

Cash in Checking:
Beginning Balance 9-1-07	$1,042.00
September Activity	+ 1,156.52
Ending Balance 9-30-07	$2,198.52

The Profit & Loss Statement for the month of September 2007 for Cakes by Claire would be as follows:

Cakes by Claire
Profit & Loss Statement
September 30, 2007

Sales Income:
Birthday Cakes	$430.00
Wedding Cakes	1,050.00

continues

(continued)

Anniversary Cakes	350.00
Miscellaneous Cakes	280.00
Total Sales	2,110.00
Cost of Sales:	
Baking Ingredients	175.91
Decorating Supplies	72.34
Boxes & Platters	110.00
Total Cost of Sales	358.25
Gross Profit	1,751.75
Expenses:	
Advertising	525.00
Misc. Supplies	25.93
Telephone Expense	29.35
Website Expense	14.95
Total Expenses	595.23
Net Profit (Loss)	1,156.52

One thing in particular should jump out at you. The Net Profit for this month is the difference posted to the Cash in Checking Account in the General Ledger.

Please take some time to review the check register, the recap worksheet, and the Profit & Loss Statement presented as samples. Study how the information in the check register is used to create the worksheet and the worksheet is used to post the September activity into the General Ledger to provide the data for the Profit & Loss Statement.

Current Month and Year-to-Date

The Profit & Loss Statement issued for Cakes by Claire for the month of September is what would be considered the current month on the

Financial Statements. However, most Profit & Loss Statements also have a second column that provides the *year-to-date financial information*.

 The **year-to-date financial information** reports the Profit & Loss figures from the first day of the business year to the last day of the current month.

Because Cakes by Claire operates on a calendar year, the year-to-date column on her Profit & Loss Statement would be from January 1, 2007, to September 30, 2007.

Still using Cakes by Claire as our sample company, her Profit & Loss Statement for the current month and year-to-date would be as follows:

Cakes by Claire
Profit & Loss Statement
For the Period

	September 1, 2007 to September 30, 2007	January 1, 2007 to September 30, 2007
Sales:		
Birthday Cakes	$430.00	$4,070.00
Wedding Cakes	1,050.00	9,950.00
Anniversary Cakes	350.00	2,100.00
Miscellaneous Cakes	280.00	3,880.00
Total Sales	2,110.00	20,000.00
Cost of Sales:		
Baking Ingredients	175.91	1,583.19
Decorating Supplies	72.34	472.34
Boxes & Platters	110.00	330.75
Total Cost of Sales	358.25	2,386.28
Gross Profit	1,751.75	17,613.72

continues

(continued)

Expenses:		
Advertising	525.00	1,050.00
Delivery Expense	0.00	35.00
Equipment	0.00	372.84
Office Expense	0.00	603.00
Misc. Supplies	25.93	105.93
Telephone Expense	29.35	252.15
Website Expense	14.95	134.55
Total Expenses	595.23	2,553.47
Net Profit (Loss)	1,156.52	15,060.25

Because this is a very small home-based business, some of the accounts set up in the Expense Section of the Profit & Loss Statement do not have expenses posted to them every month. When there is no expense to be reported for the current month of business activity, the account shows a zero balance in the current month, but does show a balance in the year-to-date column for prior months when expenses were posted.

The next set of Financial Statements for Cakes by Claire will show October 2007 as the current month and the year-to-date figures will be for January 1, 2007, to October 31, 2007.

Only the Profit & Loss Statement will have a column for the current month and the year-to-date. The Balance Sheet only has one column of financial information and that will always be the year-to-date figures.

Balance Sheet

The Balance Sheet for Cakes by Claire couldn't be simpler. The only assets shown on her books are her bank accounts. You may recall that Claire used $1,000. of her personal funds as capital to begin her cake business. She put $900. into the checking account and $100. into the savings account. Now after nine months of business activity, the Balance Sheet for this fictional home-based business would be as follows:

Cakes by Claire
Balance Sheet
September 30, 2007

Assets:	
Cash in Checking	$2,198.52
Cash in Savings	12,861.73
Total Assets	**$15,060.25**
Liabilities:	0.00
Total Liabilities	**0.00**
Equity:	
Capital	1,000.00
Retained Earnings	12,903.73
Net Income (Loss)	1,156.52
Total Liabilities & Equity	**$15,060.25**

As you can see, Assets equal Liabilities and Equity, and Cakes by Claire is a profitable, stable business.

Note that Retained Earnings shows the profits for January through August. The Net Income figure is for the current month of September. Next month, September's profit will be added to the Retained Earnings account balance and the October profit will be displayed on the line for Net Income (Loss).

The Financial Statements you have just reviewed are for a sample company that is a very small home-based business operating on a cash basis. Obviously, the method used for this one-person business could not be employed for the larger, more complex business operations presented as samples in other chapters. However, for bookkeepers that are running home-based businesses or doing bookkeeping for small companies, the procedures outlined in this hour work well.

GO TO ▶

Hour 17 where more complex business operations will be reviewed along with their Balance Sheets and Profit & Loss Statements.

Like every other aspect of the bookkeeping process, the basics are the same regardless of the size of the business. Now that you have reviewed these easy, uncomplicated Financial Statements, you should be ready to move forward and tackle reports for larger, more active business enterprises.

Notes to Financial Statements

Sometimes there are items on Financial Statements that need explaining. For example, if a business that has been operating at a profit suddenly experiences a significant reduction in its monthly profit or even a loss, the circumstances that led to that reversal should be noted and the notes made a part of that month's reports.

Notes to Financial Statements are especially important for bookkeepers who must present the statements at board meetings or other gatherings where interested parties will be questioning different items on the statements.

Going back to the September Profit & Loss Statement for Cakes by Claire, you can see that $525. was spent for a newspaper ad that month. This could be considered a larger than normal expense for this business. So, a brief explanation of why the ad was purchased might be in order.

The notes should be made any time a large expenditure occurs or any time situations arise that cause a reduction in sales or profits. Strangely enough, when income is higher than expected, people don't tend to question their good fortune. It's only when profits are lower than expected that explanations are expected.

However, if the income is higher due to a one-time "windfall" that will not be repeated next year, that income should also be explained, so outside observers will not expect the same income next year.

Even if the notes are only to refresh the bookkeeper's memory, it's a good habit to cultivate.

Hour's Up!

Using the samples presented in this hour, please answer the following questions.

1. Under what heading on the Financial Statements for Cakes by Claire will Accounts 1000 and 1010 be listed?
   a. Profit & Loss Income
   b. Balance Sheet Assets
   c. Balance Sheet Equity

2. Under what heading on the Financial Statements for Cakes by Claire will Accounts 4310, 4315, and 4320 be listed?
   a. Profit & Loss Expenses
   b. Balance Sheet Liabilities
   c. Profit & Loss Cost of Sales

3. The checkbook is a mini-financial statement for an accrual book-keeping system.
   a. True
   b. False

4. Retained Earnings displays what amount on the Financial Statement?
   a. Current month Profit & Loss
   b. Accumulated profits covering the first day in business to the last day of the prior month
   c. Year-to-date profit

5. Where does Account 3210 appear on the Financial Statement?
   a. Balance Sheet Assets
   b. Profit & Loss Cost of Sales
   c. Balance Sheet Equity

6. Why doesn't Cakes by Claire have any liabilities on the Balance Sheet?
   a. Cash basis business
   b. No loans or Accounts Payable
   c. No expenses

7. In smaller businesses, the checkbook balance is a good indication of the company's profitability.
   a. True
   b. False

Review

8. Why do some accounts on Cakes by Claire's Profit & Loss Statement show a zero balance for the current month?
   a. No year-to-date activity
   b. Never used
   c. No activity in the current month

9. Posting from the checkbook works for any size company.
   a. True
   b. False

10. What should be done when a situation or expenditure causes a significant reduction in profits?
    a. Nothing
    b. Note to Financial Statements
    c. Call the owner

Closing the Books at the End of the Year

Chapter Summary

In this hour you will learn about …

- Writing off outstanding checks
- The Trial Balance
- Identifying and correcting problems
- Running year-end reports
- Closing the General Ledger
- Keeping payroll records
- Balance Sheet accounts for the new year

You've already learned about the payroll reports and forms that are issued at the end of the calendar year. Now we will go through the other tasks that close out one financial year and begin a new one.

It doesn't matter whether the company operates on a calendar year or a fiscal year; the procedures to close out the old year and begin the new one are the same.

Up to this point, you have studied a number of small companies and learned the basic steps of working with the General Ledger and issuing Financial Statements. We will now move on to examine how these same basic steps are used to close the books and issue Financial Statements for larger business enterprises.

Writing Off Outstanding Checks

There are a number of different reasons why a check remains outstanding on your bank statement from month to month. Sometimes checks get lost or destroyed between the payer's bank and the vendor's bank. Sometimes the vendor loses the check.

When a check has been outstanding for more than 180 days it is considered "stale-dated" and should not be negotiated by the bank. Companies often contact the vendor and try to find out why the check has not yet been cashed. However, if the vendor has not contacted the payer claiming nonpayment of the bill the check covered, most companies simply write it off in their books.

Outstanding checks can be written off at any time during the year, but it is especially important to write off old outstanding checks at the end of the financial year, so they are not carried forward into the new year.

The procedure to write off an old outstanding check is simple. Look up the check number and determine what account was posted for the payment. For example, an outstanding check that paid for office supplies would be written off by a debit to Cash in Checking and a credit to Office Expense.

Once you have written the check off the books, enter the transaction into your checkbook in the space on the vouchers reserved for other entries. Note the check number and the amount added back into the bank account.

JUST A MINUTE

 Writing off outstanding checks should be done before the bank statement is reconciled so that the check can then be eliminated from the list of outstanding checks on the worksheet.

The Trial Balance

You may remember that the Trial Balance is a General Ledger report that displays all the accounts with their year-to-date balances. If you were to add up all the debit balances on this report and subtract all the credit balances, the net result would be zero. This proves that all the entries that were posted were in balance. That is, all the debits equaled all the credits.

It's actually a good idea to print out a Trial Balance report at the end of every month just because it is an easy way to look over all the balances in all the accounts. It is essential to examine the Trial Balance at the end of the year as this is the last opportunity to make adjustments and correct any posting errors.

The following Trial Balance report is for a fictional company, ABC Sales, and is for *its first year in business* ending 12-31-07.

As you can see, the debits equal the credits on this sample report so you know the books are in balance. To give you a better understanding of this report, let's break it down into sections.

ABC Sales
TRIAL BALANCE
December 31, 2007

GL ACCOUNT/NAME	DEBIT	CREDIT
1000 Checking Account	49,955.14	
1020 Cash Register Fund	100.00	
1050 Savings Account	109,500.00	
1100 Accounts Receivable	8,710.22	
1200 Inventory	58,325.00	
1350 Prepaid Expenses	300.00	
1500 Land	27,000.00	
1510 Buildings	232,000.00	
1511 A/D - Buildings		38,666.70
1570 Equipment	17,325.00	
1571 A/D - Equipment		3,465.00
1580 Furniture and Fixtures	6,235.00	
1581 A/D - Furniture & Fixtures		1,122.30
1650 Vehicles	37,500.00	
1651 A/D - Vehicles		11,250.00
1800 Utility Deposits	1,500.00	
1900 Organization Costs	4,000.00	
1901 Accum Amortization - Org Costs		2,400.12
2000 Accounts Payable		17,563.48
2025 Mortgage-Sunset Bank		248,000.00
2100 Employee Health Ins Payable		2,100.00
2105 Dental Insurance Payable		510.00
2110 401k Payable		2,000.00
2190 Sales Taxes Payable		1,675.52
2200 Federal Withholding Tax Payabl		3,400.00
2210 Social Security Tax Payable		2,480.00
2212 Medicare Withholding Tax Pay		580.00
2220 State Withholding Taxes Payabl		680.00
2280 Accrued FUTA		160.00
2290 Accrued SUTA		60.00
2900 Notes Payable - Officer		25,000.00
3210 Capital		57,000.00
4000 Sales		433,510.78
4280 Sales Discounts	565.00	
4290 Sales Returns & Allowances	1,800.00	
4310 Purchases	174,975.00	
4410 Purchases Discounts		3,480.00
6000 Salaries and Wages	45,000.00	
6050 Advertising	800.00	
6100 Auto Expense	4,512.64	
6120 Bank Service Charges	60.00	
6160 Depreciation Expense	4,542.03	
6180 Dues & Subscriptions	1,600.00	
6220 Utilities	4,500.00	
6230 Insurance - Employee Group	11,745.00	
6240 Insurance - General	900.00	
6255 401k Expense	9,000.00	

ABC Sales
TRIAL BALANCE
December 31, 2007

GL ACCOUNT/NAME	DEBIT	CREDIT
6260 Interest Expense	17,360.00	
6270 Legal & Accounting	1,500.00	
6280 Miscellaneous Expense	254.33	
6300 Office Expense	2,789.54	
6310 Outside Services	200.00	
6340 Postage Expense	240.00	
6380 Repairs & Maintenance	985.00	
6440 Supplies Expense	365.00	
6480 Taxes - Real estate	2,700.00	
6490 Taxes - Payroll	15,300.00	
6520 Telephone	960.00	
TOTALS:	855,103.90	855,103.90

The Trial Balance combines the Balance Sheet accounts with the Profit & Loss Statement accounts. The Balance Sheet accounts begin with Account 1000 Cash in Checking and end with Account 3210 Capital. Notice that the Retained Earnings account does not appear on the Trial Balance. That's because the Retained Earnings amount for the first year a company operates is the same as the Net Profit or Loss for that year.

If you add the debits and subtract the credits in the Balance Sheet section of the Trial Balance, the result will be the same amount that you will get by performing the same procedure with the Profit & Loss Statement section.

When the General Ledger is closed out for the current year, the profit reported on the Profit & Loss statement will be transferred to the Retained Earnings account in the Balance Sheet section. You will see how that works later in this chapter, but for now we will concentrate on some of the other things you should note on the Trial Balance report.

Take a look at Account 1350 Prepaid Expenses and see how it relates to Account 6240 Insurance-General. If the insurance premium had been paid in January 2007, the Prepaid Expense account would show a zero balance and the account for general insurance would be $1,200. As it stands now there is still $300. in the Prepaid Expense account and $900. in the Insurance-General account, which tells us that there are still three months to go before the insurance expires and the annual premium will be paid again.

Account 2025 Mortgage-Sunset Bank is related to Account 6260 Interest Expense and to Account 6480 Taxes-Real Estate. Remember that a bookkeeper separates the deductible portions of a mortgage payment, interest and taxes, from the principle amount which is the only part of the payment that is posted to the Liability account.

Also note that Account 2280 Accrued FUTA (Federal Unemployment Taxes) shows a balance of $160. That means it can be paid with the annual Federal Unemployment Report (Form 940) because it is well under the $500. limit for that report.

Last but not least, note that this company has many more accounts than any other one presented as samples in this book, but the basic structure of the Balance Sheet and the Profit & Loss Statement are the same as the smaller sample companies.

Identifying and Correcting Problems

Although the books of ABC Sales are in balance, with debits equaling credits, the Trial Balance may help you pinpoint other problems that need attention. The longer you manage the books for a specific company, the easier it will be for you to review the Trial Balance and recognize accounts that may need to be adjusted.

The following is a list of the things that could show up on the Trial Balance that will alert you to posting errors:

- A debit balance in an account that should have a credit balance
- A credit balance in an account that should have a debit balance
- A larger than usual balance in an account
- A smaller than usual balance in an account
- The appearance of an account that is rarely used

Still using the Trial Balance for ABC Sales, let's look at two accounts that could have alerted the bookkeeper to a posting error.

Account 6050 Advertising has a balance of $800., however the book-keeper knows that the company has a contract for advertising in a trade magazine for nine consecutive months at $200. per month. This should have resulted in $1,800. in the Advertising Account.

So now the bookkeeper looks for another account that may not have the expected balance. In this fictional case, Account 6180 Dues & Subscriptions has a balance of $1,600. The bookkeeper knows that the only expense posted to that account is supposed to be $50. per month in dues for the company's owner to attend a networking dinner once a month. This would result in a balance of $600. at the end of the year.

The next step for the bookkeeper is to review these two accounts in the General Ledger. Every entry made into the General Ledger is available for review and at the end of the year all entries posted for the year are displayed in the accounts where they were posted.

A review of the two accounts does indeed show that for the last five months, the $200. per month for advertising has been posted to the Dues & Subscriptions account. The balance in one account is $1,000. short while the balance in the other account is $1,000. over. Although these posting errors will not change the bottom line of the Profit & Loss Statement, it is important that the balance in each account be accurate for projecting a budget for the next year.

The entry to make this correction would be done as follows:

Date	Account	Description	Debit	Credit
12-31-07	6180	Post to # 6050		$1,000.00
	6050	Post from # 6180	$1,000.00	

Once this correcting entry has been made the bookkeeper can move onto the next step in the end of the year closing.

Running Year-End Reports

Before the Financial Statements are issued and the books are closed out for the year, a report should be run for Accounts Receivable showing the names of all the credit customers and the amounts due from each. A similar report should be run for Accounts Payable.

Another report that should be printed out for the year is a General Ledger report beginning with the first day of the year and ending with the last day of the year. This report will show every entry posted to every account in the General Ledger for the year that is ending.

PROCEED WITH CAUTION

 Although computerized systems allow the bookkeeper to go back and forth between years and access General Ledger information, the report should be run as a precautionary measure. In the event of a computer glitch or breakdown that causes files to be lost, the bookkeeper should have a hard copy of the year's transactions.

Obviously, after all the back-up reports have been run, the final reports will be the Financial Statements.

The following is the Profit & Loss Statement or Income Statement for our sample company, ABC Sales. In a computerized system the report titles are programmed into the system and either title is acceptable.

As you review the Profit & Loss Statement you should be aware that all the accounts and balances came directly from the Trial Balance report, but may seem to be displayed differently on the Income section of the Profit & Loss Statement. This can be confusing so let's take a closer look at this section and explain why some figures are in brackets indicating a minus amount when they are displayed as debits on the Trial Balance.

First of all, the debit or credit balance does not change when it is transferred to the Financial Statements. The brackets on a credit balance or on a debit balance on the Financial Statements simply mean that balance is modifying the balance of the main account in that section of the statement.

ABC Sales
INCOME STATEMENT
For The Period

January 01, 2007
to
December 31, 2007

SALES

Sales	$	433,510.78
Sales Discounts	(	565.00)
Sales Returns & Allowances	(	1,800.00)

Total SALES	$	431,145.78

COST OF SALES

Purchases	$	174,975.00
Purchases Discounts	(	3,480.00)

Total COST OF SALES	$	171,495.00

Total GROSS PROFIT	$	259,650.78

GENERAL & ADMINISTRATIVE

Salaries and Wages	$	45,000.00
Advertising		1,800.00
Auto Expense		4,512.64
Bank Service Charges		60.00
Depreciation Expense		4,542.03
Dues & Subscriptions		600.00
Utilities		4,500.00
Insurance - Employee Group		11,745.00
Insurance - General		900.00
401k Expense		9,000.00
Interest Expense		17,360.00
Legal & Accounting		1,500.00
Miscellaneous Expense		254.33
Office Expense		2,789.54
Outside Services		200.00
Postage Expense		240.00
Repairs & Maintenance		985.00
Supplies Expense		365.00
Taxes - Real estate		2,700.00
Taxes - Payroll		15,300.00
Telephone		960.00

```
                        ABC Sales
                    INCOME STATEMENT
                      For The Period

                                          January 01, 2007
                                                 to
                                          December 31, 2007


  Total GENERAL & ADMINISTRATIVE          $ _____125,313.54_

  Total NET OPERATING INCOME (LOSS)       $ _____134,337.24_

  NET INCOME (LOSS) BEFORE TAX            $ _____134,337.24_

  NET INCOME (LOSS)                       $        134,337.24
                                            ==============
```

The sales section of the Profit & Loss Statement for ABC Sales is
expected to have a credit balance. Therefore, debits that reduce the Sales
are shown in brackets. Instead of using brackets, the accounts in this
section could be labeled as follows.

Sales Income	433,510.78	(Credit)
Sales Discounts	565.00	(Debit)
Sales Returns & Allowances	1,800.00	(Debit)
Total Sales	431,145.78	(Credit)

By showing the Discounts and the Returns & Allowances in brackets on the Profit & Loss Statement, the report is indicating that these two accounts must be subtracted from the Sales figure in this section of the statement.

In other words, whenever an account balance on a Financial Statement reduces the balance of the main account in that section, it is shown in brackets to indicate that it has been subtracted from it. This is similar to the Accumulated Depreciation accounts in the Asset section of the Balance Sheet.

In the smaller, simpler companies previously used as samples, each section of the Profit & Loss Statement had accounts that were either all credits or all debits. So, it was not necessary to display any account balance in brackets.

Once you get past the Sales or Income section on the Profit & Loss Statement all the other accounts are displayed the same as they are on the Trial Balance for ABC Sales.

Before we leave the Profit & Loss Statement, please note that Advertising and Dues & Subscriptions now have accurate balances based on the entry the bookkeeper made to correct the posting errors.

Now let's take a look at the Balance Sheet for ABC Sales:

Again, note that the accounts displayed on the Balance Sheet are taken directly from the Trial Balance. Each account is displayed in the various sections of the Balance Sheet that you learned about in prior chapters. If you are having a problem identifying any of the accounts on the Balance Sheet for this bigger, more active business entity, you can go back and review the accounts introduced in the earlier chapters.

GO TO ◄

Hour 3 to review the Asset accounts followed by Accumulated Depreciation accounts that modify them in that section of the Balance Sheet.

ABC Sales
BALANCE SHEET
December 31, 2007

ASSETS

CURRENT ASSETS

Checking Account	$	49,955.14
Cash Register Fund		100.00
Savings Account		109,500.00
Accounts Receivable		8,710.22
Inventory		58,325.00
PREPAID EXPENSES		300.00

TOTAL CURRENT ASSETS $ 226,890.36

PROPERTY AND EQUIPMENT

Land	$	27,000.00
Buildings		232,000.00
A/D - Buildings		(38,666.70)
Equipment		17,325.00
A/D - Equipment		(3,465.00)
Furniture and Fixtures		6,235.00
A/D - Furniture & Fixtures		(1,122.30)
Vehicles		37,500.00
A/D - Vehicles		(11,250.00)

TOTAL PROPERTY AND EQUIPMENT $ 265,556.00

OTHER ASSETS

Utility Deposits	$	1,500.00
Organization Costs		4,000.00
Accum Amortization - Org Costs		(2,400.12)

TOTAL OTHER ASSETS $ 3,099.88

TOTAL ASSETS $ 495,546.24
                                        ================

ABC Sales
BALANCE SHEET
December 31, 2007

LIABILITIES AND EQUITY

CURRENT LIABILITIES

Accounts Payable	$ 17,563.48	
Mortgage-Sunset Bank	248,000.00	
Employee Health Ins Payable	2,100.00	
Dental Insurance Payable	510.00	
401k Payable	2,000.00	
Sales Taxes Payable	1,675.52	
PAYROLL TAXES PAYABLE	7,360.00	
TOTAL CURRENT LIABILITIES		$ 279,209.00

NONCURRENT LIABILITIES

NOTES PAYABLE - OFFICER	$ 25,000.00	
TOTAL NONCURRENT LIABILITIES		$ 25,000.00

EQUITY

Capital	$ 57,000.00	
NET INCOME (LOSS)	134,337.24	
TOTAL EQUITY		$ 191,337.24
TOTAL LIABILITIES AND EQUITY		$ 495,546.24
		================

All the amounts listed under the Liabilities section of the Balance Sheet, except for Mortgage-Sunset Bank, will be paid in full by the end of January 2008. Also note, that there is a Capital account, as well as a Loan Payable-Officer account. Both of these accounts represent money invested in the company by the owner that has not yet been withdrawn.

Although the first year of business was profitable, the owner is leaving the money in the company to make sure it can meet its obligations and continue to grow in the next few years.

Closing the General Ledger

Once all the adjustments and reports have been run for the old year, the General Ledger can be closed. Copies of the Trial Balance, the bank reconciliation report, and the Financial Statements are put aside to be transmitted to the company's CPA to prepare the tax return.

When the General Ledger is closed for the year, all the balances in the Profit & Loss section are zeroed out. The Net Profit of $134,227.34 is transferred to the Retained Earnings account in the Balance Sheet section. The other balances in the Balance Sheet section of the General Ledger are carried over into the new year.

The accounting periods for the new year would begin on January 1, 2008, and end 12 months later on December 31, 2008. The files for the old year should be packed up and stored away to make room for the new files that will begin accumulating for the new business year. The IRS requires that business entities keep their records for four years. That would be the current year and three years prior.

Keeping Payroll Records

All of a company's business records are important, but payroll records should top the list as they contain vital information on employees and taxes.

The IRS says that payroll records should be available for review. The following list details some of the records the IRS expects employers to keep for at least four years.

- Copies of W-2s and W-3s
- Amounts and dates of all wage payments
- Amounts of tips reported by employees
- Names, addresses, Social Security numbers, and occupations of employees
- Any employee copies of W-2 forms that were returned to you by the post office as undeliverable (keep these sealed in the envelopes they were mailed in)

- Dates of employment for each employee
- Copies of employees' W-4 forms
- Copies of employees' Earned Income Credit Advance Payment Certificates
- Dates and amounts of tax deposits made and acknowledgment numbers for deposits made through EFTPS
- Copies of quarterly reports filed
- Records of any fringe benefits paid to employees

FYI For more detailed information on the payroll records that should be retained, visit the IRS website at www.irs.gov, or call the IRS business help line: 1-800-829-4933.

In short, any information that applies to employees, wages, and taxes should be filed properly and stored in a safe place for easy access. Also, all information that applies to outside service people who were issued 1099s by the company should be kept for four years.

Balance Sheet Accounts for the New Year

Our sample company, ABC Sales, has closed its books for the year ending December 31, 2007. All the accounts in the Profit & Loss section of the Financial Statements have therefore been zeroed out.

The new year will be the second year of business operations for this sample company. Before any deposits or checks have been posted into the General Ledger for 2008, let's take a look at the Trial Balance report.

GO TO ▶

Hour 20 where you will learn more about computerized accounting and the reports that can be issued.

Note that only the Balance Sheet accounts remain on the Trial Balance. Also, there is now a Retained Earnings account on the Trial Balance report that contains the profit from 2007 of $134,337.24. The report is dated January 31, 2008, because it is computer-generated. No matter what time of the month you access some reports, most computerized systems will date it for the last day of the month you have requested.

ABC Sales
TRIAL BALANCE
January 31, 2008

GL ACCOUNT/NAME	DEBIT	CREDIT
1000 Checking Account	49,955.14	
1020 Cash Register Fund	100.00	
1050 Savings Account	109,500.00	
1100 Accounts Receivable	8,710.22	
1200 Inventory	58,325.00	
1350 Prepaid Expenses	300.00	
1500 Land	27,000.00	
1510 Buildings	232,000.00	
1511 A/D - Buildings		38,666.70
1570 Equipment	17,325.00	
1571 A/D - Equipment		3,465.00
1580 Furniture and Fixtures	6,235.00	
1581 A/D - Furniture & Fixtures		1,122.30
1650 Vehicles	37,500.00	
1651 A/D - Vehicles		11,250.00
1800 Utility Deposits	1,500.00	
1900 Organization Costs	4,000.00	
1901 Accum Amortization - Org Costs		2,400.12
2000 Accounts Payable		17,563.48
2025 Mortgage-Sunset Bank		248,000.00
2100 Employee Health Ins Payable		2,100.00
2105 Dental Insurance Payable		510.00
2110 401k Payable		2,000.00
2190 Sales Taxes Payable		1,675.52
2200 Federal Withholding Tax Payabl		3,400.00
2210 Social Security Tax Payable		2,480.00
2212 Medicare Withholding Tax Pay		580.00
2220 State Withholding Taxes Payabl		680.00
2280 Accrued FUTA		160.00
2290 Accrued SUTA		60.00
2900 Notes Payable - Officer		25,000.00
3040 Retained Earnings		134,337.24
3210 Capital		57,000.00
TOTALS:	552,450.36	552,450.36

Once again, the important thing to remember about closing out the accounting year is that the balances in Assets, Liabilities, and Equity are carried forward into the new year. The accounts in the Profit & Loss section are totaled and posted to Retained Earnings, leaving the Profit & Loss accounts empty and ready to receive the transactions for the new year's business activities.

Hour's Up!

Please try to answer the following questions that deal with closing the books at the end of the year.

1. How long should an outstanding check be kept on the books before it is written off?
   a. 30 days
   b. 180 days
   c. 90 days

2. What entry would be made to write off an outstanding check for office supplies?
   a. Debit Cash in Checking/Credit Office Expense
   b. Debit Cash in Checking/Credit Accounts Payable
   c. Credit Cash in Checking/Debit Accounts Payable

3. The Trial Balance report displays year-to-date balances of all the accounts in the General Ledger.
   a. True
   b. False

4. When the General Ledger is closed for the year, what happens to the Net Profit or Loss?
   a. It is posted to Cash in Checking
   b. It is posted to the Retained Earnings account
   c. It is posted to the Cash in Savings account

5. What portions of a mortgage payment are tax deductible?
   a. Principle and Interest
   b. Principle and Taxes
   c. Interest and Taxes

6. What could indicate a problem when reviewing the Trial Balance report?
   a. A credit balance in an Asset account
   b. A zero balance in an account
   c. A debit balance in an Income account

7. Returns and Allowances are often shown in brackets in the Income section of the Profit & Loss Statement.
   a. True
   b. False

Review

8. How long should financial data be kept?
   a. Five years
   b. Four years
   c. Seven years

9. W-2s returned by the post office as undeliverable can be discarded.
   a. True
   b. False

10. What happens to the balances in the Asset accounts at year-end?
   a. Zeroed out
   b. Posted to Cash in Savings
   c. Carried forward to the new year

Individual Tax Returns

Chapter Summary

In this hour you will learn about …

- Tax extensions
- Tracking income and deductions
- Tax help
- Tax forms

Unless you're expecting a big refund, filing a personal tax return is probably not your idea of a good time. However, it doesn't have to be a painful experience.

Whether you file your own return, use a computerized tax program, or rely on a tax professional to prepare and file the return for you, the information must be gathered and properly organized. In this hour, you will learn how to set up a bookkeeping system for your personal finances that will make filing your return easier.

Tax Extensions

You may be one of those people who takes every scrap of paper deemed to be tax-related, dumps it into a box or a paper sack and carries it over to your local tax professional.

The last few days before the filing deadline, tax preparers interview a steady stream of clients. For many there is not enough time to prepare and file a tax return on time, so an application must be filed after requesting an extension from the IRS.

There are two problems for the people who do not have their tax data organized or must file for a tax extension. Both problems involve money. First of all, the tax professional who receives your box or bag of papers will have to sort through and organize all those papers in order to prepare your tax return. You will be charged for the additional time it takes to do that. Secondly, an automatic extension does not give you additional time to pay any tax liability. It only extends the time you have to file the return. So, when *Form 4868* is filed, it must be accompanied by a payment of at least 90 percent of any tax liability not already paid through employee withholding taxes or estimated tax payments.

STRICTLY DEFINED

 Form 4868 is the Application for Automatic Extension of Time to File U.S. Individual Income Tax. Proper filing of this form before the tax deadline gives an individual a six-month extension.

Keeping your personal books updated will help you avoid problems at tax time. Don't let a tax liability be an unexpected expense that costs you more dollars in penalties and interest.

Tracking Income and Deductions

If you are a wage earner, you will receive a W-2 from your employer reporting the income you earned in the tax year that just ended and the amount of Federal Withholding Taxes you paid in for that income.

In Hour 14, you learned that paying in too much Federal Withholding Tax may result in a big refund at the end of the year, but that because the IRS doesn't pay interest, you are better off putting those additional funds into a savings account. However, at the end of the next tax year, you don't want to have to withdraw your savings to pay a tax liability because you reduced your withholding taxes too much.

The way to avoid paying in too much or too little is to monitor your income and taxes all year long. Based on your paychecks, you know what your base salary is and how much is deducted for taxes on your Gross Wages. What most people overlook is the other income that flows into their household during the year.

The following is a list of other sources of income you may have to consider:

- Interest on Savings Accounts
- Prizes/gambling winnings
- Dividends or interest from stocks, bonds, annuities, or Mutual Funds
- Capital Gains

- Alimony
- Distributions from retirement accounts, pensions, or annuities
- Royalties
- Rents

Most of this information is put into your hands or delivered right to your mailbox every month. You should be receiving monthly statements on savings accounts, income on rentals, and any miscellaneous earnings from investments. You can use those to estimate what your annual income from these accounts will be for the year.

Individuals may also receive 1099s at the end of each tax year from the payers of royalties on books and patents and the majority of the other income sources just listed. For example, if you win an automobile, you will have to pay taxes on the value of the vehicle.

Capital Gains on the sale of assets may also be reported to you on a 1099. This is especially true regarding the buying and selling of stocks and bonds through a stockbroker or through a Mutual Fund account. The sale of an asset, like your personal residence, could trigger Capital Gains tax. However, up to $250,000. for a single person and $500,000. for a married couple is excluded from Capital Gains for the sale of a personal residence, with the following provisions:

- The home was used as your main residence for at least two of the five years prior to the sale.
- You have not sold or exchanged another main residence for the two year period ending on the date of the sale.

PROCEED WITH CAUTION

 Consult a tax professional for advice on the sale of personal property that will result in a profit. This is especially important if the property has been held one year or less.

You can make up a worksheet to estimate all the income you expect to receive during the current year. Start with all the income listed on last year's tax return and increase or decrease the amounts based on the information you are receiving for the new year. For example, if you receive a raise in salary increase or if the interest rate on your savings is increased, adjust that figure for the coming year.

Once your income is estimated, subtract the amount claimed for personal exemptions and either the standard deduction from your prior return or the itemized deduction you claimed. This will provide you with your estimated taxable income for the new year. Tax rates are available all the time on the IRS website (www.irs.gov) so you can look at a tax table and, based on your estimated income, see what the tax will be on the current's years projected income. Compare the tax amount to the withholding taxes being deducted from your paychecks, and you will know whether to adjust the withholding taxes up or down.

When estimating your tax liability, don't forget to take any tax credits for children, education, or disability into consideration. With a worksheet that lays out all your income and deductions, you can simply make adjustments if your income drops, deductions increase, or any other financial event comes up during the year that changes your projected taxable income.

This may sound like a long involved project, but in reality the time factor is minimal and well worth the effort if it saves you from a tax bill at the end of the year. If you don't have to be concerned with a tax bill when you file your return, or if you are not disciplined enough to make up a worksheet and keep it updated, consider the next best thing. Set up files to hold all your tax information. If you have savings accounts and other income that filters in through out the year, separate folders are essential. If you just throw everything into one folder, it is the same as the box or bag that the tax preparers have to sort through at the end of the year.

What works for many people is one folder for each type of income and any expenses that pertain to that income. For example, people who have rental income also have expenses related to that income that must be itemized on a tax return. If you don't want to keep a ledger, at least set up a file to hold all the information so that it can be easily accessed when needed.

TIME SAVER

 If you pay cash for any expense, remember to get a receipt or at the very least write a note with the date, the amount, and the reason for the expenditure. There will still be some sorting to do at the end of the year, but it will be a lot easier sorting through individual folders than sorting through a year's worth of combined receipts and statements.

If you don't want to do worksheets or set up files, there is one more method that can be used. You may recall that duplicate checks were discussed for personal bank accounts in Hour 2. The carbon copies automatically filled in whenever you write a check can be stored during the year. When tax time rolls around you can go through the check copies and sort out anything that is tax deductible. Things like charitable donations, medical expenses such as doctor's visits and prescriptions, educational expenses, and out-of-the-pocket employee expenses are all deductible.

You may think that you don't have enough expenses to itemize deductions on your federal tax return, but you don't know for sure unless you actually take the time to organize and total your expenditures. Also, some items that are not deductible on your federal tax return can be deducted on your state return. So monitor your income and expenses during the year and be prepared to file an accurate tax return. Any major change in income or lifestyle can affect your taxable income. First time home buyers, for instance, find that the interest and taxes on a home mortgage make it possible for them to itemize deductions which allows them a larger write-off than the standard deduction afforded.

Understand that the bookkeeping you do to track your income and expenses for taxes does not mean you should try to prepare your own tax return. It is simply a way to ensure that you have gathered all the information necessary to result in an accurate return.

Tax Help

A tax professional should always be consulted for any questions you may have about income or deductions. There are also a number of low-cost or free places to go to get tax help. Visit www.irs.gov/help and click on one of the following:

- *Frequently Asked Questions* is a section that contains an extensive list of questions and answers.
- *Tax Trails* is an interactive section that asks questions that you can answer with a "yes" or "no."
- *Tax Topics* contains 17 main categories. Each topic has a link to more topics and to a discussion of the topics.

Free help in preparing your tax return is available from IRS-sponsored programs. The Volunteer Income Tax Assistance program is designed to help low-income taxpayers. Tax Counseling for the Elderly is a program for taxpayers age 60 or older. More information is available on these programs at the IRS website or by calling 1-800-829-1040.

Seniors can also request help from the AARP Tax-Aide program. For more information visit the website: www.aarp.org/taxaide or call 1-888-227-7669.

Help for people with disabilities is available by calling 1-800-829-4059.

You can also get face-to-face help solving tax problems every business day in IRS Taxpayer Assistance Centers. Employees there will explain letters and notices from the IRS, request adjustments to your account, or help you set up a payment plan on a tax liability.

Tax Forms

Each year new tax forms are issued and sent out to people who filed hard copies of the forms the year before. People who filed electronically do not usually receive tax forms in the mail. Computer programs used to figure and file taxes are updated each year with the latest forms and the system automatically prints out copies of the completed forms for the taxpayer and files the return electronically with the IRS.

Professional tax preparers also supply all the forms needed to prepare your return. Tax forms and instructions can also be accessed, downloaded, and printed from the IRS website.

The most commonly used tax form for individuals is Form 1040. Often this is the only tax form that needs to be completed because it has been designed to accommodate the majority of taxpayers. Form 1040 has lines where taxpayers can report all their exemptions, various forms of income, adjustments to income, deductions, tax credits, and more.

One thing to note as you review Form 1040 is that there are a number of places on this form that instruct you to submit another form in connection with income, adjustments, or credits. For example, for interest income over $1,500. you must also complete Schedule B and attach it to the 1040. If you itemize deductions you will have to complete and file Schedule A. You will find lines on Form 1040 where the credits mentioned earlier can be entered and subtracted from your tax liability.

Form **1040** Department of the Treasury—Internal Revenue Service **2006**

U.S. Individual Income Tax Return (99) IRS Use Only—Do not write or staple in this space.

For the year Jan. 1–Dec. 31, 2006, or other tax year beginning , 2006, ending , 20

OMB No. 1545-0074

Label
(See instructions on page 16.)
Use the IRS label.
Otherwise, please print or type.

Your first name and initial	Last name
If a joint return, spouse's first name and initial	Last name
Home address (number and street). If you have a P.O. box, see page 16.	Apt. no.
City, town or post office, state, and ZIP code. If you have a foreign address, see page 16.	

L A B E L H E R E

Your social security number

Spouse's social security number

▲ **You must enter your SSN(s) above.** ▲

Checking a box below will not change your tax or refund.

Presidential Election Campaign ▶ Check here if you, or your spouse if filing jointly, want $3 to go to this fund (see page 16) ▶ ☐ You ☐ Spouse

Filing Status

Check only one box.

1 ☐ Single
2 ☐ Married filing jointly (even if only one had income)
3 ☐ Married filing separately. Enter spouse's SSN above and full name here. ▶
4 ☐ Head of household (with qualifying person). (See page 17.) If the qualifying person is a child but not your dependent, enter this child's name here. ▶
5 ☐ Qualifying widow(er) with dependent child (see page 17)

Exemptions

6a ☐ **Yourself.** If someone can claim you as a dependent, **do not** check box 6a
b ☐ **Spouse**

c Dependents:

(1) First name Last name	(2) Dependent's social security number	(3) Dependent's relationship to you	(4) ✓ if qualifying child for child tax credit (see page 19)
			☐
			☐
			☐
			☐

If more than four dependents, see page 19.

d Total number of exemptions claimed

Boxes checked on 6a and 6b ____
No. of children on 6c who:
• lived with you ____
• did not live with you due to divorce or separation (see page 20) ____
Dependents on 6c not entered above ____
Add numbers on lines above ▶ ☐

Income

Attach Form(s) W-2 here. Also attach Forms W-2G and 1099-R if tax was withheld.

If you did not get a W-2, see page 23.

Enclose, but do not attach, any payment. Also, please use Form 1040-V.

7 Wages, salaries, tips, etc. Attach Form(s) W-2	7	
8a **Taxable** interest. Attach Schedule B if required	8a	
b **Tax-exempt** interest. **Do not** include on line 8a	8b	
9a Ordinary dividends. Attach Schedule B if required	9a	
b Qualified dividends (see page 23)	9b	
10 Taxable refunds, credits, or offsets of state and local income taxes (see page 24)	10	
11 Alimony received	11	
12 Business income or (loss). Attach Schedule C or C-EZ	12	
13 Capital gain or (loss). Attach Schedule D if required. If not required, check here ▶ ☐	13	
14 Other gains or (losses). Attach Form 4797	14	
15a IRA distributions 15a	b Taxable amount (see page 25)	15b	
16a Pensions and annuities 16a	b Taxable amount (see page 26)	16b	
17 Rental real estate, royalties, partnerships, S corporations, trusts, etc. Attach Schedule E	17	
18 Farm income or (loss). Attach Schedule F	18	
19 Unemployment compensation	19	
20a Social security benefits 20a	b Taxable amount (see page 27)	20b	
21 Other income. List type and amount (see page 29)	21	
22 Add the amounts in the far right column for lines 7 through 21. This is your **total income** ▶	22	

Adjusted Gross Income

23 Archer MSA deduction. Attach Form 8853	23	
24 Certain business expenses of reservists, performing artists, and fee-basis government officials. Attach Form 2106 or 2106-EZ	24	
25 Health savings account deduction. Attach Form 8889	25	
26 Moving expenses. Attach Form 3903	26	
27 One-half of self-employment tax. Attach Schedule SE	27	
28 Self-employed SEP, SIMPLE, and qualified plans	28	
29 Self-employed health insurance deduction (see page 29)	29	
30 Penalty on early withdrawal of savings	30	
31a Alimony paid b Recipient's SSN ▶	31a	
32 IRA deduction (see page 31)	32	
33 Student loan interest deduction (see page 33)	33	
34 Jury duty pay you gave to your employer	34	
35 Domestic production activities deduction. Attach Form 8903	35	
36 Add lines 23 through 31a and 32 through 35	36	
37 Subtract line 36 from line 22. This is your **adjusted gross income** ▶	37	

For Disclosure, Privacy Act, and Paperwork Reduction Act Notice, see page 80. Cat. No. 11320B Form **1040** (2006)

1040 (2006) U.S. Individual Income Tax Return.

Form 1040 (2006)   Page **2**

Tax and Credits	38	Amount from line 37 (adjusted gross income)	38	
	39a	Check if: ☐ **You** were born before January 2, 1942, ☐ Blind. } **Total boxes** checked ► 39a		
Standard Deduction for—		☐ **Spouse** was born before January 2, 1942, ☐ Blind. }		
	b	If your spouse itemizes on a separate return or you were a dual-status alien, see page 34 and check here ►39b ☐		
• People who checked any box on line 39a or 39b **or** who can be claimed as a dependent, see page 34.	40	**Itemized deductions** (from Schedule A) **or** your **standard deduction** (see left margin) . .	40	
	41	Subtract line 40 from line 38	41	
	42	If line 38 is over $112,875, or you provided housing to a person displaced by Hurricane Katrina, see page 36. Otherwise, multiply $3,300 by the total number of exemptions claimed on line 6d	42	
	43	**Taxable income.** Subtract line 42 from line 41. If line 42 is more than line 41, enter -0-	43	
	44	**Tax** (see page 36). Check if any tax is from: a ☐ Form(s) 8814 b ☐ Form 4972 . . .	44	
• All others:	45	**Alternative minimum tax** (see page 39). Attach Form 6251	45	
Single or Married filing separately, $5,150	46	Add lines 44 and 45 . . . . ►	46	
	47	Foreign tax credit. Attach Form 1116 if required [47]		
	48	Credit for child and dependent care expenses. Attach Form 2441 [48]		
Married filing jointly or Qualifying widow(er), $10,300	49	Credit for the elderly or the disabled. Attach Schedule R . [49]		
	50	Education credits. Attach Form 8863 . . . . [50]		
	51	Retirement savings contributions credit. Attach Form 8880 . [51]		
	52	Residential energy credits. Attach Form 5695 . . . . [52]		
Head of household, $7,550	53	Child tax credit (see page 42). Attach Form 8901 if required [53]		
	54	Credits from: a ☐ Form 8396 b ☐ Form 8839 c ☐ Form 8859 [54]		
	55	Other credits: a ☐ Form 3800 b ☐ Form 8801 c ☐ Form___ [55]		
	56	Add lines 47 through 55. These are your **total credits**	56	
	57	Subtract line 56 from line 46. If line 56 is more than line 46, enter -0- . . . . . ►	57	
Other Taxes	58	Self-employment tax. Attach Schedule SE	58	
	59	Social security and Medicare tax on tip income not reported to employer. Attach Form 4137 . .	59	
	60	Additional tax on IRAs, other qualified retirement plans, etc. Attach Form 5329 if required .	60	
	61	Advance earned income credit payments from Form(s) W-2, box 9	61	
	62	Household employment taxes. Attach Schedule H	62	
	63	Add lines 57 through 62. This is your **total tax** . . . . ►	63	
Payments	64	Federal income tax withheld from Forms W-2 and 1099 . . [64]		
	65	2006 estimated tax payments and amount applied from 2005 return [65]		
If you have a qualifying child, attach Schedule EIC.	66a	**Earned income credit (EIC)** . . . . [66a]		
	b	Nontaxable combat pay election ► [66b]		
	67	Excess social security and tier 1 RRTA tax withheld (see page 60) [67]		
	68	Additional child tax credit. Attach Form 8812 . . . . . [68]		
	69	Amount paid with request for extension to file (see page 60) [69]		
	70	Payments from: a ☐ Form 2439 b ☐ Form 4136 c ☐ Form 8885 . [70]		
	71	Credit for federal telephone excise tax paid. Attach Form 8913 if required [71]		
	72	Add lines 64, 65, 66a, and 67 through 71. These are your **total payments** . . . . ►	72	
Refund Direct deposit? See page 61 and fill in 74b, 74c, and 74d, or Form 8888.	73	If line 72 is more than line 63, subtract line 63 from line 72. This is the amount you **overpaid**	73	
	74a	Amount of line 73 you want **refunded to you.** If Form 8888 is attached, check here ► ☐	74a	
	►b	Routing number		
	►d	Account number ► c Type: ☐ Checking ☐ Savings		
	75	Amount of line 73 you want **applied to your 2007 estimated tax** ► [75]		
Amount You Owe	76	**Amount you owe.** Subtract line 72 from line 63. For details on how to pay, see page 62 ►	76	
	77	Estimated tax penalty (see page 62) . . . . [77]		

Third Party Designee	Do you want to allow another person to discuss this return with the IRS (see page 63)? ☐ **Yes.** Complete the following. ☐ **No**
	Designee's name ► _____ Phone no. ► ( ) _____ Personal identification number (PIN) ► □□□□□

Sign Here
Joint return? See page 17.
Keep a copy for your records.

Under penalties of perjury, I declare that I have examined this return and accompanying schedules and statements, and to the best of my knowledge and belief, they are true, correct, and complete. Declaration of preparer (other than taxpayer) is based on all information of which preparer has any knowledge.

Your signature	Date	Your occupation	Daytime phone number ( )
Spouse's signature. If a joint return, **both** must sign.	Date	Spouse's occupation	

Paid Preparer's Use Only

Preparer's signature ►		Date	Check if self-employed ☐	Preparer's SSN or PTIN
Firm's name (or yours if self-employed), address, and ZIP code ►			EIN	
			Phone no. ( )	

Form **1040** (2006)

GO TO ►

Hour 19 where more information will be found about Partnerships and S Corporations.

Another form that is used by many taxpayers is Schedule E, Supplemental Income and Loss. Report income or loss from rentals, royalties, partnerships, S Corporations, estates, and trusts on Schedule E which is then attached and filed with Form 1040.

There are, of course, many other tax forms that must be filed depending on the taxpayer and his or her financial activities. Please take some time to review Form 1040 and see what other forms may apply to your income or deductions. Even if you have a tax professional prepare your return, you need to be aware of what information the government expects you to provide.

After reviewing Form 1040 you will understand how developing some type of bookkeeping system to keep track of your income and deductions during the year can save you time and money at tax time.

Hour's Up!

Answering the following questions may help you remember the information presented in this chapter.

1. An extension gives you six extra months to pay your tax liability.
    a. True
    b. False

2. What form is filed to obtain an income tax extension?
    a. 1040
    b. 941
    c. 4868

3. How are prize winnings reported on a tax return?
    a. Other Income
    b. Capital Gains
    c. Itemized Deductions

4. How much profit on the sale of a personal residence may be exempt from Capital Gains for a single taxpayer?
    a. $100,000.
    b. $250,000.
    c. $500,000.

5. Tax rate tables are available all year long.
    a. True
    b. False

6. What is the most commonly used tax form for individuals?
    a. 1165
    b. 1120
    c. 1040

Review

7. Schedule B must be filed if interest income exceeds what amount?
   a. $1,000.
   b. $1,500.
   c. $500.

8. Disabled taxpayers may be eligible for a tax credit.
   a. True
   b. False

9. What tax schedule is used to report rental income or loss?
   a. Schedule A
   b. Schedule B
   c. Schedule E

10. Distributions from retirement accounts are never taxable.
    a. True
    b. False

Business Taxpayers

Chapter Summary

In this hour you will learn about …

- Sole proprietors
- Partnerships
- S Corporations
- Corporations
- Limited Liability Companies

The basics of bookkeeping you have learned so far will not change. These standard procedures can be adapted to suit the needs of any company. What may be different is the way the business entity has been created and structured. In this chapter, we will discuss the different types of business entities and how the initial formation and structure of the business determines how it will operate and how it will be recognized and taxed by the U.S. government.

As a bookkeeper, you will not be required to file income tax returns, but you will be responsible for providing a great deal of the information needed for the tax return. Therefore, understanding the various ways a company can be structured will be beneficial.

Sole Proprietors

You have already learned that this business entity is often a small, home-based business run by one person or a married couple. However, there are larger firms that operate as sole proprietors. They may have employees, run factories, service businesses or retail establishments, and earn large profits.

The income or loss for sole proprietors is the Net Profit or Loss of the business that is reported on their personal tax return. One of the advantages of the sole proprietorship is that profits are not shared with anyone else and income is taxed at the personal tax rate. You also know that the sole proprietor is required to pay Self-Employment Taxes on the Net Profit of the business.

GO TO ◀

Hour 14 to review the information on sole proprietors and Self-Employment Taxes.

The sole proprietor usually operates on a calendar year because he or she is required to file the Form 1040 U.S. Individual Tax Return that you have just reviewed. On line 12 of that form, the sole proprietor reports the income or loss generated by his or her company for the past year and attaches Schedule C or Schedule C-EZ.

SCHEDULE C (Form 1040) Department of the Treasury Internal Revenue Service (99)	**Profit or Loss From Business** (Sole Proprietorship) ▶ Partnerships, joint ventures, etc., must file Form 1065 or 1065-B. ▶ Attach to Form 1040, 1040NR, or 1041. ▶ See Instructions for Schedule C (Form 1040).	OMB No. 1545-0074 2006 Attachment Sequence No. **09**

Name of proprietor | Social security number (SSN)

A	Principal business or profession, including product or service (see page C-2 of the instructions)	B Enter code from pages C-8, 9, & 10 ▶
C	Business name. If no separate business name, leave blank.	D Employer ID number (EIN), if any

E   Business address (including suite or room no.) ▶
    City, town or post office, state, and ZIP code

F   Accounting method: **(1)** ☐ Cash   **(2)** ☐ Accrual   **(3)** ☐ Other (specify) ▶
G   Did you "materially participate" in the operation of this business during 2006? If "No," see page C-3 for limit on losses   ☐ Yes   ☐ No
H   If you started or acquired this business during 2006, check here   .   .   .   .   ▶ ☐

Part I   **Income**

1	Gross receipts or sales. **Caution.** If this income was reported to you on Form W-2 and the "Statutory employee" box on that form was checked, see page C-3 and check here . . . . . ▶ ☐	1	
2	Returns and allowances	2	
3	Subtract line 2 from line 1	3	
4	Cost of goods sold (from line 42 on page 2)	4	
5	**Gross profit.** Subtract line 4 from line 3	5	
6	Other income, including federal and state gasoline or fuel tax credit or refund (see page C-3) . . .	6	
7	**Gross income.** Add lines 5 and 6 . . . . ▶	7	

Part II   **Expenses.** Enter expenses for business use of your home **only** on line 30.

8	Advertising	8			18	Office expense	18	
9	Car and truck expenses (see page C-4)	9			19	Pension and profit-sharing plans	19	
10	Commissions and fees . .	10			20	Rent or lease (see page C-5):		
11	Contract labor (see page C-4)	11				**a** Vehicles, machinery, and equipment .	20a	
12	Depletion	12				**b** Other business property . .	20b	
13	Depreciation and section 179 expense deduction (not included in Part III) (see page C-4)	13			21	Repairs and maintenance . .	21	
					22	Supplies (not included in Part III)	22	
					23	Taxes and licenses . . .	23	
					24	Travel, meals, and entertainment:		
						a Travel	24a	
14	Employee benefit programs (other than on line 19). .	14				**b** Deductible meals and entertainment (see page C-6)	24b	
15	Insurance (other than health) .	15			25	Utilities	25	
16	Interest:				26	Wages (less employment credits) .	26	
	a Mortgage (paid to banks, etc.) .	16a			27	Other expenses (from line 48 on page 2)	27	
	b Other	16b						
17	Legal and professional services	17						

28	**Total expenses** before expenses for business use of home. Add lines 8 through 27 in columns . ▶	28	

29	Tentative profit (loss). Subtract line 28 from line 7	29	
30	Expenses for business use of your home. Attach **Form 8829**	30	
31	**Net profit or (loss).** Subtract line 30 from line 29. • If a profit, enter on both **Form 1040, line 12,** and **Schedule SE, line 2,** or on **Form 1040NR, line 13** (statutory employees, see page C-6). Estates and trusts, enter on Form 1041, line 3. • If a loss, you **must** go to line 32.	31	
32	If you have a loss, check the box that describes your investment in this activity (see page C-6). • If you checked 32a, enter the loss on both **Form 1040, line 12,** and **Schedule SE, line 2,** or on **Form 1040NR, line 13** (statutory employees, see page C-6). Estates and trusts, enter on Form 1041, line 3. • If you checked 32b, you **must** attach **Form 6198.** Your loss may be limited.	32a ☐ All investment is at risk. 32b ☐ Some investment is not at risk.

For Paperwork Reduction Act Notice, see page C-8 of the instructions.   Cat. No. 11334P   Schedule C (Form 1040) 2006

Schedule C 1040 (2006) Profit or Loss From Business (Long Form).

Schedule C (Form 1040) 2006   Page **2**

Part III   **Cost of Goods Sold** (see page C-7)

33 Method(s) used to value closing inventory: **a** ☐ Cost   **b** ☐ Lower of cost or market   **c** ☐ Other (attach explanation)

34 Was there any change in determining quantities, costs, or valuations between opening and closing inventory?
If "Yes," attach explanation . . . . ☐ **Yes**   ☐ **No**

35 Inventory at beginning of year. If different from last year's closing inventory, attach explanation . .	**35**	
36 Purchases less cost of items withdrawn for personal use	**36**	
37 Cost of labor. Do not include any amounts paid to yourself	**37**	
38 Materials and supplies	**38**	
39 Other costs	**39**	
40 Add lines 35 through 39	**40**	
41 Inventory at end of year	**41**	
42 **Cost of goods sold.** Subtract line 41 from line 40. Enter the result here and on page 1, line 4 . .	**42**	

Part IV   **Information on Your Vehicle.** Complete this part **only** if you are claiming car or truck expenses on line 9 and are not required to file Form 4562 for this business. See the instructions for line 13 on page C-4 to find out if you must file Form 4562.

43 When did you place your vehicle in service for business purposes? (month, day, year) ▶ ....../....../......

44 Of the total number of miles you drove your vehicle during 2006, enter the number of miles you used your vehicle for:

a Business .... **b** Commuting (see instructions) .... **c** Other ....

45 Do you (or your spouse) have another vehicle available for personal use?. . . . . ☐ **Yes**   ☐ **No**

46 Was your vehicle available for personal use during off-duty hours? . . . . ☐ **Yes**   ☐ **No**

47a Do you have evidence to support your deduction? . . . . ☐ **Yes**   ☐ **No**

b If "Yes," is the evidence written? . . . . ☐ **Yes**   ☐ **No**

Part V   **Other Expenses.** List below business expenses not included on lines 8–26 or line 30.

48 **Total other expenses.** Enter here and on page 1, line 27	**48**	

Schedule C (Form 1040) 2006

Schedule C-EZ has a number of stipulations that limit its use, so most sole proprietors would have to file the longer form, Schedule C.

If the sole proprietor has employees, an EIN would have been obtained, but for the sole proprietors that do not have employees, their social security numbers are used at the top of the form as a means of identification.

Note that line F on Schedule C is where the owner would specify whether his bookkeeping records are set up on a cash or accrual basis. The rest of the form is similar to a Profit & Loss Statement, and filling it out should be a simple matter of transferring the figures from the company's books to the form. However, if the proprietor claims certain deductions on Part II of Schedule C, additional forms have to be filed in connection with those deductions.

Section 179 Expense, Depreciation Expense, and Amortization Expense all require that Form 4562 be completed and filed also. Expensing business property under Section 179 is an option that should be discussed with the owner's professional tax advisor regardless of the size of the company.

STRICTLY DEFINED

Section 179 of the Internal Revenue Code allows business owners to expense the total cost of business property up to a set limit in one tax year rather than depreciating the cost over a longer period of time.

Form 8829, Expenses for Business Use of Your Home, is used by many home-based businesses. If the business is profitable, the taxpayer can claim a tax deduction for the business use of the home. However, this deduction is limited to companies that are reporting a profit and cannot be used to increase a business loss. Don't attempt to complete Form 8829 without reading the instructions available at www.irs.gov and making sure you understand its limitations.

Other business deductions listed on Part I, Income, and Part II, Expenses, of Schedule C require that related information be completed on the reverse side of the form:

- Cost of Goods Sold
- Other Income
- Car and Truck Expenses
- Contract Labor
- Rentals
- Travel, Meals, and Entertainment Expenses
- Other Expenses

When Schedule C and the supporting schedules have been completed, the Net Profit or Loss is transferred to Form 1040, Line 12. Remember that Form SE must also be completed for the proprietor's FICA taxes. Fifty percent of that tax can be deducted from Gross Income on Line 27 of 1040, but the total amount of the tax must be entered on Line 58 to be added into the taxpayer's tax liability for that year.

Please remember that the tax forms and explanations in this book are not meant to provide tax advice or encourage you to complete and file a tax return without the assistance of a tax professional. This is simply a preliminary introduction to the forms and the process of completing them so that you are aware of the information that must be gathered for the tax return.

Partnerships

According to the IRS, a partnership is the relationship existing between two or more persons who join to carry on a trade or business. Each person contributes money, property, labor, or skill and expects to share in the profits and losses of the business. There are as many partnerships as there are different types of trades and businesses. Sometimes, one partner actually runs the business while the other partners supply the funding for it. Partners buy and sell property in the real estate markets, invest in stocks and bonds, or run law firms, retail stores, construction companies, art galleries, and various entertainment venues.

A partnership is considered one entity by the IRS and is usually assigned an EIN even if it does not have employees. Of course many partnerships do have employees and so must follow all the rules and regulations on payroll and payroll taxes.

The partners in any venture should have an underlying agreement that specifies how it will operate, how the workload and investments will be divided, and how the profit or loss will be distributed. It doesn't have to be an even split. There are working partners and silent partners and the proceeds of the business can be divided any way the partners decide to do under their agreement. However, when it comes to reporting income or loss to the IRS, the split of proceeds among the partners must equal 100 percent of the profit or loss when totaled.

Partnerships must file an annual information return to report the income, deductions, gains, and losses from its operations, but it does not pay taxes on its profits. Instead, profits or losses are passed through to the partners. Note that when a partner leaves a firm, the partnership is dissolved and a new partnership must be formed.

The partnership return is filed on Form 1065 and, once the information on that return is completed, each partner receives a copy of Form 1065-K-l which is a schedule showing the partner's share of the current year's income or loss. The income or loss on the K-1 is then transferred to the partner's personal tax return and reported on line 17 Schedule E, which was discussed in Hour 18.

FYI For more information on Partnerships and Form 1065 read IRS publication 541. This publication and the partnership tax forms can be accessed via the website (www.irs.gov) or can be ordered by calling 1-800-829-3676.

Again, the tax forms discussed regarding partnerships are intended to provide information only to give you a better understanding of the taxation process and the information needed for the forms. A legal advisor should be consulted when drawing up a partnership agreement and a financial advisor should be consulted to prepare tax returns for the entity.

Partnerships and sole proprietors have two things in common. One is that the profit or loss of the business entity they are involved in is reported on their personal tax return and may be subject to Self-Employment Tax. Two is the fact that sole proprietors and partners are liable for any problems the business operation encounters. This includes debts and other financial losses. Also, if someone sues the business, they are actually suing the partners or the sole proprietor. In other words, both the business assets and the personal assets of the partners and sole proprietors are at risk for any problems encountered by the company.

The liability factor for partners and sole proprietors of business operations often prompts them to incorporate the company.

S Corporations

An S Corporation is a smaller version of a regular corporation. It is a way to avoid personal liability from the activities and actions of the business entity. It is also a way to be exempt from the tax liabilities a regular corporation incurs.

The business assets and liabilities belong to the S Corporation, limiting any risk factors to the S Corporation rather than the shareholders' personal assets.

Like the partnership, the profits and losses of the S Corporation are passed through to the principles of the organization that own the stock and run the company. This is a tax advantage not available to the larger "C" Corporation.

Smaller businesses, such as one or two person law firms and accounting practices, are often structured as S Corporations. The principles of the S Corporation can be employees as well as employers. At the end of the tax year, they receive a W-2 form for the wages earned and taxed and they report their portion of the profit or loss of the S Corporation on Line 17 of the 1040 tax return they file.

Bookkeeping systems for S Corporations are set up and managed as they would be for any other company. S Corporations are subject to federal laws and to the laws of the states where they are incorporated.

The Corporation Commission of each state must approve the incorporation of any company within its jurisdiction. Annual Reports on stockholders, meetings, and finances must be filed with the state commissions to keep the S Corporation in operation and licensed. Form 1120-S (S Corporation) is used to file the tax return for this type of business entity.

Corporations

A regular corporation operates like any other business and its bookkeeping system is based on the standard procedures you have studied in this book. However, a corporation has shareholders who may or may not be principles or officers of the company. The shares issued by public corporations can be bought, sold, and traded on the stock market. The price of the stock is based on the assets and the overall profitability of the corporation.

The shareholders are actually considered the owners of the company and, as owners, expect to receive reports on the business operations and finances and hope to share in the profits of the company through *dividends* paid on their stock holdings. Unlike sole proprietorships and partnerships, corporations have an unlimited lifetime.

Dividends are distributions of the prorated profits of a corporation issued to the stockholders for each share of stock owned.

As mentioned several times in this book, large corporations often have departmentalized bookkeeping systems.

Corporations can operate on a calendar or fiscal year, and the tax returns are due within a few months after the end of the annual financial periods. The tax return is filed on Form 1120 and can be very long and complex. Taxes are based on a corporate rate structure different from the individual rates.

Limited Liability Companies

Limited Liability Companies or LLCs are a relatively new business structure allowed by state statute. This business structure has become popular because the owners of an LLC have limited personal liability for the actions and debts of the business.

Generally, the owners of an LLC are called members. Most states do not restrict ownership, so members can be individuals, corporations, and other LLCs. Also, most states allow single owner LLCs, giving the owner some legal protection on his or her personal assets while not having to go through the legal process and expense of forming a corporation. Frequently, two companies may form an LLC to manage a project in which both companies are a part.

Some types of businesses—banks, insurance companies, and nonprofit organizations—cannot be structured as LLCs. LLCs can also have employees and are subject to the same rules and regulations as any other employer.

Single member LLCs do not have to file a tax return for the LLC. Instead the income or loss is reported on Form 1040 using Schedule C or E. The individual may also have to file Form SE and pay self-employment taxes. LLCs with multiple members are more like partnerships that have management flexibility and pass-through taxation. These LLCs can file Partnership returns.

Keep in mind that losses for LLCs on a tax return may be limited because the member's liability for debts is limited.

FYI For more information on LLCs refer to IRS publication 3402, available on their website (www.irs.gov) or by calling 1-800-829-3676.

The business structures covered in this hour should give you a general idea of the different types of companies that you may encounter as a bookkeeper. This information will help you understand how the business was created.

Although the bookkeeping systems will be virtually the same regardless of the initial structure of the company, there may be some extra steps or procedures needed to suit the needs of a specific business. For example, a corporation may require additional reports and information to keep the stockholders informed.

Hour's Up!

Please try to answer the following questions without looking back at the text in this chapter.

1. Sole proprietors usually operate on a calendar year.
   a. True
   b. False

2. What would a sole proprietor indicate on Line F of Schedule C?
   a. EIN
   b. Cash or accrual bookkeeping method
   c. Cost of sales

3. What tax form is used to report depreciation expense?
   a. 1040
   b. 4868
   c. 4562

4. What do sole proprietors and partners have in common?
   a. Bookkeeping methods
   b. Liability for business debts
   c. Pass-through taxation

5. What tax form is filed by a partnership?
   a. 1065
   b. 1040
   c. 1120

Review

6. An S Corporation cannot have employees.
   a. True
   b. False

7. Who approves the formation of a corporation?
   a. The IRS
   b. Federal Trade Commission
   c. State Corporation Commissions

8. LLCs must have more than one member
   a. True
   b. False

9. What tax form is filed by corporations?
   a. 1065
   b. 1040
   c. 1120

10. What type of business cannot be an LLC?
    a. Banks
    b. Retail stores
    c. Law firms

Computerized Bookkeeping Programs

Chapter Summary

In this hour you will learn about ...

- Initial set-up
- Automatic postings
- Receivables and payables
- Reports, reports, reports

There are many choices when it comes to choosing a computerized program for bookkeeping. Some versions are generic software programs that can be used for almost any type of business. Some allow the user to set up multiple companies so that several businesses can be served at the same time.

There are also software companies that program the bookkeeping system around the needs of a particular business. This doesn't mean that the basics of bookkeeping are different in these programs, it just means there are added features, like job costing for construction companies, or hourly billing calculations for lawyers, that are built into the program.

The advantages of using a computer program for bookkeeping have been mentioned throughout this book. In this chapter, we will take a closer look at the standard bookkeeping programs and how they are initialized and operated.

Initial Set-Up

For most bookkeeping programs, the following steps must be completed before you can post transactions into the General Ledger:

1. Enter company information.
2. Establish accounting periods.
3. Create a Chart of Accounts.
4. Enter bank account information.
5. Create ledger cards.
6. Enter beginning balances.

Usually, the program will lead the user through the process, but let's take the steps one at a time and explain why they are necessary.

Enter Company Information

The company information requested by the computer program varies but generally it is the name, address, phone number, and tax identification number. Remember that the tax identification number is the EIN assigned by the IRS or it is the owner's Social Security number. The EIN number will be used on any payroll reports generated by the program.

Once the company information has been entered and saved, the program will automatically set up the computer files needed to store the bookkeeping information.

Establish Accounting Periods

The next step is establishing the monthly accounting periods that will be used for the company. Most programs bring up another screen where the user enters the first day of the business year, either calendar or fiscal, and the last day of the year.

Even if the company operates on a calendar year and it is May 15th, the user must enter January 1st and December 31st as the beginning and ending dates for that year so that the computer will set up the periods correctly for the current year and any subsequent years.

TIME SAVER

 When switching from a manual bookkeeping system to a computerized system, you can enter the year-to-date totals into the computer as the opening entry for the prior month, instead of entering each month individually into the program.

Create a Chart of Accounts

As you have learned, a Chart of Accounts must be created for all bookkeeping systems. Computerized programs require the same thing. The difference is that most programs already have a number of different Chart of Accounts built into the software that include the most common accounts needed for a variety of different businesses.

The following standard Charts are already in many software programs:

- General Business
- Medical/Dental
- Contractor/Builder
- Farm/Agriculture
- Church/Synagogue
- Service Business
- Legal Practice
- Manufacturing
- Nonprofit Organization
- Real Estate
- Personal Finance

Each Chart of Accounts can be reviewed by the user before it is chosen for the company. Keep in mind, that account titles can be changed and accounts can be added to suit the company's specific needs. Control accounts such as Accounts Receivable and Accounts Payable usually cannot be deleted from the Chart of Accounts. However, there are some software programs that allow the user to set preferences for control accounts. Unless the company has specific needs, this is not necessary. Remember if you don't use the control accounts, they will not print out on the Financial Statements.

Note that the last Chart of Accounts on the list is for Personal Finance. This enables individuals to set up their household bookkeeping system on the computer. This Chart of Accounts can also be used as a guideline to monitor your income and deductions throughout the tax year.

GO TO ◄
Hour 3 where there is an example of a personal financial statement showing the Net Worth of a married couple.

The following Chart of Accounts is for a sample household from a computerized bookkeeping program.

Note how the accounts in the Balance Sheet section of this sample cover the assets and liabilities that you would find in an individual's household. Instead of the Retained Earnings account you would find for a business, there is a Net Worth account.

Blake's Household
CHART OF ACCOUNTS

ACCOUNT NUMBER	NAME	TYPE	BALANCE SHEET SECTION / INCOME STATEMENT SECTION
1000	Checking Account	Asset	ASSETS
1050	Savings Account	Asset	ASSETS
1060	Money Market Account	Asset	ASSETS
1080	Marketable Securities	Asset	ASSETS
1085	Cash Value Life Insurance	Asset	ASSETS
1088	Interest in Net Asset Business	Asset	ASSETS
1098	Undeposited Cash	Asset	ASSETS
1099	Cash Transfers	Asset	ASSETS
1100	Accounts Receivable	Asset	ASSETS
1200	Residence	Asset	ASSETS
1220	Automobiles	Asset	ASSETS
1240	Jewelry	Asset	ASSETS
1260	Paintings	Asset	ASSETS
1280	Silver	Asset	ASSETS
1300	Collections	Asset	ASSETS
1320	Household Furnishings	Asset	ASSETS
1340	Vested Interest - Pension Plan	Asset	ASSETS
1360	Investments in Real Estate	Asset	ASSETS
1380	Contingent Assets	Asset	ASSETS
2000	Accounts Payable	Liability	LIABILITIES
2010	Credit Card - Visa	Liability	LIABILITIES
2020	Credit Card - Mastercard	Liability	LIABILITIES
2030	Credit Card - American Express	Liability	LIABILITIES
2090	Notes Payable - Short Term	Liability	LIABILITIES
2100	Accrued Expenses	Liability	LIABILITIES
2105	Dental Insurance Payable	Liability	LIABILITIES
2110	401k Payable	Liability	LIABILITIES
2120	Customer Security Deposits	Liability	LIABILITIES
2140	Unsecured Note Payable	Liability	LIABILITIES
2180	Mortgage Note Payable	Liability	LIABILITIES
2190	Installment Note Payable	Liability	LIABILITIES
2200	Federal Withholding Tax Payabl	Liability	LIABILITIES
2210	Social Security Tax Payable	Liability	LIABILITIES
2212	Medicare Withholding Tax Pay	Liability	LIABILITIES
2220	State Withholding Taxes Payabl	Liability	LIABILITIES
2240	Secured Note Payable	Liability	LIABILITIES
2250	Local Withholding Taxes Payabl	Liability	LIABILITIES
2280	Accrued Income Taxes Payable	Liability	LIABILITIES
3040	Net Worth	Equity	NET WORTH
3098	Initial Credit Card Offset	Equity	NET WORTH
3099	Initial Cash Balance Offset	Equity	NET WORTH
4000	Salaries & Bonuses	Income	INCOME AND OTHER GAINS
4100	Dividends	Income	INCOME AND OTHER GAINS
4110	Interest Income	Income	INCOME AND OTHER GAINS
4120	Drawings	Income	INCOME AND OTHER GAINS
4150	Gain on Sale of Securities	Income	INCOME AND OTHER GAINS
4190	Gain on Sale of Other Assets	Income	INCOME AND OTHER GAINS
4200	Increase - Value of Securities	Income	INCOME AND OTHER GAINS
4210	Increase - Value of Residence	Income	INCOME AND OTHER GAINS

Blake's Household
CHART OF ACCOUNTS

ACCOUNT NUMBER	NAME	TYPE	BALANCE SHEET SECTION / INCOME STATEMENT SECTION
4220	Increase - Value of Business	Income	INCOME AND OTHER GAINS
4280	Sales Discounts	Income	INCOME AND OTHER GAINS
4290	Increase - Value of Other Asse	Income	INCOME AND OTHER GAINS
5000	Real Estate Taxes	Expense	TAX DEDUCTIBLE EXPENDITURE
5020	State Income Taxes	Expense	TAX DEDUCTIBLE EXPENDITURE
5040	Sales Taxes	Expense	TAX DEDUCTIBLE EXPENDITURE
5060	Other Taxes	Expense	TAX DEDUCTIBLE EXPENDITURE
5080	Interest on Home Mortgage	Expense	TAX DEDUCTIBLE EXPENDITURE
5100	Interest on Consumer Debt	Expense	TAX DEDUCTIBLE EXPENDITURE
5120	Interest on Bank Loans	Expense	TAX DEDUCTIBLE EXPENDITURE
5140	Other Interest	Expense	TAX DEDUCTIBLE EXPENDITURE
5160	Contributions - United Way	Expense	TAX DEDUCTIBLE EXPENDITURE
5180	Contributions - Church	Expense	TAX DEDUCTIBLE EXPENDITURE
5200	Contributions - Other	Expense	TAX DEDUCTIBLE EXPENDITURE
5300	Medical - Hospitals	Expense	TAX DEDUCTIBLE EXPENDITURE
5320	Medical - Physicians	Expense	TAX DEDUCTIBLE EXPENDITURE
5340	Medical - Dentists	Expense	TAX DEDUCTIBLE EXPENDITURE
5350	Medical - Prescriptions	Expense	TAX DEDUCTIBLE EXPENDITURE
5360	Medical - Insurance	Expense	TAX DEDUCTIBLE EXPENDITURE
5380	Medical - Other	Expense	TAX DEDUCTIBLE EXPENDITURE
5400	Other Deductible Expenses	Expense	TAX DEDUCTIBLE EXPENDITURE
5660	Freight and Delivery	Expense	TAX DEDUCTIBLE EXPENDITURE
6010	Employer Social Security Exp	Expense	TAX DEDUCTIBLE EXPENDITURE
6015	Employer Medicare Expense	Expense	TAX DEDUCTIBLE EXPENDITURE
6020	Family Entertainment	Expense	NON-DEDUCTIBLE EXPENDITURE
6040	Vacations	Expense	NON-DEDUCTIBLE EXPENDITURE
6060	Clothing	Expense	NON-DEDUCTIBLE EXPENDITURE
6080	Automobile Expenses	Expense	NON-DEDUCTIBLE EXPENDITURE
6100	Home Improvement & Maintenance	Expense	NON-DEDUCTIBLE EXPENDITURE
6120	Bank Service Charges	Expense	NON-DEDUCTIBLE EXPENDITURE
6125	Food	Expense	NON-DEDUCTIBLE EXPENDITURE
6140	Tuition	Expense	NON-DEDUCTIBLE EXPENDITURE
6160	Other Personal Expenses	Expense	NON-DEDUCTIBLE EXPENDITURE
6200	Income Taxes	Expense	NON-DEDUCTIBLE EXPENDITURE
6250	Provision for Inc Tax on Appre	Expense	NON-DEDUCTIBLE EXPENDITURE
6255	401k Expense	Expense	NON-DEDUCTIBLE EXPENDITURE
6300	Decrease in Value of Assets	Expense	NON-DEDUCTIBLE EXPENDITURE
6550	Bad Debts	Expense	NON-DEDUCTIBLE EXPENDITURE
6560	Purchases Discounts Expense	Expense	NON-DEDUCTIBLE EXPENDITURE
9999	Temporary Distribution	Expense	NON-DEDUCTIBLE EXPENDITURE

In the Profit & Loss section of the sample Chart of Accounts, notice that the expenses are categorized as either Tax Deductible Expenditures or Nondeductible Expenditures. Whether you set up your personal finances on a computer or not, this Chart of Accounts is a good reference list for individuals.

Enter Bank Account Information

Once the Chart of Accounts has been set for the new bookkeeping system, the next task is to enter the information for the bank accounts. This is especially important if the program will be used to write checks as the computer will set up a check register for the account and all deposits and disbursements will be posted to the computerized check register.

PROCEED WITH CAUTION

The bookkeeping program will update the computerized check register whenever a deposit or disbursement is done through the program. However, if a deposit is made manually or a check is handwritten, the bookkeeper must remember to post these transactions into the computer.

Create Ledger Cards

Another task to be completed in the initial set-up of a company is the creation of ledger cards. The type of ledger cards set up in the program depends on the business operation. A company similar to ABC Sales used as a sample in Hour 17 would have ledger cards created for inventory, vendors, customers, and employees.

Inventory cards have to be created for every item the company sells. The following is a list of the main information that would be entered for every item in the company's inventory:

- Item ID
- Item Description
- Name of vendor that supplies the item
- Purchase Account Number
- Sales Account Number
- Quantity on Hand
- Part number assigned by vendor for reordering
- Unit of measure for the item i.e., each, pair, dozen

Depending on the capabilities and features of the bookkeeping program, other information may be entered into the system such as *unit price codes*.

STRICTLY DEFINED

Unit price codes are for customers that have been assigned a special price for an item. When the bookkeeper enters the code, the special price is automatically entered on the customer's invoice.

Vendor cards will require the following information:

- Vendor ID
- Vendor name, address, phone, fax, and contact person
- Payment terms
- Expense account number

An important thing to remember about the account numbers programmed into the computer on ledger cards is that they automatically come up when the bookkeeper is posting a transaction, but can be overridden with another account number.

A ledger must be created in the bookkeeping system for every customer that buys merchandise on credit. The following information should be entered for each one:

- Customer ID
- Billing name and address
- Phone and fax numbers
- Shipping name and address
- Sales account
- Payment terms/credit limit

Employee ledgers should be created even if the payroll is not going to be processed in-house through the computerized program. The paychecks will still have to be posted into the computer when they are issued and the employees' ledgers will have to be updated each pay period.

The information to be entered on the employee cards is as follows:

- Employee ID
- Employee's name, address, and phone number
- Social Security Number
- Status: active or terminated
- Marital status
- Salary or hourly rate
- Withholding exemptions

Other information can be included on the employee cards as needed.

JUST A MINUTE

 Most systems allow the user to use numbers or letters or a combination of the two to create IDs for the cards. Using letters that pertain to the name of the item or person will make it easier for the bookkeeper to identify and find the correct ledger cards when necessary.

When all the necessary information and ledgers are set up in the program, you can enter the beginning balances.

Enter Beginning Balances

Most computers have an icon called "Setup," and when you click on that, it will lead you through the process of entering the beginning balances for the company.

Use the company's Trial Balance from the bookkeeping period prior to the date you will start entering actual transactions into the system. Those ending balances are the beginning balances for the next period. If the date you will start using the computer program is January 1st, enter the figures from the Trial Balance of December 31st of the prior year. If the start date is May 1st, use the Trial Balance from the period ending April 30th. As you are entering the beginning balances, you can add any accounts that are not in the computer's General Ledger.

TIME SAVER

 Before you start posting the beginning balances, you can note the account numbers in the computer's Chart of Accounts/General Ledger next to each amount to be posted from the Trial Balance. Then, if accounts need to be added, you can do it before you start posting.

If you have an amount in Accounts Payable that was posted from the Trial Balance, you will have to access the Vendor Ledger cards from the "Setup" menu and enter the outstanding balances on the respective cards that make up the Accounts Payable balance in the General Ledger. You will have to do the same for Customer Ledgers with an unpaid balance so that they equal the amount posted to Accounts Receivable from the Trial Balance. Lastly, if you have Employee Ledgers each one will have to be updated with the totals for the current year if you are in the midst of a calendar year.

The time it takes to enter all of the company information and create the ledger cards in the bookkeeping program depends on the size of the business you are converting to a computerized system. However, the time it takes to set up the bookkeeping system in the computer will be quickly recaptured once you start using it and experiencing the miracle of automatic postings.

Automatic Posting

As the bookkeeper posts the daily financial activity into the General Ledger of a computerized bookkeeping system, the program automatically distributes the information to the accounts that are affected by the transactions entered. Most programs today lead the user through the process based on the area of the bookkeeping system that has been accessed. The user is prompted to enter the information needed for the program to perform the automatic postings. Because the computerized program allows the user to go back and forth between monthly bookkeeping periods, remember to check the date and make sure you are in the correct month before you begin posting entries into the system.

Let's look at the standard postings that are programmed into the system and occur automatically.

Cash sales are posted as credits to the income accounts and debits to the Cash in Checking account. In addition, a Deposit Slip is initiated and prepared as the cash postings are entered. Credit sales are posted as credits to the income accounts and debits to Accounts Receivable and to the customers' ledger cards.

If the inventory item numbers are in the system, the program will prompt the user to enter them as the sales are posted and the program will then access the item numbers and reduce them by the amount sold. This occurs with both cash and credit sales.

Keep in mind that posting to the inventory item cards is simply a control method and generally does not affect the General Ledger Inventory account balance which will have to be adjusted at the end of the month after the physical inventory count has been completed and verified.

Purchases also affect the inventory items if the details of the purchase invoice are entered. Cash purchases are debited to the Cost of Sales account indicated while Cash in Checking is credited. Purchases made on credit are debited to the Cost of Sales account and credited to Accounts Payable and to the vendors' individual ledger cards.

If payroll is done in-house, the computer issues the paychecks and posts them to employees' ledger cards. It also posts the payroll taxes and employer expenses to the proper accounts.

The banking section of the program issues deposit slips for cash receipts and issues checks. Many programs display the balance in Cash in Checking account on the bottom of the screen and it increases or decreases as the transactions are completed. At the end of the month when the bank statement is received, the banking section can automatically reconcile it.

PROCEED WITH CAUTION

It is up to the user to determine what automatic functions the computerized bookkeeping system will perform as they may vary depending on the software program being utilized. Always review the instruction manual and features of the program before posting transactions.

As you learned in Hour 5, end-of-the-month Journal Entries can be set up to post automatically. These would include postings for Prepaid Expenses, Depreciation Expenses, and Amortization Expenses.

If you are working with a small company, you can use the method outlined in Hour 16 for posting from the checkbook. This is done by accessing the prompt for posting Journal Entries. You will enter the account numbers and the amounts and the computer will post the income and expenses to those accounts and then post net debit or credit to the Cash in Checking account. Any other adjustments that need to be made to accounts in the General Ledger can also be posted in this way. Also, if a posting error has occurred, the user can void the entry and the program will automatically delete the postings from the accounts where they were distributed.

Receivables and Payables

When it comes to issuing checks and billing customers, the computerized program will do it automatically. However, most programs allow the user to choose the way the computer will print the checks and documents. This is done through a section of the program for preferences and usually has a separate area for any reports, invoices, billing statements, or checks generated by the computer.

Most programs will automatically issue the invoices and statements for customer billings with one prompt. Because the program has all the information for both receivables and payables in the system, you can also print out reports for each before billing or issuing checks to vendors to make sure the balances on the cards agree with the total balance in the General Ledger accounts.

Reports, Reports, Reports

There are so many different reports a computerized bookkeeping system can generate, it is mind-boggling. The following is a list of the reports that most computerized bookkeeping systems will issue whenever prompted. Some of them, like budgets and prior year comparisons, require that additional information be input into the system.

- Current Month and Year-to-Date Financial Statements
- Comparative Financial Statements, i.e., this year to last year
- Cash Flow Statements and Cash Flow Projections
- Budgets and Statements showing current income and expenses compared to the budget for that year and whether the current activity is over or under the budget figure
- Banking Reports on Deposits or Checks Issued
- Accounts Receivable Reports by customer or by invoice
- Aged Accounts Receivable Reports
- Accounts Payable Reports by vendor or purchase invoice
- Aged Accounts Payable
- General Journal Reports
- Trial Balance Report
- General Ledger Reports
- Job Costing Reports
- Inventory Reports
- Sales Reports
- Purchase Reports

The list could go on and on depending on the program you are using. Again, review the features of any computerized bookkeeping program before purchasing it to make sure it will do what you want it to do for yourself or your company.

If you contract with a software company to create a program for the specific needs of your company, be sure that the software provider has a good support team in place that you can go to whenever you have questions or problems.

Hour's Up!

Review the information presented in this chapter by answering the following questions.

1. What information does a software program need to set up the accounting periods?
   a. Current month
   b. 1st and last day of prior year
   c. 1st and last day of current year

2. Standard Charts of Accounts are programmed into most computerized bookkeeping systems.
   a. True
   b. False

3. What is the Personal Finance Chart of Accounts in a computerized system used for?
   a. Secret expenses
   b. Household bookkeeping
   c. Tracking stocks and bonds

4. What account replaces Retained Earnings on the Balance Sheet for household bookkeeping?
   a. Net Worth
   b. Capital
   c. Profit & Loss

5. What ledger cards have to be created for Accounts Payable?
   a. Customer
   b. Vendor
   c. Inventory

6. Unit price codes are used for all customers.
   a. True
   b. False

7. What figures should be used for the beginning balances for a set-up date of May 1st of a calendar year.
   a. Trial Balance figures of 12-31
   b. Trial Balance figures of 3-31
   c. Trial Balance figures of 4-30

8. What function allows the user to customize invoices and checks?
   a. Set-up
   b. None
   c. Preferences

9. What function and report may be included in a bookkeeping program designed specifically for a contractor/builder?
   a. Job costing
   b. Accounts Receivable
   c. Budgets

10. Some reports in a computerized bookkeeping program require that additional information be entered.
    a. True
    b. False

Adapting the Basics of Bookkeeping to Different Businesses

Part V

Retail, Restaurants, and Entertainment Venues

Chapter Summary

In this hour you will learn about …

- Retail outlets
- Restaurants
- Theaters
- Membership organizations

The fact that the basics of bookkeeping do not change regardless of the size of the company or whether the system is manual or computerized has been stressed several times throughout this book.

Although this is true, different types of businesses require small adjustments and additions to the basic tasks associated with the bookkeeping system. In some business operations, certain aspects of the financial system may need more attention than others.

Retail Outlets

You have already absorbed a good deal of information regarding retail operations, but there are so many different kinds of retail outlets you should be aware of some of the ways they differ from one another. Some of the main differences depend on the products or services that are sold and how their employees are paid.

A car dealership would not generally be considered a store, but it is a retail outlet that sells one big product. The dealership usually has a contract with one particular auto manufacturer and purchases all vehicles from that manufacturer.

Sales and leasing people at an auto dealership usually work on a commission basis. Sometimes they receive weekly or monthly draws against future earnings; sometimes they do not. Also, as the salespeople work their way up in the dealership, they not only receive commissions on the autos they personally sell but also receive a percentage of the commissions for the salespeople they supervise.

Any one who has ever purchased a car at a dealership knows about the managers and closers who often move in and help the salesperson finalize the deal. Some of these people manipulate the numbers on the vehicle being sold, the trade-in of a used vehicle, down payments, and other payment options. These managers and closers may be on salary, or they may also get a cut of the original salesperson's commission.

Because most auto dealerships also have service departments, that is another area that will generate work for the bookkeeper. Most mechanics earn an hourly rate that is based on the amount of time it is supposed to take to do a certain repair. For example, a repair job is supposed to take four hours. If the mechanic finishes the job in three hours or takes five hours to do it, the customer is still charged for four hours and the mechanic gets paid accordingly.

JUST A MINUTE

Most auto repair garages use the Chilton Automotive Manual to determine how much time it should take to do certain repairs. This book sets the standard for estimating costs and billing customers.

There will also be people on the dealership's payroll who earn a set salary or do jobs like detailing cars and cleaning the showroom that are paid on an hourly basis.

The payroll alone at an auto dealership requires additional work and calculations for the bookkeeper. Depending on the size of the dealership, a payroll service may be used, but anyone who is contemplating employment as a bookkeeper at a car dealership needs to study payroll methods and how to calculate paychecks for each category of employee.

Also, in addition to the income earned on sales and servicing and repairing vehicles, the dealership will be selling auto parts needed for servicing and repairing the automobiles. Therefore, a separate Inventory Account for auto parts will be set up in the General Ledger that will have to be monitored and adjusted like the main inventory account for the automobiles on the dealer's lot.

Large automobile dealerships may employ more than one bookkeeper to handle the different areas of their business operation.

Products sold by retail outlets can include one expensive item like automobiles or they can sell a variety of smaller, less expensive items. Stores that sell a variety of products may require that the bookkeeper concentrate a good deal of effort on inventory and inventory control. This is especially true if the operation is not large enough to have separate inventory and purchasing departments.

Lumberyards and hardware stores are another area of the retail business that require special bookkeeping tasks. Lumber is sold by the board foot, nails by the package or pound, and other products by inches. Customers at lumberyards are contractors who pay wholesale prices for merchandise and other people who pay retail prices.

All the invoices eventually end up on the bookkeeper's desk and must be checked and entered into the General Ledger. Usually the income accounts for this type of company are set up separately for wholesale goods and retail goods.

The physical inventories are also more difficult because of the way the individual products have to be counted. However, if the bookkeeper is lucky, he or she won't be required to take part in the inventory count but will have to total the inventory sheets or enter the counts into the computer and make the adjustments.

Because retail outlets are major employers, a bookkeeper should give some thought to the type of products sold by a potential employer and the extra tasks and procedures those products and the people that sell those products may require within the bookkeeping system.

Restaurants

One of the main concerns of restaurant owners, regardless of the size of the establishment, is food cost. Food cost in a restaurant often determines the profit or loss each month. Food cost is determined by the amount purchased during the month and by the physical inventory of the food products in stock at the end of the month. The chef, kitchen manager, or restaurant owner usually takes the inventory. Once everything is counted, the figures are turned over to the bookkeeper to make the inventory adjustment and figure the food cost for the month.

The desired food cost varies from restaurant to restaurant, depending on the menu items and the number of customers the restaurant serves. Keep in mind that the food cost determines the Gross Profit of the restaurant, and all the other expenses must be covered by that.

Remember that if the inventory has been reduced, the entry to adjust it to actual is a credit to Inventory and a debit to Purchases in the Cost of Sales section. That entry automatically reduces the Gross Profit.

The food cost percentage is obtained by dividing the balance in the Purchase account into the Gross Sales figure:

> $10,000. (Purchases) divided by $ 25,000. (Sales) = 40 percent Food Cost

Of course, most restaurants have computerized bookkeeping systems that calculate the food costs and other percentages such as wages and expenses for the Profit & Loss Statements.

In some venues, like retirement homes where three meals a day are served to residents, the desired food cost is often obtained by multiplying the number of people served by a set amount. For example, if there are 100 residents and the cost per person per day is supposed to be $3.15, the monthly cost of food purchased is not supposed to exceed $9,450.00.

The other concern for bookkeepers and owners of large food and beverage establishments is the IRS requirement to file Form 8027, Employer's Annual Information Return of Tip Income and Allocated Tips. The purpose of this bookkeeping procedure is to allocate tips based on the Gross Sales of the restaurant to employees that are deemed to be under reporting the tips they earn to the employer. The wait staff in a restaurant are considered to be directly tipped employees, while other employees are *indirectly tipped*.

STRICTLY DEFINED

 Indirectly tipped employees in restaurants are people who assist the wait staff and receive a percentage from the wait staff for their assistance. They might include bus people and the host and hostesses at the front desk that seat customers.

If the employee is under reporting tips, then he or she is not paying taxes on the actual amounts earned each year. All employees receiving $20. or more a month in tips are required to report 100 percent of their tip income to their employers so that taxes can be reported and paid.

In general, a large food and beverage establishment is one to which the following criteria apply:

- Food or beverage is provided for consumption on the premises.
- Tipping is a customary practice.
- More than 10 employees who work more than 80 hours were normally employed on a typical business day during the preceding calendar year.

These criteria would eliminate fast-food restaurants from the establishments that are required to allocate tips, because there is generally no wait staff in a fast food place and tipping is not customary.

A bookkeeper in a large food and beverage establishment will be responsible for keeping track of the tips reported by employees and for calculating which members of the wait staff should have tips allocated to them. The IRS has currently set the allocation percentage at 8 percent of the Gross Receipts of the establishment. However, restaurants can contact the IRS and possibly get a lower rate.

Form 8027 is an annual report, but the record-keeping may be easier if it is done on a monthly basis. The following worksheet provided by the IRS can be used to determine tip allocations to employees. For this sample worksheet, it is assumed that the restaurant has Gross Receipts of $100,000. in the pay period and has tips reported of $6,200. Directly tipped employees reported $5,700. and indirectly tipped employees reported $500.

The sample worksheet should give you a good idea of how the allocation of tips would be determined if you were the bookkeeper in a large food and beverage establishment.

Another thing to consider in regard to Form 8027 is that the allocation of tips must be done before the end of the calendar year so the allocation amounts and taxes can be added into the employees' payroll figures before the W-2s are issued.

FYI For more information on allocating tips and completing Form 8027, access the form, the instructions, and other information available on the IRS website at www.irs.gov or order it by phoning 1-800-829-3676.

Directly tipped employees	Gross receipts for payroll period	Tips reported
A	$18,000	$1,080
B	16,000	880
C	23,000	1,810
D	17,000	800
E	12,000	450
F	14,000	680
Totals	$100,000	$5,700

1. $100,000 (gross receipts) x .08 = $8,000
2. $8,000 - $500 (tips reported by indirectly tipped employees) = $7,500

3.

Directly tipped employees	Directly tipped employee's share of 8% of the gross	(Times) Gross receipts ratio	Employee's share of 8% of gross
A	$7,500	18,000/100,000 =	$1,350
B	$7,500	16,000/100,000 =	1,200
C	$7,500	23,000/100,000 =	1,725
D	$7,500	17,000/100,000 =	1,275
E	$7,500	12,000/100,000 =	900
F	$7,500	14,000/100,000 =	1,050
		Total	$7,500

4.

Directly tipped employees	Employee's share of 8% of the gross	(Minus) Tips Reported	Employee shortfall
A	$1,350	$1,080 =	$270
B	$1,200	880 =	320
C	$1,725	1,810 =	—
D	$1,275	800 =	475
E	$ 900	450 =	450
F	$1,050	680 =	370
		Total shortfall	$1,885

5. $8,000 less $6,200 (total tips reported) = $1,800 (amount allocable among employees who had a shortfall)

6.

Shortfall employees	Allocable amount	(Times) Shortfall ratio	Amount of allocation
A	$1,800	270/1,885 =	$258
B	$1,800	320/1,885 =	306
D	$1,800	475/1,885 =	454
E	$1,800	450/1,885 =	430
F	$1,800	370/1,885 =	353

Since employee C has no shortfall, there is no allocation to C.

Like retail outlets, restaurants are major sources of employment for bookkeepers. Full-Charge Bookkeepers employed at CPA firms often have restaurant owners as clients and may be required to calculate allocated tips and complete Form 8027.

Theaters

Movie theaters work with the distributors of motion pictures and pay a fee to show films. The distributors also supply posters and trailers, short clips of the films, that the theaters can use to advertise the films to the theater patrons. The income accounts for a movie theater would include things like admission fees and the sales of food products at the concession stands. Many theaters today sell a lot more than popcorn, soda, and candy. Patrons at some theaters can have dinner there while seeing the film. Most theater employees are hourly workers hired to sell tickets, work in the concession stands, clean the theater after each showing of each film, and serve as projectionists.

There are very few movie theaters that operate independently these days. They are owned by corporations, but still must have people at the theater to count cash receipts, accept inventory, and perform a number of other tasks that could be considered bookkeeping. Sometimes, depending on the size of the theater, there are managers and assistant managers at the site that handle the bookkeeping chores as well as supervise the employees and make sure the overall operation runs smoothly.

Although the individual theater may or may not have its own set of books and General Ledger, there are still reports that would have to be completed and sent on to the corporate offices.

Theaters that produce works for the stage operate much differently than movie theaters and are usually much less profitable. Many theaters must supplement the income from their ticket sales with donations and by applying for grants from various corporations and organizations that support the arts. This of course requires the establishment of accounts in the General Ledger to record donations and grant money in addition to the income from ticket sales. The bookkeeper is usually not the person writing grant proposals but may be expected to supply financial information to the person that is applying for the grant money on the theater's behalf.

Theater expenses include things like royalties on the plays performed, construction of sets, and the purchase of props and costumes. Sometimes expenses for food and housing are paid for a playwright called in to help with a production of his or her work. Once in a while, a playwright is commissioned to write a particular play for a particular theater, generating another account to be added to the General Ledger. In addition, accounts for General Expenses such as rent, utilities, advertising, and telephone must be set up and monitored by the bookkeeper.

Monthly accounting reports will be issued for the theater in general. Also, reports detailing the income and expenses of the individual plays staged that season may be required.

While the actors that perform in the plays are not employees of the theater, they must be paid for each performance and often for rehearsal time as well. If the venue is what is known as an Equity theater, there are a number of rules that must be followed including the use of players that belong to *Actors Equity*. Equity actors must be paid standard rates higher than nonequity actors.

STRICTLY DEFINED

 Actors Equity is a union for professional actors and stage managers that sets the amounts their members must be paid and provides other benefits such as health insurance and pension plans.

The theater will also have an Artistic Director who chooses the plays and hires directors and actors as well as a number of staff people on the payroll.

The bookkeeper would be responsible for making sure the theater had the proper paperwork and tax identification numbers for each actor in each play and for any other people contracted to work on sets, provide music, and take care of the sound and lights for each performance.

Some theaters have employees who handle the lights and sound equipment but often they are outside service people that move from theater to theater. Of course you know that means many 1099s must be issued by the bookkeeper at the end of every calendar year.

Membership Organizations

There are many membership organizations that exist for various purposes. Some are social, some are charitable, and some are both. There are also organizations and support groups for acting, writing, bird watching, reading, hiking, teaching, political awareness, and anything else one can think of doing. Many of these membership organizations are nonprofit entities, which means that they have a special classification with the IRS that allows them to be exempt from taxes. These groups earn income by charging membership fees. The amount of the dues doesn't really matter to a bookkeeper, as tracking the dues is the same regardless of its amount.

Every dues check that comes into the organization should be photocopied and filed for easy access. This may be an extra step in the bookkeeping process but worth the time, because members are famous for not knowing if or when they paid their dues.

In addition to dues, these membership groups sponsor numerous other activities. An Elks Lodge is a social organization as well as a charitable operation. Many lodges own buildings, run restaurants, hold dances, picnics, and other events to fund their charitable donations. All of the income and expenses for the lodge itself, the restaurants and all of the other activities, must be recorded in the bookkeeping system along with the dues.

A popular fund raising activity for many groups is bingo. While this might not sound like a big deal for the bookkeeper, bingo is a form of gambling and states have stringent rules and regulations about these games. A license must be obtained for the bingo operation. Reports and forms have to be completed and submitted to the state on a regular basis.

Except for bingo games, the bookkeeping for a membership organization is not much different than any other business operation. However, keep in mind that these types of organizations change officers every year or so. That means the bookkeeper may have a different boss each year and have to make some adjustments in his or her daily routine and procedures.

Hour's Up!

Assess how much information you have retained from this hour by answering the following questions.

1. What is one of the main sources of income for an auto dealership?
    a. Financing
    b. Auto service and repairs
    c. Investments

2. The Chilton Automotive Manual lists the current prices of vehicles.
    a. True
    b. False

3. How is lumber sold?
    a. By the inch
    b. By the foot
    c. By the board foot

4. What reduces the Gross Profit at a restaurant?
    a. Less purchases
    b. Higher food costs
    c. Lower food costs

5. What IRS form is filed annually by large food and drink establishments?
    a. 8122
    b. 2780
    c. 8027

6. What is the purpose of form 8027?
    a. To report sales information
    b. To report food costs
    c. To allocate unreported tips

7. What is the current percentage set by the IRS for Form 8027?
    a. 8 percent
    b. 10 percent
    c. 15 percent

8. What is Actors Equity?
    a. Casting agent
    b. Bank
    c. Actors union

9. Who regulates bingo games?
   a. The IRS
   b. State
   c. FTC

10. Membership organizations can be both social and charitable.
    a. True
    b. False

Review

Personal and Professional Services

Chapter Summary

In this hour you will learn about …

- Hairdressers
- Law firms
- Accountants
- Agents

Businesses that offer personal and professional services are important to our economy and to the millions of people that seek their services. Most of these businesses use the standard bookkeeping accounts and files you have been learning about throughout this book. However, there are a few variations in the way the income is earned, the employees are paid, and the way the clients are billed that is worth exploring.

While many of these service providers are large corporate entities, just as many are smaller operations, even home-based businesses, that may need information on managing their own bookkeeping systems.

Hairdressers

Hairdressers can work in beauty salons, barber shops, spas, theaters, movie studios, and out of their homes. The place where they work often determines how they get paid and how the bookkeeping system that pays them is structured and managed. Another factor that affects their pay scale and their bookkeeping practices is whether they are employees, employers, or self-employed.

Hairdressers who have set up shop in their own homes have the simplest set of books to manage. As sole proprietors, the profit or loss of the hairdressing business becomes their personal gross income or loss at the end of the year. A review of Schedule C and the other tax forms it could generate will give you the basic information needed to set up a viable bookkeeping system. These tax forms can be viewed on the IRS website (www.irs.gov).

The next category to consider is the hairdresser who works at a theater or a movie studio. Some may be employees, but most will be contract workers. You know that employees receive a W-2 at the end of the tax year; contract workers receive a 1099. Both individuals need to monitor their income and taxes for the year. In addition, the contract worker needs to set up accounts and files to track all the expenses related to the income reported on the 1099. Again, a look at Schedule C will be helpful in organizing tax data.

Working in a salon, barber shop, or spa does not always mean that the hairdresser is an employee. Many of these business operations rent space to hairdressers and, depending on how their agreement is structured, the hairdressers may still be self-employed and responsible for keeping his or her own set of books and paying his or her own taxes. Self-employed hairdressers pay the salon a weekly or monthly fee for the use of a work station and the hairdressers set their own schedules and pay for any supplies they need for their clients.

GO TO ◄

Hour 11 for information on the IRS rules that determine whether a person is an employee or not.

Salons and other establishments that employ hairdressers usually have them work on a commission basis, but the employer sets the work hours, the prices for services, and supplies all the necessary equipment. The only difference in the bookkeeping system would be in the way the Gross Wages are computed. Most places give the employee 70 percent of the amount the hairdresser earns for the shop each pay period. That means that a separate bookkeeping tally must be kept every day for each person working in the shop. The daily sales become the Gross Income for the shop and the commissions paid to employees can be classified as Cost of Sales or Selling Expenses or can simply be expensed as Salaries and Wages.

Law Firms

Lawyers usually specialize in a particular area of the law. Even a large law firm that handles any type of case is able to do so because its staff includes a number of different lawyers that are deemed experts in various legal categories.

One thing that all law firms have in common is that they all have Trust Accounts. You may recall that a Trust Account is a bank account that is separate from a company's operating account. In any type of law practice, from a criminal attorney to a patent attorney, the Trust Account is where funds that have been collected for clients of the firm are deposited and held.

The bookkeeper at a law firm usually is responsible for making sure the proper funds are deposited into the Trust Account. Legally, client funds should not be commingled with other funds on the law firm's books. Monitoring the Trust Account and reconciling it with the bookkeeping records is imperative as Trust Accounts are subject to audits. In addition to the Trust Account, the General Ledger for a law firm should have an account set up in the Liability section of the Balance Sheet accounts titled, Client Funds Held in Trust.

Most attorneys collect a retainer from clients before any legal work is performed. The retainer is simply an advance payment against the legal fees that will be assessed as the case progresses. Retainers are posted as a credit to Accounts Receivable and as a payment to the ledger card made up for the client. The other side of the entry is a debit to Cash in Checking. No posting is made to an income account because the lawyer has not actually earned any income yet.

A file folder should be made up for every client of the law firm. This would generally be done by the lawyer or the lawyer's secretary, but sometimes the bookkeeper performs this task. Many bookkeepers make a copy of each retainer check and put it in the client's file. Any other information relating to the client or the client's case would be placed in the file also.

As the attorney works on lawsuits, patents, or other legal matters for clients, he or she keeps track of the hours expended on each client's behalf. At some point, the attorney turns his time sheets over to the bookkeeper. This can happen daily, weekly, or monthly depending on the volume of work and how many clients the lawyer is servicing. In some cases, there will be a time sheet for each client, in others the hours on the time sheets will be for any number of different clients and the bookkeeper will have to sort out and total the billable hours for each person. Also, there are legal assistants and researchers employed by some law firms that will also have billable hours for work they do for clients and those time sheets will also be transmitted to the bookkeeper for handling.

Once the billable hours have been determined for each client, the bookkeeper multiplies the billable hours by the hourly rate the lawyer charges for his work.

PROCEED WITH CAUTION

If the attorney handles a variety of legal matters, there may be a different hourly rate for each type of case or a set fee for some assignments. The bookkeeper will have to keep some sort of rate information to refer to when working on the client billings.

The bookkeeper then posts the legal fees and any expenses incurred on behalf of the clients to the General Ledger. The entry would be a credit to the Income account and debit to Accounts Receivable and the ledgers for each client. In some larger law firms, there may be a computerized program for time sheets and billable hours that will automatically post to the General Ledger and the clients' ledger cards.

At the end of the month or the billing period, the clients' bills or statements would be made up and mailed based on the balance in Accounts Receivable and the clients' ledger cards.

When funds are received from an outside source for a client such as proceeds from a lawsuit, the funds are deposited into the Trust Account. The entry in the General Ledger is a debit to the Trust Account and a credit to the Client Funds Held in Trust Account. These funds are a liability to the law firm because they belong to the client and must be paid to the client in a timely manner.

There are times when the lawyer receives a percentage for getting a settlement for a client. In that case, the bookkeeper might post only the client's portion of the settlement to the Trust Account and the liability account while the rest of the funds would be posted to Income and to the Cash in Checking Account. If the transaction is handled this way, be sure that documentation including the attorney's agreement and the settlement papers are properly filed in the client's file. Also, a photocopy of the check issued to pay the client for his or her share of the proceeds should be placed in the file along with the other documents.

Doing the books at a law firm often requires more attention to detail and more paperwork than other business employers. That's because all lawyers will tell you, if it's not in writing it doesn't count.

Accountants

Just like lawyers, accountants and their staff keep time sheets where they enter the hours they have worked on the clients' books or tax returns. The professional accounting office will usually have a bookkeeper who just handles the books for the accounting firm itself. That bookkeeper gets the time sheets and posts the billings to the clients and the General Ledger accounts.

The accounting firm will also have Full-Charge Bookkeepers on staff who perform much of the work for the clients. The CPA handles work for some of the bigger clients and also reviews all the work done by the staff before it leaves the office. Work for clients at a CPA firm is usually done on a monthly basis and includes basic tasks like reviewing and posting the income and expenses for the month, posting adjustments, calculating FTDs, and preparing payroll reports.

GO TO ◄

Hour 13 to review the information on calculating and remitting Federal Tax Deposits (FTDs).

During tax season, everyone at a CPA firm usually works overtime as the regular work increases because clients often have their accountants issue W-2s and 1099s for their companies. Then, after January 31st when everyone has received their W-2s and the business books are closed for the year, there is a steady flow of clients coming into the office to have their tax returns prepared. It's no wonder, that most CPA firms close their offices on the day after the tax deadline. They need the break!

Some professional accounting firms have clients who turn over all their business and personal financial matters to the accountant. This is a common practice for celebrities who are too busy to handle their own financial affairs. Hopefully, they are not too busy to review the Financial Statements and other information the accountant supplies, so they have a general idea of their monetary status. Letting someone else have complete control of your finances is never a smart idea no matter how wealthy you are.

At the accounting firm that offers personal financial management, bank accounts are set up and funded by the client. All the bills incurred by the client are then delivered or mailed directly to the accounting firm for payment from the client's funds. The bookkeeping system for this type of client is set up like any other business entity and every transaction is posted and handled according to standard procedures. The only difference is that the accountant is not an employee of the client. He or she is simply providing a service and charges a set fee or bills the client an hourly rate depending on how much work has been done.

JUST A MINUTE

 These bank accounts set up to pay the bills of a client are not Trust Accounts. They are usually regular checking accounts. The accountant estimates the monthly expenses, and the client provides the funds for the checking account.

Accounting offices may use the computerized bookkeeping programs that allow multiple companies to be set up in the system. That way each client has its own set of books and the staff can go back and forth between companies to post transactions and adjustments.

Bookkeepers at law firms and accounting offices handle privileged and very confidential information about the clients the firms service. Therefore, they need to be trustworthy, discreet, and ethical to protect their employers, the clients, and themselves.

Agents

Agents is a very broad category, but because this chapter is about personal and professional services, we will limit agents to the people who manage careers.

Actors, sports figures, and writers all use agents to help them further their careers. While agents perform different functions depending on the profession of the client, they all have one thing in common as far as bookkeeping is concerned. The monies earned by the clients are paid to the agents; the agents deduct their commissions and any other pertinent fees from the cash received and then send the balance on to the client.

All monies collected for clients pass through the agent's bank account. Usually, the agents deposit the checks and make sure they clear the bank. As you know, with electronic processing this only takes a day or two at the most. When the check is received, it can posted as a debit to Cash in Checking, a credit to a liability account for the client's funds, and a credit to an income account for commissions earned.

Of course, files must be set up for all the clients represented by an agent with notations on the people or companies that have been contacted on the client's behalf. Actors supply professional photos, called headshots, and resumés of their acting experience for the agent to submit to producers. Writers supply manuscripts for the agents to submit to publishers and producers.

Some agents charge fees for photocopying and other administrative expenses and accounts for those charges could be set up in the income and expense sections of the General Ledger. Of course the agent also has a number of other expenses such as rent, utilities, telephone, payroll, and taxes.

The money that a client earns during the year through the agent's efforts is paid directly to the agent. Therefore, the agent is the one that issues the 1099 statement to the client at the end of the tax year.

Many agencies are incorporated and have a number of agents who handle a variety of clients on their staffs.

As a bookkeeper, you are included in the category of professional service providers, and the advantage of that is that you can work in any type of business environment.

Hour's Up!

Please answer the following questions regarding personal and professional service providers.

1. Hairdressers are seldom self-employed.
    a. True
    b. False

2. How do most salons pay the hairdressers they employ?
    a. Hourly rates
    b. Salaries
    c. Commission

3. Where do law firms deposit client funds?
    a. Checking account
    b. Trust Account
    c. Savings account

4. What is a retainer?
    a. Advance payment
    b. An Equity account
    c. A Capital account

5. How are retainers posted in the General Ledger?
    a. Credit Income/Debit Accounts Receivable
    b. Debit Cash in Checking/Credit Income
    c. Debit Cash in Checking/Credit Accounts Receivable

6. How do lawyers track billable client hours?
    a. Client Time Sheets
    b. Expense Accounts
    c. Payroll Time Sheets

Review

7. How are client funds held in trust classified?
    a. Assets
    b. Liabilities
    c. Capital

8. Wealthy people do not need to read the financial reports issued by their accountants.
    a. True
    b. False

9. What IRS form can be a guideline for a self-employed person to use for bookkeeping?
    a. 1040-A
    b. 1040-E
    c. 1040-C

10. How often do most clients bring their books into their accountants' offices to be reviewed?
    a. Daily
    b. Weekly
    c. Monthly

Real Estate

Chapter Summary

In this hour you will learn about …

- Contractors
- Real estate sales
- Property management

Real estate is an industry that includes a multitude of income-producing activities. Real property is developed, constructed, and bought and sold every hour of every day all over the world. All of this activity must be recorded and financed. So, it is easy to understand why real estate provides many employment opportunities for bookkeepers.

In this hour, we will discuss three of the busiest and most lucrative business operations in the real estate field and explain the procedures and tasks required by each.

Contractors

General Contractors (GCs) often purchase large parcels of land to develop into residential areas. Everyone is familiar with these housing developments that start with the contractor making the improvements to the vacant land that are required by the city or county before actual construction of homes can begin. Sometimes, contractors must guarantee the construction of a school and a park if the area is totally undeveloped and the homes they will be building and selling are for families.

Once the basic improvements have been completed and all the licenses and building permits have been obtained, the contractor is allowed to build a few model homes to use as sales' offices. Potential buyers inspect the model homes and choose the model they want to purchase. The buyer also chooses a location in the development where the house should be built. Financial arrangements include cash down payments and qualifying and obtaining a mortgage for the balance of the cost of the house.

General Contractors often do more than just build new homes. They also build commercial property, such as shopping centers, office buildings, apartment complexes, and schools. They also develop parks and build recreation centers. In addition, a General Contractor may remodel properties, buy and sell properties, and own rental properties.

The Chart of Accounts for a General Contractor can be several pages long. This is because in addition to the standard accounts found in the General Ledger of most companies, contractors have a number of other accounts that are specific to their business activities.

The following is a list of accounts in the Asset section of the Balance Sheet that you would probably find in the General Ledger for a contractor:

- **1120-Mortgages Receivable:** A loan secured by property where the contractor is the lender. Usually these mortgages have what is called a *stop* on them, so the term of the loan is shorter than a regular mortgage is expected to be.

STRICTLY DEFINED

 A **stop** on a mortgage loan is the date that the mortgage must be paid in full or refinanced through another lender.

- **1200-Inventory Land:** This account would hold the values of land purchased and held for development in the future.
- **1210-Inventory Buildings:** Completed buildings that have yet to be sold.
- **1220-Construction in Progress:** The value of buildings that are not yet completed.
- **1910-Escrow Deposits:** In the Asset section, this account would be used to record deposits the contractor has put on land or other real property being purchased for future development. Escrow is the legal process by which ownership is transferred from one person to another.
- **1920-Municipal Tax Liens and Deposits:** Until properties are sold and ownership is transferred to the buyers, the contractor must pay taxes and deposits required by the cities and counties where the property is located.

One thing to consider when reviewing some of the assets on a General Contractors' books is that the contractor is usually applying for construction loans to finance the building of properties that will be resold.

The more Assets that appear on the Balance Sheet, the better the company looks to potential lenders.

In the Liability section of the Balance Sheet, General Contractors also have additional accounts that reflect the particulars of their business activities. The following are some of those accounts you might find listed under Liabilities on the Balance Sheet:

- **2115-Commissions Payable:** Real estate salespeople earn commissions on the new houses they sell. Those commissions would be accrued on the contractors' books until the property is actually transferred to the buyer.

Contractors usually have their own sales staff on site at a housing development. However, the contractors also cooperate and pay commissions to Realtors from other firms that bring clients to the development and successfully negotiate a sale for the contractor.

- **2120-Customer Security Deposits:** Money collected from buyers that will eventually be returned to the buyer or paid out to a utility company or other vendor.
- **2130-Escrow Deposits Payable:** Deposits the contractor collected from buyers that will be turned over to the escrow agent that is handling the sale. Sometimes this money is held pending the buyer's approval for a mortgage to finance the purchase.
- **2300-Short Term Notes-Payable:** Construction loans that are scheduled to be paid off within a year. These loans usually have a higher than normal interest rate as well.

The Income and Cost of Sales accounts in a contractors' General Ledger are pretty standard. It is in the Direct/Selling Expenses and General Expenses sections of the Profit & Loss accounts that you will find the extra accounts that are needed by the contractor.

Keep in mind that a General Contractor performs some of the basic work done on a development depending on the type of equipment and the construction workers employed by the company. However, many facets of the construction process are done by *subcontractors*.

STRICTLY DEFINED

Subcontractors are experts in their particular area of construction, such as carpenters, electricians, plumbers, and painters. Subcontractors are not employees, but outside service providers the contractors use to complete specific work on their projects.

This leads us to a list of the accounts that are included in the General Ledger to record the expenses for subcontractors and other work that the contractor may be required to do by the cities and counties where the development is being built. The titles of the following accounts explain their purpose in the General Ledger:

- 5000-Roads and Curbs
- 5100-Water Mains
- 5120-Engineering
- 5140-Surveys
- 5160-Legal & Municipal Costs
- 5180-Land Fill
- 5510-Masonry
- 5525-Carpentry
- 5530-Plumbing
- 5535-Heating & Air Conditioning
- 5540-Sheet Metal
- 5545-Electrical
- 5550-Appliances
- 5555-Other Subcontractors
- 5820-Permits
- 5840-Cleaning
- 5850-Landscaping

The bookkeeping system for a General Contractor has more accounts that must be monitored, but it doesn't really change the procedures for posting transactions. The big difference in working for a General Contractor instead of another type of business may be the workload. However, with a good understanding of the business and a computerized system, a bookkeeper could manage quite nicely.

Real Estate Sales

Real estate sales is a fairly easy profession to get into. In most states, it does not require a college degree or any prior experience. Real estate people are usually licensed by the state where they reside. They obtain a license by completing a prescribed educational course and passing a test administered by the state Real Estate Board.

Before the salespeople can be licensed, they must find a real estate broker to sponsor them. A broker is an experienced professional who has completed the additional schooling required by the state and has passed a more stringent examination. The licenses issued to the brokers allow them to supervise the work of the salespeople that they sponsor. However, a salesperson working for a broker is not usually considered an employee.

Unless the broker has formed a corporation where he or she can be considered an employee, the broker is also self-employed. The broker gets a percentage of all the commissions earned by the salespeople that are under his broker's license. Of course, the brokers also earn commissions on their own real estate sales.

Currently the standard commission earned on the sale of residential property is 7 percent of the sales price. The commission is divided between the *listing agent* and the *selling agent*.

STRICTLY DEFINED

 The **listing agent** contracts with the property owner to list the property for sale. The **selling agent** actually sells the property.

Some brokers pay a franchise fee to be part of a nationwide real estate corporation, like Century 21. It affords them the use of a recognizable name and other benefits like group insurance and nationwide advertising campaigns.

The income accounts for real estate salespeople and brokers are usually limited to commissions. On the expense side, auto expenses are probably one of the largest expenditures. Real estate salespeople should use Schedule C as a guideline for setting up their accounts. Remember, like all self-employed people, they may also have to pay estimated taxes on the income that accumulates during the tax year.

If you are thinking about doing bookkeeping for a real estate company that just handles sales, it will be much like any other company that derives its income from sales. The broker usually rents office space and provides desks, telephones, computers, and marketing assistance for the sales staff. Regular payroll would only be done for the administrative people in the office and the brokers if they are employees of a corporation. The sales staff receives commission checks issued whenever the escrow process on a sale is completed. At the end of the escrow process, the escrow agent pays the commissions earned on the sale to the listing broker and the selling broker. The brokers retain their share of the commission and pay the remainder to their agents.

Property Management

Real estate companies sometimes house a separate department that manages income property for clients. Property managers are usually divided into two categories:

- Residential property managers supervise the rental and maintenance of houses and apartment buildings for residential tenants.
- Commercial property managers supervise the rental and oversee the maintenance of office buildings, stores, warehouses and any other building used for business purposes.

All property management companies must have a Trust Account where security and cleaning deposits and the rents collected on behalf of their clients are deposited and held.

Bookkeepers at property management companies work closely with the Realtors who actually contract with owners to handle the rental of their properties. The Realtors screen tenants, negotiate leases and rental agreements, and arrange for any necessary maintenance or repairs on the properties in their care. The bookkeepers handle all the funds, set up files for the property owners, and keep a separate accounting for each owner of every monetary transaction related to the property.

Fortunately, there is computer software created specifically for property management companies. It allows the bookkeeper to set up an account for every property managed by the company. Because these accounts are created and coded alphabetically and numerically for each individual property, a client that has three properties with the management company would have three accounts set up in the software system, one for each property. This computer software creates individual bookkeeping systems that will track all the income and expenses for the property. Reports similar to a Profit & Loss Statement can be generated at any time on any property.

The bookkeeper enters the daily transactions into the system using the account code assigned to each property. When rental checks are received, they are photocopied and coded for posting before being deposited into the company's Trust Account. The total of all the checks posted must equal the total amount deposited into the Trust Account.

As the month progresses the bookkeeper receives invoices from the property managers for utilities, repairs, and maintenance to the properties in their care. The invoices are coded with the account number of the property as a reference number. The bookkeeper enters the invoices into the computer and the system automatically posts the expense to each individual property. When all the invoices have been entered, the program will print the checks to the vendors. The checks are drawn on the Trust Account from the clients' funds that are deposited there.

At some point, the bookkeeper has the system generate a report showing the management fees that the company has earned from the rents collected that month. When the check is issued the fees are posted to each owner's account as an expense.

After all the owners' expenses have been paid for the month, the bookkeeper prompts the system to issue reports for the owners showing their rental income and expenses for the period. Lastly, the bookkeeper commands the system to issue checks to the owners for the net income shown on their reports. The report, the check, and copies of any invoices or bills relating to the property are mailed to each owner.

The property management software also issues a report that lists every property in the system and the balance in the account. The total of that report must equal the total amount in the Trust Account. Remember that Security Deposits and Cleaning Deposits are also posted to the owners' accounts, but the monies are held in the Trust Account until the current tenants leave the property.

Besides the work involved in keeping the records for the property owners, the bookkeeper must do the books and pay the bills for the property management department. The department will have an operating account where the fees it earns on its management activities are deposited each month. This will be the Cash in Checking Account in the management department's General Ledger. All transactions pertaining to the property management business will be posted in the General Ledger and Financial Statements will be issued and reviewed.

PROCEED WITH CAUTION

 Bank statements for the operating account and the Trust Account must be reconciled as soon as possible. Remember that a Trust Account is subject to audit, so keeping it in balance with the clients' accounts is imperative.

If doing bookkeeping for a property management company sounds like a lot of work, it is. Of course, the actual workload depends on the number of properties that are being managed by the company. However, bookkeepers for companies that manage more than a hundred properties usually have assistants and clerical people to help them.

Hour's Up!

The following questions are a review of the information presented in this chapter.

1. What is a "stop" clause in a mortgage contract?
   a. An extension
   b. A date specified when the mortgage must be paid
   c. An interest reduction

2. Contractors must complete certain improvements on vacant land before buildings can be constructed.
   a. True
   b. False

3. What is a contractor's inventory?
   a. Completed buildings
   b. Work in progress
   c. Vacant land
   d. All of the above

4. Where are Escrow Deposits received from buyers posted in a contractor's General Ledger?
   a. Assets
   b. Capital
   c. Liabilities

5. Subcontractors are employees of General Contractors.
   a. True
   b. False

6. What is a listing agent?
   a. Agent who sells the property
   b. Agent who shows the property
   c. Agent who contracts with the owner to sell the property

7. Who rents properties at a property management company?
   a. Property owner
   b. Property manager
   c. Bookkeeper

8. A separate account must be set up for each property managed.
   a. True
   b. False

9. Who pays for the repairs of managed properties?
   a. Bookkeeper
   b. Property manager
   c. Property owner

10. There is special bookkeeping software that is written specifically for property managers.
   a. True
   b. False

Review

Finance and Insurance

Chapter Summary

In this hour you will learn about …

- Banks
- Mortgage brokers
- Insurance

Finance and insurance often go together. That's because banks and mortgage companies want collateral for the loans they fund, and they expect that the property used for collateral be insured against loss or damage.

Both industries offer employment opportunities for bookkeepers with varying degrees of skill and experience. In other words, there are entry-level positions in banking and insurance that will allow the novice to gain valuable experience. Learning a little more about how these businesses operate may also help you make informed decisions when you are applying for personal loans or mortgages.

Banks

As you know, every General Ledger begins with the Balance Sheet accounts, and the first accounts listed on a Balance Sheet are always the bank accounts. The reason for this is obvious. Cash in Checking and Cash in Savings are considered to be the primary strengths of a business operation. The banking industry itself also recognizes the strength of bank accounts. That's why banks and credit unions are always offering incentives, like free services or gifts, to coax people into opening new checking and savings accounts with them.

The money that is on deposit at a financial institution is money the banks use to earn income for the bank. The funds of their depositors are used for investments and for the loans and mortgages they process on a daily basis.

Most banks distribute the workload associated with the services provided into departments. The up front people are the tellers and customer service people who deal face to face with the depositors. In the background are all the people in the other departments. Together bank employees handle the following services:

- New Accounts/Customer Service
- Change Funds and Night Drop Deposits
- Credit Cards
- Administrative/Wire and Electronic Transfers
- Investments
- Loans

Working in any one of these banking areas is good experience for anyone who wants to learn more about the financial industry. All of them require good people skills and some knowledge of bookkeeping.

Tellers must know how to count money and post it correctly into the computer. At the end of the day, the teller's cash drawer must balance with the entries that have been posted to the accounts belonging to the customers that he or she has assisted that business day.

The customer service people are also visible in the bank lobby. These employees assist new customers with opening bank accounts and help others who have questions or problems with their existing accounts.

Some bookkeeping skills are required for most banking jobs. Consider the customers who have made a mess of their checking accounts and can't get them to reconcile to the bank statement. Many are distressed because their checks are being returned for insufficient funds, and they are accruing more and more bank charges. The banker works with these people, analyzes their checking account, explains the errors, and helps the customers resolve the problems so that their accounts are once more in balance.

GO TO ◄
Hour 2 where you will find information on the services banks offer to customers in the retail business.

There are also bank employees who work in a secure area to count the money in the night deposit bags and make up the change funds requested by customers. This job is very similar to what the tellers do in the bank lobby area as money must be handled, counted, and then posted to the customers' accounts. The same is true of the change funds that are assembled and then deducted from the customers' accounts.

Large banking establishments have credit card departments that work with customers applying for a bank-issued card. The employees in this area often have to assess the customers' financial condition and determine the limit that will be assigned to the credit card. Remember that credit card debt is normally an unsecured loan. However, people with poor credit histories are often required to deposit money in a bank account in order to obtain a credit card.

Qualified bookkeepers work behind the scenes in a bank's administrative offices. The first task of the day is to review all the wire transfers and electronic transfers that have been delivered overnight and make sure they have all been correctly posted. In addition to managing the bank's bookkeeping system, the administrative people may be responsible for making sure bank statements are issued and mailed promptly. Corporate customers are serviced, tax reports are reviewed, and financial research is conducted to improve customer relations and solve problems.

Some bank managers and other employees are trained to handle investments such as *Mutual Funds* for their customers. This job requires an understanding of the stock market so the process can be explained to customers interested in this banking service. The investment representative must be licensed by the National Association of Securities Dealers (NASD) and pass a rigorous examination to acquire the license. He or she is also monitored by the Securities and Exchange Commission (SEC).

STRICTLY DEFINED

 Mutual Funds are investment opportunities where groups of people pool their money and allow the fund administrator to buy and sell stocks and bonds on their behalf. The profits or losses on these investments are shared by the members of the Mutual Fund group based on the amount of money they have contributed to it.

Once people have chosen to participate in the Mutual Funds offered by their bank, the bank manager is required to be available to answer any questions or explain the monthly statements issued by the fund administrators.

The loan department of a bank handles all the requests and paperwork required for the loan applicants. As you've learned, every time you complete a loan application, you are presenting a Balance Sheet to the lender. Therefore, the employees in the bank's loan department must be adept at helping customers complete the applications, assessing their Net Worth, checking their credit history, evaluating the collateral they are using for the loan, and determining their ability to repay the loan. Banks finance homes, autos, business expenses such as inventory or equipment acquisitions, and a multitude of other necessities and luxuries for their customers.

As you can see, most positions in banking require some type of bookkeeping skill or at the very least a desire and aptitude to work with figures.

Mortgage Brokers

Mortgage brokers work for companies that only finance real property such as land, commercial buildings, and residential housing. Most commercial properties require large mortgages and the companies or brokers that finance these properties must be able to assess the financial stability of the buyer, the value of the property, and its income producing potential. A background in bookkeeping and accounting is required for this type of financing.

In the home-buying market, the mortgage brokers should also have some bookkeeping knowledge, but basically they will be working with individuals and simpler loan requirements.

The General Contractors discussed in the last hour often make arrangements with a specific mortgage company or broker to be on site at their developments to screen potential buyers. Sometimes, the contractors are able to get the mortgage companies to offer special discount rates on loans in exchange for the opportunity to be at the development and connect with buyers.

Real estate agents also establish relationships with mortgage professionals because most sales hinge on the ability of the buyer to procure a mortgage on the property they want to purchase.

In today's market, buyers are usually prequalified by the mortgage companies. That means the mortgage company interviews the buyers and reviews their financial information and credit history to determine the amount of money the mortgage company will loan to them. That gives the buyer a price range to explore in the housing market.

Keep in mind that there are a lot of different kinds of mortgages. Some loans sponsored by the government require no down payments and have reduced closing costs. One of the responsibilities of the mortgage broker or company is to find the loan that best suits the needs of the buyer. To do that, mortgage brokers must be able to accurately appraise the financial status and the current and future income of the buyers.

FYI For more information on low cost home loans guaranteed by the Federal Housing Administration visit their website: www.fha.com.

Mortgage people have computer systems that can check credit ratings and analyze financial information very quickly, but the accuracy of the information it generates depends on the mortgage broker's expertise in accumulating the necessary data to enter into the computer.

A very important part of prequalifying buyers is the closing cost statement that the mortgage broker is required by law to provide to the buyers. This is a detailed document that lists all the costs associated with securing a mortgage. The mortgage broker must have a working knowledge of bookkeeping and financial statements to complete the qualification process and to produce an accurate estimate of the costs the buyer will have to pay in order to get the loan.

Second mortgages are another large facet of the industry. These loans tap into the equity of an owners' property and require the mortgage broker to closely examine the owners' financial status and thoroughly research the value of the home being used to secure the second mortgage.

Using bookkeeping skills in the mortgage industry may be a good alternative for some people. Instead of managing a set of books, mortgage brokers are constantly reviewing financial information and making decisions based on their analysis of it. This career choice can be lucrative and personally rewarding.

Insurance

Lenders, like banks and mortgage companies, may have their own insurance departments. If not, they have agents and companies that will provide immediate coverage on any property that these lenders have a lien on. If a loan customer fails to provide verification of insurance on property that secures the debt, the lenders obtain their own insurance on the property and charge the premium to the property owner. Regardless of who obtains the coverage on collateral, the lending institution will be listed on the insurance policy as the *Loss Payee*.

STRICTLY DEFINED

 The **Loss Payee** on the insurance policy that insures your home or personal auto is the bank or mortgage company that has financed the purchase. Even though you are paying the premiums for the coverage, in the event of loss or damage to the property, the lender receives the proceeds, not you.

Insurance policies are issued by insurance companies, but most companies have agents that actually deal with the consumer. The agents may be employed by a specific insurance company or just contracted to sell policies issued by one or more companies. The following is a list of some types of insurance coverage that can be purchased by individuals and business owners:

- Life insurance
- Disability insurance
- Auto insurance
- Health insurance
- Homeowners insurance
- Fire insurance
- Liability insurance

There are also what are called Umbrella Policies that are designed to protect all aspects of a person's life, personal property, and business holdings.

Some insurance companies specialize in one particular area of coverage, like life insurance or health insurance. Other companies sell many different kinds of insurance policies, but separate the insurance classifications by dividing them among auxiliary companies that they own.

Insurance companies employ administrative people, called underwriters, who actually rate and issue policies based on the amount of coverage the consumer needs or requests. Before the advent of computers, underwriters had to manually calculate insurance premiums. Now they simply enter the policy information into the computer and receive an instant rate quote. However, some bookkeeping skills are still required by insurance underwriters. As you know, the reports a computer generates are only as good as the information keyed into it.

The employees who manage the bookkeeping system at an insurance company would have income accounts set up in the General Ledger for the types of policies the company collects premiums on. For example, a company that sells life insurance may also sell disability insurance and medical insurance.

All insurance companies would have Accounts Receivable, as many policy holders pay premiums on a monthly basis. In the Liability section of the Balance Sheet there would be an account set up for Commissions Payable and in one of the expense sections there would be an account for Commissions Paid.

The commissions that insurance companies pay out go to the various insurance agents that represent the company to the public.

Insurance agencies can be small one-person operations, large corporations, or any size in between. All insurance agents basically work on commission, but like the companies, they often specialize in one or two types of coverage. Some agents only handle commercial insurance and deal strictly with businesses. Others handle what is called Personal Lines, which includes auto, home, health, and life insurance for individuals. It does not include commercial coverage for business operations.

Depending on their relationship with the insurance companies, agents could be considered employees, but many are self-employed individuals.

Agents usually have computer programs that provide rate information on different types of coverage. Some programs are connected to the insurance company's computers. Obviously, the agents must have certain bookkeeping knowledge and skills to service their clients.

A general insurance agency would have contracts with a number of different companies, making their bookkeeping system a little more complex depending on how many companies they represent. This type of agency sometimes collects the premiums from their clients and transmits it to the insurer. This, of course, involves Accounts Receivable and Accounts Payable and all the underlying ledger cards for each.

Working in an insurance agency can be stressful. There will be claims that have to be filed, adjusted, and paid. While the companies usually have claims adjusters that handle the claims, many people contact the agent that sold them the policy first and come back to the agent with any problems or questions about the claim. In spite of this, the insurance business can be profitable and often provides excellent benefits.

Review

Hour's Up!

Please take a few minutes to answer the following questions as a review of this chapter.

1. How do banks use depositors' funds?
   a. Investments
   b. Loans
   c. Salaries

2. What are Mutual Funds?
   a. Insurance policies
   b. Bank accounts
   c. Investment groups

3. What does an individual's Balance Sheet report?
   a. Retained Earnings
   b. Net Worth
   c. Profit or Loss

4. What is a mortgage broker required to provide to applicants?
   a. Loan cost statement
   b. Good interest rates
   c. Good loan terms

5. No bookkeeping skills are required to prequalify buyers.
   a. True
   b. False

6. What is a second mortgage?
   a. Homeowners insurance
   b. Equity loan
   c. Unsecured loan

7. Most insurance agents are self-employed.
   a. True
   b. False

8. What are insurance company employees that provide rate information and issue policies called?
   a. Claim adjusters
   b. Insurance agents
   c. Underwriters

9. How are lenders listed on insurance policies covering collateral?
   a. Beneficiaries
   b. Loss Payees
   c. Lien Holders

10. Credit card balances are normally classified as what type of debt?
    a. Unsecured
    b. Secured
    c. Equity loans

Review

Hour 1: Bookkeeping Job Titles, Duties, and Responsibilities

This hour introduces you to the various jobs that require bookkeeping knowledge and skills. It explains the tasks performed by cashiers, clerks, and Full-Charge Bookkeepers who actually manage bookkeeping systems and supervise assistant bookkeepers. In addition, it offers advice and suggestions for keeping your personal financial records updated and in order.

Hour 2: Organization and Bank Accounts

Before a bookkeeping system can be initiated, it is prudent to think about the specific needs of the company or individual that will be using it. This basic information enables the bookkeeper to set up the proper files and accounts for the system. This hour also explains how to choose a bank and open the bank accounts that will become the heart of the bookkeeping system.

Hour 3: The Balance Sheet Accounts

The next step in learning how to keep a set of books is to study the accounts that make up the General Ledger where all transactions will be recorded. In this hour the Balance Sheet accounts are introduced and explained. Once the Assets, Liabilities, and Equity accounts are in place, the lesson continues by demonstrating how these accounts can be used to report the financial stability of a company or an individual.

Hour 4: The Profit & Loss Accounts

In this hour, the Profit & Loss area of the General Ledger is covered. All five sections of this part of the bookkeeping system are examined so that you will understand how the financial data recorded in each account combines with the figures posted to the other accounts in this section to produce a Profit & Loss Statement.

Hour 5: Working Within the Bookkeeping System

The basic procedures for working with the General Ledger to record income and expenses are explained in this hour. It includes instructions on adding and deleting accounts, debits and credits, and posting daily and monthly transactions. Explanations are provided for books that are kept on a cash or accrual basis and the relationships of some accounts to other accounts in the system.

Hour 6: Cash Receipts and Sales Tax

In this hour, you learn more about the daily transactions every book-keeper must record in the General Ledger. This lesson includes information on cash sales, balancing the cash register, and how to handle and post Sales Tax. Depositing cash receipts into the bank account and the procedures and accounts used to make adjustments to the sales' accounts are also presented.

Hour 7: Credit Sales and Customer Information

Credit sales require an understanding of Accounts Receivable and the customer ledgers that carry the balances posted there. Instructions and information for billing credit sales to the customers, collecting payments, and reviewing the charge accounts to make sure the balances are correct and agree with the total posted to Accounts Receivable.

Hour 8: Inventory Control, Vendors, and Credit Terms

All the tasks related to inventory are explained in this hour. The lesson continues with information on purchases that affect inventory, and how the invoices are posted to Accounts Payable and to the underlying vendor ledgers that must be created. It ends with explanations of physical inventories and the various methods used to count and evaluate inventory items.

Hour 9: Paying the Bills

In this hour you study the proper procedures for managing Accounts Payable and issuing checks to vendors. In addition, information on monitoring the other accrual and loan accounts is provided. An explanation of credit ratings, how they can be reviewed, and how they affect a company or individual's purchasing power is also presented.

Hour 10: Updating and Balancing the Checkbook

An elementary lesson that explains how to make bank deposits, write checks, and handle work papers and audits is offered in this hour. There are also step by step instructions for reviewing the bank statement and reconciling business and personal bank accounts.

Hour 11: Employees, Wages, and Taxes

Hour 11 begins the lessons on payroll and payroll taxes by outlining the rules and the forms that must be completed when employees are hired. Basic information on wages and salaries leads into explanations of the various taxes associated with wages. Finally, instructions on handling employee expense accounts are presented with samples showing how they are posted into the General Ledger.

Hour 12: Gross Payroll and Deductions

The second lesson on payroll procedures teaches you how to compute wages for a variety of payroll types and schedules. Federal and State payroll deductions are explained along with other employee deductions. The payroll taxes an employer must pay are explained and the procedure for posting payroll and taxes is presented in detail.

Hour 13: Payroll Tax Reports and Payments

The third and final lesson on payroll and taxes explains the rules and regulations the IRS imposes on employers for making Federal Tax Deposits through banks and through the IRS electronic processing system. Instructions for completing and filing Federal and State payroll tax reports are presented along with information on using payroll services.

Hour 14: Wage Earners and the Self-Employed

This hour provides information on adjusting your federal withholding taxes to keep more money in your pocket during the year without creating a tax liability. It includes tips on retirement savings that may be tax deductible. The lesson goes on to explain how to issue W-2s to employees and 1099s to outside service providers. Lastly, it has instructions on how and when the self-employed report and pay their tax liabilities.

Hour 15: Closing the Books at the End of the Month

The end of the month process is explained with an emphasis on the adjustments that have to be calculated and posted to the General Ledger. There are also instructions for reconciling and reimbursing the Petty Cash Fund, balancing customer and vendor ledgers, and writing off bad debts.

Hour 16: Issuing Financial Statements

In this hour, a time-saving method that can be used by small businesses to update the General Ledger and issue Financial Statements is presented. You will also find information on generating Financial Statements for different time periods and advice on how and when you should include notes with financial reports.

Hour 17: Closing the Books at the End of the Year

A Trial Balance report for a more complex business operation is presented along with information on how to identify problems in the General Ledger and correct them. Instructions on running end of the year reports and advice on what financial records must be stored for future reference. The lesson ends with the Balance Sheet accounts that carry their balances forward into the new year.

Hour 18: Individual Tax Returns

This hour concentrates on individuals and how they can track their income and expenses so that there are no unpleasant surprises at tax time. The most commonly used tax forms are presented along with information on the type of financial data that is needed to complete them. There is also a section that explains where individuals can go for tax help if needed.

Hour 19: Business Taxpayers

The way businesses are structured in the United States and how that affects their tax status with the IRS is the focus of this hour. You will learn about sole proprietors, partnerships, large and small corporations, and limited liability companies. The tax forms that must be completed and filed for each different business type are also presented and explained.

Hour 20: Computerized Bookkeeping Programs

In this hour, you will study computerized bookkeeping programs and their many time-saving features. The process of setting up a Chart of Accounts and General Ledger is explained in detail. Also information on automatic postings, receivables, payables, and all the reports the programs can generate to help bookkeepers and business owners with financial planning.

Hour 21: Retail, Restaurants, and Entertainment Venues

This is the first of four hours that presents information on a variety of business operations and how the basic bookkeeping procedures are adapted to their needs. There is a look at auto dealerships, restaurants, theaters, and membership organizations with advice on the accounts that must be set up and maintained in their General Ledgers.

Hour 22: Personal and Professional Services

Service businesses can be small one-person operations or huge corporations. Both will be examined and explored in this hour. You will learn about hairdressers, law firms, accounting firms, and agents and study how they operate and what bookkeeping accounts and procedures work best for each of these businesses.

Hour 23: Real Estate

This hour provides an overview of the fast paced real estate industry and studies contractors, real estate agents, and property managers. Some of the rules and regulations that govern these businesses are presented. You will also review the special accounts that their specific business activities require.

Hour 24: Finance and Insurance

Financial institutions, including banks and mortgage companies, are visited in this last hour along with insurance agents and the companies that they represent. Discussions of the bookkeepers that keep this industry running and the knowledge and skills they must possess are presented with advice on other qualifications these companies may be looking for in employees.

Bookkeeping Terms

account   A place within a bookkeeping system used to record and hold financial data.

Accounts Payable   The account set up to record expenses that are owed but not yet paid.

Accounts Receivable   The account set up to record income on sales or services that will be collected at a later date.

accrual basis   Recognizing income on sales or services that has not yet been collected and recognizing expenses that have not yet been paid out. This method puts Accounts Payable and Accounts Receivable into use.

amortization   The process by which the value of intangible business assets is reduced and written off the books.

asset   Something of value that is owned by a business or individual.

Balance Sheet   The financial report that presents the year-to-date values of Assets, Liabilities, and Equity.

bottom line   The Net Profit or Loss.

capital   Cash or something of value that is invested in a business enterprise.

canceled check   One that has been processed and canceled by the bank.

Cash disbursements   Payments issued for purchases and other expenses.

Cash receipts   Revenue or income received.

Chart of Accounts   A listing of accounts established to record financial data.

credit   An offset to a debit.

debit   An offset to a credit.

depreciation   The reduction in value of a tangible asset.

entry   The method by which financial data is recorded.

equity   The value that is retained.

Financial Statements   Reports that present the financial condition of a business.

General Journal Entry   An adjustment made to accounts in the General Ledger.

General Ledger   The place in a bookkeeping system that holds all the accounts and the entries that have been posted to them.

Gross Profit   The amount of income remaining after direct costs have been deducted from the revenue generated by sales or service.

Income Statement   Another term for the Profit & Loss Statement.

liabilities   Debts or expenses.

Mutual Funds   Investment opportunities where groups of people pool their money and allow the fund administrator to buy and sell stocks and bonds on their behalf. The profits or losses on these investments are shared by the members of the Mutual Fund group based on the amount of money they have contributed to it.

Net Loss   The amount that exceeds the income from sales or services after costs and expenses have been deducted.

Net Profit   The amount of income remaining after direct costs and expenses have been deducted from the revenue generated by sales or service.

Profit & Loss Statement   The report that presents the Income, Costs, and Expenses of a business.

Retained Earnings   The amount of profit or loss that is carried over from month to month and year to year on the Balance Sheet of a business.

Trial Balance   A report that lists all the accounts in the General Ledger with their year-to-date balances.

Hour 1

1. b
2. c
3. b
4. a
5. c
6. b
7. a
8. a
9. d
10. b

Hour 2

1. c
2. a
3. a
4. b
5. b

6. a
7. c
8. b
9. b
10. a

Hour 3

1. a
2. c
3. b
4. c
5. a
6. c
7. a
8. b
9. c
10. b

Hour 4

1. a
2. b
3. c
4. b The IRS has restricted these deductions.
5. a
6. b
7. a
8. a
9. c
10. b

Hour 5

1. a
2. b
3. c
4. c
5. b
6. a
7. a
8. c
9. b
10. c

Hour 6

1. b
2. b
3. a
4. a
5. d
6. b
7. a
8. a
9. a & b
10. b

Hour 7

1. c
2. a
3. c
4. b
5. a
6. c
7. c
8. a
9. a
10. c

Hour 8

1. b
2. c
3. a
4. b
5. b
6. c
7. b
8. c
9. a
10. c

Hour 9

1. c
2. b
3. a
4. c
5. a
6. b
7. a
8. a
9. c
10. b

Hour 10

1. b
2. c
3. a
4. c
5. a
6. b
7. b
8. c
9. c
10. a

Hour 11

1. b
2. b
3. c
4. a
5. c
6. a
7. c
8. b
9. b
10. a

Hour 12

1. b
2. a
3. a
4. c
5. b
6. b
7. a
8. a
9. b
10. a

Hour 13

1. c
2. a
3. b
4. b
5. c
6. a
7. b
8. c
9. a
10. b

Hour 14

1. c
2. a
3. c
4. c
5. c
6. a
7. c
8. b
9. b
10. a

Hour 15

1. b & c
2. a
3. a
4. c
5. b
6. c
7. b
8. b
9. c
10. a

Hour 16

1. b
2. c
3. b
4. b
5. c
6. a & b
7. a
8. c
9. b
10. b

Hour 17

1. b
2. a
3. a
4. b
5. c
6. a & c
7. a
8. b
9. b
10. c

Hour 18

1. b
2. c
3. a
4. b
5. a
6. c
7. b
8. a
9. c
10. b

Hour 19

1. a
2. b
3. c
4. b
5. a
6. b
7. c
8. b
9. c
10. a

Hour 20

1. c
2. a
3. b
4. a
5. b
6. b
7. c
8. c
9. a
10. a

Hour 21

1. b
2. b
3. c
4. b
5. c
6. c
7. a
8. c
9. b
10. a

Hour 22

1. b
2. c
3. b
4. a
5. c
6. a
7. b
8. b
9. c
10. c

Hour 23

1. b
2. a
3. d
4. c
5. b
6. c
7. b
8. a
9. c
10. a

Hour 24

1. a & b
2. c
3. b
4. a
5. b
6. b
7. a
8. c
9. b
10. a

IRS Help

IRS live telephone assistance is available Monday through Friday 7:00 A.M. to 10:00 P.M. (your local time) Alaska and Hawaii (Pacific Time). You may ask questions about preparing your tax return or about any notices you have received from the IRS.

Individuals call: 1-800-829-1040.

Businesses call: 1-800-829-4933.

Forms and publications are available at the IRS website (www.irs.gov) or by calling 1-800-829-3676.

Employer Identification Numbers

EINs can be obtained by applying online at the IRS website (www.irs.gov) or by calling 1-800-829-4933 Monday through Friday.

Credit Bureaus

Equifax Credit Information Services, Inc.
P.O. Box 740241
Atlanta, GA 30374
1-888-202-4025
www.equifax.com

TransUnion
P.O. Box 6790
Fullerton, CA 92834
1-800-813-5604
www.transunion.com

Experian
P.O. Box 9701
Allen, TX 75013
1-888-397-3741
www.experian.com

Free credit reports can be obtained by visiting the Federal Trade Commission website (www.ftc.gov) and clicking on Free Annual Credit Reports.

Books

Bragg, Steven M. *Inventory Accounting.* John Wiley & Sons, 2005.

Costa, Carol, and C. Wesley Addison, CPA. *Teach Yourself Accounting in 24 Hours, Second Edition.* Alpha Books, 2006.

Fraser, Lyn M., and Aileen Ormiston. *Understanding Financial Statements.* Pearson Education, 2006.

Internal Revenue Service. *Depreciation and Amortization* (including information on listed property). IRS tax Form 4562, 2006.

Little, Ken. *Teach Yourself Investing in 24 Hours.* Alpha Books, 2000.

Salek, John G. *Accounts Receivable Management.* John Wiley & Sons, 2005.

Slesnick, Twila, John C. Suttle, and Amy Delpo. *IRAs, 401(k)s & Other Retirement Plans.* NOLO, 2006.

Index